Virtual Sovereignty

VIRTUAL SOVEREIGNTY

Nationalism, Culture and the Canadian Question

ROBERT WRIGHT

Canadian Scholars' Press Inc.
Toronto

Virtual Sovereignty: Nationalism, Culture and the Canadian Question
Robert Wright

First published in 2004 by
Canadian Scholars' Press Inc.
180 Bloor Street West, Suite 801
Toronto, Ontario M5S 2V6
www.cspi.org

Chapter Two, "Dream, Comfort, Memory, Despair: Canadian Musicians and the Dilemma of Nationalism," by Robert Wright, was originally published in *Journal of Canadian Studies* 22:4 (Winter 1987–88). Reprinted by permission of the publisher.

Chapter Three, "Gimme Shelter: Cultural Protectionism and the Canadian Recording Industry," by Robert Wright, was originally published as "Gimme Shelter: Cultural Protectionism and the Recording Industry in Canada" in *Cultural Studies* 5:3 (October 1991). www.tandf.co.uk. Reprinted by permission of the publisher.

Chapter Four, "Historical Underdosing: Pop Demography and the Crisis in Canadian History," by Robert Wright, was originally published in *Canadian Historical Review* 81:4 (December 2000), pp. 646–667. Reprinted with permission of the University of Toronto Press.

Every reasonable effort has been made to identify copyright holders. CSPI would be pleased to have any errors or omissions brought to its attention.

Canadian Scholars' Press Inc. gratefully acknowledges financial support for our publishing activities from the Government of Canada through the Book Publishing Industry Development Program (BPIDP) and the Government of Ontario through the Ontario Book Publishing Tax Credit Program.

National Library of Canada Cataloguing in Publication

Wright, Robert A. (Robert Anthony), 1960–
   Virtual sovereignty : nationalism, culture and the Canadian question / Robert Wright.

Includes bibliographical references and index.
ISBN 1-55130-258-6

   1. Nationalism—Canada. 2. Canada—Civilization—20th century.
3. Canada—Cultural policy. 4. Conservatism—Canada. I. Title.

FC95.5.W75 2004   971.064'8   C2004-900177-9

Cover design and typeset by Zack Taylor Design, www.zacktaylor.com.

05 06 07 08 5 4 3 2

Printed and bound in Canada by AGMV Marquis Imprimeur, Inc.

Canadä

For Laura, Helena, Anna and Michael.

TABLE OF CONTENTS

PREFACE AND ACKNOWLEDGEMENTS

Virtual Sovereignty is a collection of essays on aspects of modern Canadian culture, ideology, history and identity. This wonderful title I owe to *Toronto Star* columnist Richard Gwyn, who despaired in the aftermath of the September 11th terrorist attacks on the United States that Canadians had "entered the virtual sovereignty phase of our national story." In my view Canadian sovereignty has always been virtual, which is precisely why obsessing about it has been so important to intellectual life in this country since Goldwin Smith first broached "the Canadian question" in 1891. This book is my modest contribution to that obsession.

Though the chapters in this book are linked thematically, most were conceived as self-contained essays and may still be read that way. Three of these pieces are, in fact, revised and expanded versions of articles first published elsewhere. Chapter Two, "Dream, Comfort, Memory, Despair: Canadian Musicians and the Dilemma of Nationalism," first appeared in the *Journal of Canadian Studies* (Winter 1987-8); Chapter Three was originally published in *Cultural Studies* as "Gimme Shelter: Cultural Protectionism and the Recording Industry in Canada" (October 1991); and Chapter Four, "Historical Underdosing: Pop Demography and the Crisis in Canadian History," first appeared in the *Canadian Historical Review* (December 2000). For their permission to reprint copyright material, I would like to express my gratitude to the editors of these journals.

It is a great pleasure for me to acknowledge the many individuals without whose contributions this book would never have seen the light of day. My old friend and comrade Craig Walker read a draft version of this book in its entirety, taking me to task on some of its more contentious minutiae as well as its broader claims. For his uncompromising intellectual rigour, for his commanding knowledge of Canadian culture, and especially for his personal allegiance over the better part of a lifetime, I am greatly indebted. Jim Struthers also read an early draft of this book, graciously piloting me through the labyrinth of Canadian social policy and, more subtly, buoying me up with his indomitable passion for the social-democratic tradition in Canada. I cannot begin to repay my debt to this exemplary scholar, teacher and friend—a debt that dates from my days as a undergraduate and has been accumulating ever since. My deepest thanks go out as well to my brother, Dan Wright, and my father, R.K. Wright, both of whom contributed more than they might have imagined to my thinking about modern Canada over the years in which this book was written.

Other friends and colleagues whose ideas about culture and ideology have directly shaped my own include Jody Berland, Jonathan Bordo, Simon Frith, Jane Harrison, Ian McLachlan, Karen Pegley, John Shepherd, Geoff Smith, Will Straw, John Wadland and Keith Walden. Thanks to Jack Wayne, Althea Prince, Renée Knapp and Rebecca Conolly of Canadian Scholars' Press for providing me with such a pleasant publishing environment. Christine McLaughlin helped to organize and index this book, for which I am grateful. I would like to make a special point of thanking my undergraduate students at the Durham University Centre, who continue to generously indulge my intellectual obsessions in their tutorials and seminars, as well as those friends and colleagues at Julian Blackburn College whose tireless efforts make my work not only possible but utterly pleasurable: Joan Milovick, Sandra Gunn, Nancy Maguire, Rita Bode, Margaret Steffler, Murray Genoe, and especially Tui Menzies.

As always, my greatest debt is to my wife, Laura. And as always, it is impossible for me to put into words the depth of my gratitude for her support for my work and, more generally, for anchoring everything I do with her love, loyalty and strength of character. Our beautiful children—Helena, Anna and Michael—are still too young to fully understand what keeps Daddy glued to his computer, but one day they will. For their love and affection, their good humour and their forbearance, I am grateful beyond measure.

INTRODUCTION

Virtual Sovereignty owes much of its inspiration to my academic mentor, the late George A. Rawlyk, professor of history at Queen's University from the mid-1960s until his death in 1996. My relationship with George Rawlyk began in 1983 when I entered his graduate seminar on comparative colonial ideologies and when, in the same year, I began my teaching career as a TA in his second-year undergraduate course on Canadian-American relations. In those days, despite his disappointment that Canada and other Western nations were opting for what he saw as the political palliative of neo-conservatism, Rawlyk was still energized by some of the questions that had marked much of his academic career and most of his writing: what, exactly, was the nature of the relationship of Canada and the United States, in all of its historic dynamism? What was the meaning, and what were the contexts for the changing meanings, of terms such as *republicanism, democracy, individualism, puritanism, loyalism, liberalism, conservatism* and *nationalism?* Although he was an extremely complex and, by his own admission, introspective scholar, Rawlyk's pedagogical gift lay in his ability to inspire his students to consider historical material always in the context of their own ideas and prejudices. He constantly challenged his students to rethink even their most deeply held convictions in the face of contradictory evidence, and he insisted that they "squeeze" historical documents for their hidden and perhaps ambiguous meanings, even though this could be a disconcerting process. This determination to challenge oneself was the measure of his own scholarly work—he never missed an opportunity to remind his students that all writing is autobiography—and it produced a corpus of writing that tells us as

13

much about George Rawlyk and what he saw as the temper of his times as it does about the various historical subjects that concerned him.

In the late 1980s and early 1990s, by which time I had ceased to have the close relationship with Rawlyk of graduate student to thesis supervisor, it was evident that he had become disillusioned with contemporary politics and disenchanted with the academic project of Canadian-American relations, a transition he confirmed bluntly when, in my capacity as book review editor of the *Journal of Canadian Studies*, I asked him to contribute a review article on the state of Canadian-American studies. The article explored, with characteristic honesty and self-awareness, Rawlyk's change of heart about many of the ideas that had for decades anchored his understanding of — and love for — Canada. What he wrote is worth excerpting at length, for it seems even now to encapsulate the identity crisis through which many Canadian intellectuals were passing:

> It seemed so easy in the late 1960s to impose a straightforward "Whig" organizational framework on the historical material covered in [my graduate seminar] — a framework which gave shape and substance to an emerging contemporary sense of Canadian identity. My class and I loved to read George Grant's *Lament for a Nation*, regarding it as a ringing clarion call for all of us to try to preserve the Canadian nation — despite the odds.... At the core of what had quickly become our collective neo-Canadian nationalism was a powerful critique of almost all things American as well as an understandable desire to exaggerate the uniqueness of the Canadian experience. I stressed in my class the fact that Canada had "rejected" the American Revolution and all that it represented; it had turned back military imperialism during the War of 1812.... In 1867, Canadian "peace, order and good government" had easily defeated the forces of American republican "life, liberty and the pursuit of happiness"; and despite the Liberal Party's enthusiasm for reciprocity, Canadian good

sense had prevailed in the federal elections of 1891 and 1911 and throughout the long political night of W.L. Mackenzie King....

By the late 1980s, I found that my students were no longer really interested in Canadian-American relations. Most of them found Grant's *Lament for a Nation* to be too pessimistic and totally irrelevant. My own reading of the historical past, moreover, was being contradicted by Canadian political and economic realities. The Mulroney electoral victory in 1988 seemed to deliver a death blow to my interpretation of the Canadian-American relationship.... For me Grant had been right after all and his *Lament* became my lament.[1]

Like many Canadian nationalists, Rawlyk found the re-election of the free-trading Tories in 1988 demoralizing and even incomprehensible. Thereafter, he shifted his research focus entirely towards the study of Canadian religiosity, and of Protestant evangelicalism in particular, where he believed the scholarship was more robust, the field understudied and, above all, the questions more resonant for himself personally. This was a courageous decision, for it resulted in accusations from colleagues and even friends that he had abandoned the social-democratic principles with which he had always been identified, charges that hurt him deeply but did not surprise him.

In retrospect, though I have no doubt about the depth of Rawlyk's disillusionment, I think he overstated his own commitment to a "Whig" interpretation of the Canadian experience. Few of his students will forget his thunderous condemnation of American "Whig" scholars like Bernard Bailyn, or his injunction that "Whig" history is always written from the vantage point of the winners! Indeed, if there is a term that for me embodies George Rawlyk's scholarly and even personal style, it is *ambivalence*, a complex idea defined succinctly by *Webster's* as "simultaneous conflicting feelings toward a person or thing, as love and hate." Whether in the life of an individual like the evangelist Henry Aline or in the life of a nation like Canada, Rawlyk was always open to the idea that competing forces co-existed, usually uneasily and often "morbidly"—a claim he made openly about the currents that shaped his own life.

Ambivalence is not a word that has entered the popular North American lexicon. This is in some ways puzzling, especially given that the term *paradox*, like the term *irony* before it, has now been fully popularized. *Webster's* defines *paradox* as "a statement that seems contradictory, unbelievable or absurd but that may be true in fact." I think there is good reason why the term *paradox* has gained such wide currency and the term *ambivalence* has not. It is easier to perceive internal contradiction than to explain it or, worse yet, to embrace it. To say something is *paradoxical* is arguably to make a tough-minded statement, one that points a knowing finger at the existence of self-contradiction, much as the terms *hypocrisy* or *sanctimony* have done historically. *Ambivalence*, on the other hand, seems to carry connotations of pensiveness, immobilization, failure of will, and perhaps even cowardice. In a world replete with contradiction—which is patently the world of early twenty-first century North American life—it is, in fact, safer to identify and proclaim the existence of paradox than it is to actually be ambivalent. George Rawlyk was both tough-minded and ambivalent. By word and also by deed, he taught his students that ambivalence was not only a common human response to conditions of rapid change, confusion and institutional complexity, but that it may in fact be the only salient option for people whose lives are riddled with apparent contradiction.

Ambivalence is an idea that permeates this book. It is my contention that Canadians' understanding of notions such as "art," "culture," "unity," "identity" and "sovereignty" have virtually always been informed by conflicting forces, most of them beyond the control of "ordinary" citizens, many beyond the control even of governments. I take the view, therefore, that Canadians are not timid fence-sitters or apathetic victims of situational forces, but rather that they have developed remarkably sophisticated cultural and political strategies for deriving pleasure, prosperity and peace of mind out of conditions of contradiction, paradox and irony. *Ambivalence* constitutes for me a uniquely Canadian response to lived social, cultural and economic conditions which are themselves uniquely Canadian. Living with contradiction has always been a fact of Canadian life; *ambivalence* has been the critical framework that has made this living not only possible but the envy of the world. *Ambivalence* has allowed, and perhaps even fostered, a Canadian propensity for pragmatism, flexibility and adaptability; yet, equally remarkably, it has done so for the most part without damaging Canadians' longstanding sense of moral certitude.

Like George Rawlyk, I am ambivalent about Canadian nationalism, as this collection of essays undoubtedly shows. My ambivalence is rooted in part in the formative experiences of my youth, something I have come to appreciate the more so as I contemplate the kind of Canada my children will inherit. Born in 1960, I absorbed the nationalist obsession of the Trudeau era as if by osmosis. As Catherine Annau showed in her film, *Just Watch Me: Trudeau and the '70s Generation*, my experience of Canada was far from unique. Many Canadians of my vintage came to share a deep and abiding passion for this country and some continue to believe, as Trudeau himself put it, that Canada's disappearance would be a crime against humanity. Yet, like Trudeau, we are also decidedly post-nationalist in some important respects, suspicious of the tendency of nationalism to draw lines in the sand and even more wary of its incendiary destructiveness in the hands of political opportunists. In an era in which the mere mention of Bosnia or Rwanda connotes the worst sort of ethnic-nationalist excess, Samuel Johnson's remark in 1775 that "patriotism is the last refuge of a scoundrel" seems to ring eternally truc.

My ambivalence also stems, of course, from my experience of the highly charged, some would say revolutionary, times through which we are now living. Globalization and neo-conservatism have downsized and dismantled the Canada of my youth, a Canada of social-democratic consensus, of generous state support for public education, cultural production and the social safety net, a Canada that pursued an independent foreign policy, a Canada that cared deeply about young people and understood them to be central to the project of nation-building. Culture critic Jody Berland has described this world and its demise angrily but eloquently, and she speaks for many disillusioned Canadian intellectuals, myself included:

> Canadians raised with public institutions like the CBC, the Canada Council, and the public school system learned to picture a national community sharing a benign, good-humoured mythic space continuous with a naturalized collective past. The symbolic association of territoriality and public good—making Canada synonymous with (relative) compassion—acquired over time a genuine affectivity. One wanted to be the beaver, not the eagle; the Mountie, not the Green Beret; to be the kind of person who waited in line, looked after the old and the poor, and respected picket lines and trees as a matter of course. As symbols, these were myths in every sense: they reshaped history and imposed a unifying narrative on very heterogeneous subjects. They also symbolized compassionate, democratic, and anti-imperialist values whose political defeat is now reflected in and exacerbated by the cynical marginalization of these shared meanings. What we are supposed to value now in the ebb and flow of everyday life—kindness, altruism and compassion, fairness, civility, respect for difference—is no longer represented as a legitimate basis for public morality. Instead, governments, cities, old-age homes, film productions, galleries, and schools must all be run like businesses (for is not that their true nature?) and business people must run them. We are witnessing no less than a fundamental redefinition of the concept of democracy in the public sphere.[2]

Today, as the postwar Canadian consensus recedes from view, we are left with little more than the symbolic traces of the "national community" described by Berland, cynically deployed. Canadians recognize the syndrome and rightly resent it. This was the unambiguous meaning of the "flag fiasco" in the wake of the 1995 referendum in Quebec: the Chrétien Liberals had proved incapable of articulating any sort of national vision to counter the separatists; instead Heritage Minister Sheila Copps spent

$20 million on a "One Million Flags Challenge." The same cynical sleight of hand obtains in matters of culture. In 1999, after six years of Finance Minster Paul Martin's "hell or high water" cuts to federal spending, the CRTC quietly raised the Cancon quota for commercial radio from 30 per cent to 35. Jody Berland had been right: the social, cultural and political fabric of the country had been ravaged but we got to hear even more Shania Twain. Seldom has public discourse in Canada been as impoverished as it has become in the era of neo-conservatism, as old-fashioned notions of *citizenship*, *belonging* and *the public good* recede before a *laissez-faire*, essentially consumerist model of civic life. One may agree or disagree with the claims of Canadian nationalists — in these pages, I do both — but there can be no disputing their absolutely vital role in the maintenance of a "national conversation" in which all Canadians have a stake.

Virtual Sovereignty is comprised of four groups of thematically related chapters, each of which discloses my admittedly idiosyncratic preoccupation with "the Canadian question" as it has evolved over almost two decades. The first group concerns the institutional mediation of Canadians' cultural tastes in the twentieth century, focusing specifically on the manner in which patterns of representation and consumption were informed by officially sanctioned state nationalism. Chapter One examines the nationalist "doctrine" of the Group of Seven and its extraordinarily successful promulgation throughout the twentieth century at the hands of those who believed, with Group co-founder Lawren Harris, that "an Art must grow and flower in the land before the country will be a real home for its people." Chapter Two surveys the ideas of Canadian popular musicians in the highly celebrated Centennial era, suggesting that many of the most accomplished artists of the period were ambivalent about state-imposed "Canadian content" on commercial radio and loathe to be pedestalized as national symbols. Chapter Three examines the longer-term implications of state intervention in the private-sector broadcasting and recording industries, suggesting that policies designed to privilege Canadian music in the domestic marketplace have in fact served to homogenize it along lines dictated by the multinational music business.

The second group of chapters explores the crisis in Canadian history that is believed by Professor J.L. Granatstein and others to have contributed to Canada's current national malaise. Chapter Four challenges the Granatstein thesis directly, arguing that a powerful new paradigm for understanding the organization of the past—something I call *pop demographics*—has disrupted not only the formal study of history but Canadians' understanding of tradition, custom and narrative as the organizing principles of their own individual and collective past. Chapter Five challenges the related claim that corporate-controlled, profit-driven *History Television* has become a fun and entertaining surrogate for professional historiography in Canada.

The third group of chapters addresses what have been, to my mind, the most striking yet unacknowledged casualties of the neo-conservative revolution in Canada: young people. Chapter Six argues that in contrast with the Trudeau era, when young Canadians were central to nationalist formations, full participants in the organizations they inspired, and immediate beneficiaries of the massively expanded state apparatus they produced, youth today are silent on the great national issues of our time, their citizenship status is precarious, they are demonized rather than celebrated in the popular imagination, and they have been singularly disadvantaged by the retreat of the welfare state. Chapter Seven extends this analysis by showing how Liberal policies in the Chrétien era have contributed directly to the disaffection and marginalization of young Canadians.

The final group of chapters examines the Canadian question as it exists today, against the backdrop of George W. Bush's post-September 11th dictum that "[e]very nation in every region now has a decision to make: either you are with us, or you are with the terrorists." Chapter Eight assesses the Canadian response to September 11th, suggesting that the crisis provided the pretext for an offensive against Canadian nationalists unprecedented since the free trade election of 1988. The Conclusion extends this analysis with some thoughts on the new "sovereignty" debate in Canada that has arisen in concert with the American war in Iraq—evidence, to borrow George Grant's memorable phrase, that even at this late hour Canadians are not yet ready to "rejoice in the disappearance of Canada."[3]

NOTES

1. George A. Rawlyk, "Lament for Canadian-American Relations?" *Journal of Canadian Studies* 26:2 (Summer 1991), pp. 169–172.

2. Jody Berland, "Politics after Nationalism, Culture after 'Culture'," *Canadian Review of American Studies* 27:3 (1997), p. 45.

3. George Grant, *Lament for a Nation* (Toronto: McClelland and Stewart, 1965), p. 88.

CHAPTER ONE

THE MAKING OF A MYSTIQUE

NATIONALISM, WILDERNESS AND
THE ORIGINS OF THE GROUP OF SEVEN

"I'm stunned each time I see the extraordinary power of
these artists to extract the very essence from the subjects
we have all seen. How much more clearly we see it and
feel it through their marvellous interpretations."

VINCENT MASSEY (1965)

"They sure caught the moods and spirit of the country.
Somehow in the paintings I see the forests and lakes with
greater clarity than when I was right there."

JOHN ROBARTS (1964)

"In our travels, Signe and I feel that we now see these scenes
more clearly through the artists' eyes. We often point out to
each other a Carmichael sky, a Jackson hill, or a Thomson pine."

ROBERT McMICHAEL (1986)[1]

As a child growing up in suburban Toronto in the 1970s, I was
taken to see the paintings of Tom Thomson and the Group of Seven
long before I had ever seen Algonquin Park or Georgian Bay or Algoma.
Though the paintings are commonly thought to embody the majesty of
the northern Ontario landscape, for me, even now, it is the landscape that
embodies the majesty of the paintings. The evidence suggests that my
experience of this powerful association is far from unique. Since at least

1965, when the McMichael Collection in Kleinburg, Ontario, became a public art gallery, millions of Canadians living in the industrial "golden horseshoe" region of southern Ontario have had more convenient access to the original landscape paintings of Thomson and the Group of Seven than to the land itself. According to McMichael officials, the number of school children who tour the gallery on class field trips now exceeds 30,000 per year, while the number of visits to the McMichael website exceeds 10,000 per week.[2] This is to say nothing of Canadians' virtually constant exposure to the posters, prints, cards, postage stamps and other Group of Seven paraphernalia that have proliferated throughout the country (and well beyond) since the Group was inaugurated.[3]

In *Ways of Seeing*, John Berger observes that "a work of art… suggests a cultural authority, a form of dignity, even of wisdom, which is superior to any vulgar material interest; an oil painting belongs to the cultural heritage; it is a reminder of what it means to be… cultivated." For Berger, this "cultural authority" arises from processes of *mystification*, in which privileged élites strive to "invent a history" which can justify their own ideological claims. Thus, he urges, "[i]n order to avoid mystifying the past," we must "examine the particular relation which now exists, so far as pictorial images are concerned, between the present and the past."[4] Mystification is a useful concept for the study of the paintings of Tom Thomson and the Group of Seven, insofar as they were deployed more or less consistently between the 1920s and the 1990s in the service of a well-developed English-Canadian nationalist ideology. Canadian art historian Scott Watson has put the case bluntly:

> As the Group's landscape images spread across the country via the medium of silkscreen reproductions designed for the post office and school room, they became enmeshed in a symbolism of a different order. Reduced to icons in the flat, matte colours of silkscreen, they became signs of obedience to a bureaucracy that had appropriated the Group's myth to the extent that their images stood simply for the state order.[5]

Following Berger, the purpose of this chapter is to de-mystify the work of Tom Thomson and the Group of Seven by exploring its formative nationalist elements—those which, in a sense, predisposed Canadian officials in the 1920s and beyond to appropriate the paintings in the cause of "nation-building and the establishment of a common heritage."[6] I am less interested in aesthetic questions than in questions of context: how did the work of Tom Thomson and the Group of Seven fit into the Western landscape tradition? How did the art establishment and ordinary Canadians respond to the work? How was this work popularized and monumentalized? What was its perceived relationship to the land? How did it figure in the articulation of a modern Canadian nationalist mythology? And, perhaps above all, how were Canadians' experience of the work mediated by ideology, institutions, inherited wisdom, and the contexts of their own everyday lives?

I argue that the Group of Seven sought and achieved its own mystique. It did so, firstly, by obscuring its debts to an earlier generation of Canadian landscape painters—notably those of the Canadian Art Club—and by knowingly exaggerating its declaration of a radically new conception of Canadian painting. Secondly, as art historian Roald Nasgaard has argued, the Group appropriated the *leitmotifs* of certain late nineteenth-century Scandinavian painters virtually intact, including their romantic assertion of a uniquely northern nationalist ideal, and later "obfuscated" these seminal debts as well. Lastly, the Group collaborated with its patrons and boosters in the 1920s—most notably Dr. James MacCallum and "outdoorsman" F.B. Housser—in the creation of a largely fictional epic narrative in which its members were said to have discovered and claimed the Canadian North aesthetically, in the virile and selfless tradition of the early explorers. In the end, of course, even the most aggressive self-promotion would not have raised the Group of Seven to heroic status had its work not resonated powerfully for Canadians. This chapter concludes, therefore, with some thoughts on what I consider to be the essential element in the Group of Seven mystique as it took shape in the years after the Great War: the articulation of an imaginative new "wilderness myth" for a modern, industrial and urban Canada in which the "real" wilderness had largely ceased to exist.

THE UNPAINTED LAND

Notwithstanding the powerful claim that the paintings of Tom Thomson and the Group of Seven arose spontaneously out of their encounter with the land, it is clear that virtually everything about the Group, from its conception, to its visual styles, to its knack for publicity, to what would become its historical legacy, was conceived with reference to what art historian and curator Dennis Reid has somewhat casually called its "doctrine."[7] Like many of their European contemporaries—Cubists, Futurists, Dadaists—the Group of Seven set for itself the lofty goal of overthrowing what they claimed was an ossified, self-important art establishment.[8] In the Canadian context, this meant refusing to "ape" tired European styles in favour of indigenous themes and the robust techniques they demanded. Lawren Harris, for example, openly mocked "so-called Art lovers" in Canada who "refuse[d] to recognize anything that does not come up to the commercialized, imported standards of the picture sale room," while A.Y. Jackson implored Canadians to "replace the Dutch cow with the northern bull moose."[9] The explicit ideological content of the Group's doctrine was by 1920 an aggressive, proselytizing strain of nationalism, as they noted in the catalogue for their inaugural show: "[A]n Art must grow and flower in the land before the country will be a real home for its people."[10] This nationalist ideal is commonly thought to account for the Group's initial success and, moreover, for its unrivalled hegemony in the Canadian art world for much of the twentieth century. For Robert and Signe McMichael, founders of the gallery that now bears their name, the genius of Tom Thomson and the Group of Seven lay in their "unabashed nationalism, [their] determination to celebrate Canadian themes in a distinctively Canadian manner."[11]

Despite their initial expectation that their work would be ridiculed by the Canadian art establishment, the Group met with comparatively little opposition and, indeed, almost immediately became the dominant force—the new establishment—in Canadian painting. It now requires a colossal suspension of disbelief to conceive of the Group of Seven as the underdogs in a struggle to redefine Canadian landscape painting or as a subversive force in Canadian art. The vision that inspired the Group of Seven was grand: they conceived their own artistic mission from the perspective of a future in which they would be celebrated as both seminal and visionary.[12] Even Tom Thomson, who lacked Harris's and Jackson's gift for hyperbole, confided quietly to more than one close friend his conviction that "at some future time [his work] would receive full recognition and acclaim."[13]

Like all artistic triumphs, the Group's had everything to do with timing and good luck. In broad historical terms, it is clear that the Group of Seven was well positioned to benefit from the intellectual and artistic rebellions occasioned by the Great War. With its almost 60,000 dead and its forthright claim to an independent role in the postwar world, Canada was popularly thought to have "come of age" during the conflict, an idea that Canadian historians have routinely repeated ever since. Rather than staggering into the modern age as a "lost generation," however, many Canadian artists, poets and novelists—along with their patrons, publishers and publicists—embraced the new era as one in which, finally, a "national spirit" could flourish. As Arthur Lismer put it, "After 1919 most creative people, whether in painting, writing or music, began to have a guilty feeling that Canada was as yet unwritten, unpainted, unsung…. In 1920 there was a job to be done."[14] Some observers of this new nationalism in the Canadian arts called it a "renaissance," but far more prevalent was the view that, in fact, this was the awakening of an indigenous Canadian artistic sensibility. Historians have since reiterated this claim, suggesting that if the Twenties didn't exactly roar in Canada, "something was definitely happening in the once-somnolent world of Canadian arts and letters."[15]

Lismer's recollection that Canada was as yet "unpainted" is a subtle but highly revealing twist on the theme of awakening, for it suggests, not that there was an establishment to overthrow, but merely that there was a vacuum to fill. Here we get a glimpse at the mystique in progress, for one of the most powerful myths about the Group of Seven is that they were the first Canadian painters to show any interest in their native land. Indeed, the "guilty feeling" recalled by Lismer points to yet another enduring legacy of the Group, namely that it provided a kind of national atonement for the artistic sins of the past. Even now, there is a decidedly redemptive tone to popular writing about the Group. Commenting on Lismer's mid-1920s work, for example, Robert McMichael exclaims in his autobiography that "it had the freedom, the spirit and the power so characteristic of the band of young painters who would change Canadian art and the way Canadians saw their country forever."[16] For many observers, this redemptive quality seems somehow to reside in the paintings themselves, as if, but for the acuity of Tom Thomson and the Group of Seven, the Canadian landscape would have gone "unpainted" and perhaps even unnoticed altogether.

Creation myths die hard. Given the popular reputation of the Group of Seven for "pioneering" Canadian art, it is important to recall that Canada produced several internationally acclaimed landscape artists in the late nineteenth century, as well as a coterie of professional painters who came together in the early twentieth under the explicitly nationalist rubric of the Canadian Art Club (CAC). Of these, none was more cel-ebrated in his own time — or so quickly and thoroughly dismissed in the rush to christen the Group of Seven — than Homer Watson (1855–1936). Dubbed "the Canadian Constable" by Oscar Wilde, Watson's western Ontario-based landscapes were admired throughout the English-speak-ing world. While in his twenties, his *The Pioneer Mill* was purchased by the Marquis of Lorne as a gift for Queen Victoria, setting in motion a career that would peak at the turn of the century with one-man shows in London and New York. In Canada and abroad, collectors competed for his canvasses, which he regularly exhibited under the auspices of the Ontario Society of Artists and the Royal Canadian Academy, and in prestigious British galleries.[17]

In 1907 Homer Watson was named the founding president of the Canadian Art Club — a "private exhibiting society" created to stimulate and promote "modern" Canadian painting, which meant confronting the "tired, old-fashioned look of Canadian art" and "lur[ing] the real talent back to Canada."[18] Other internationally acclaimed Canadian artists affiliated with the CAC included James Morrice, Edmund Morris, Curtis Williamson and Horatio Walker. In a deliberate attempt to achieve national representation, the CAC recruited Franklin Brownwell from Ottawa, William Brymner and Maurice Cullen from Montreal, Clarence Gagnon from Baie-Saint-Paul, Quebec, and Marc-Aurèle de Foy Suzor-Côté, another Quebec-born painter who had enjoyed acclaim in Europe. The CAC was not only artistically progressive and politically nationalist but—in classic Canadian style—it sought to bridge the two solitudes of Canadian art by exposing Anglo-Canadian and Québécois artists and audiences to each other. There is, however, no Canadian Art Club mystique, nor is there much space alongside the Group of Seven mystique to accommodate one. Homer Watson died in 1936, poor and forgotten, amid accusations that he had lately copied the style of the Group of Seven. Similarly, when Horatio Walker died in 1938, according to Dennis Reid, his paintings were thought as "anachronistic" as the Île d'Orléans peasant folk they depicted.[19] The CAC itself failed to navigate that great cultural watershed, the Great War, formally dissolving in 1915 amid criticisms that it represented "an approach to painting that was unsuitable for Canada."[20]

The Canadian Art Club was, in one crucial respect, on the wrong side of history. Beginning in the 1860s, progressive European painters had undertaken a sustained assault on the sombre "narrative" painting styles that had long dominated not only the Paris salons but European public taste. The best known of these rebels were, of course, the Impressionists—Manet, Monet, Renoir, Pissarro—painters who openly rejected "the studio gloom of academic tonal formulas" in favour of a bold new approach emphasizing the comparatively free play of colour and light.[21] Emerging alongside this nascent Impressionist movement in the 1870s, however—and drawing on many of the same influences—was a "Dutch" or "Hague" school of landscape painting that adopted the French "Barbizon" concern with "the subdued light of the interior of the forest, of dawn, and of twilight."[22] Although some Canadian painters showed a "tentative" interest in the techniques of the Impressionists, by the 1890s the Dutch school was predominant in English Canada — partly, no doubt, because its techniques were thought appropriate to the Canadian landscape, but also because several wealthy and powerful Canadian patrons had institutionalized this bias in large private collections, generous financial support for Canadian students studying in Holland, and even books on the subject.[23] It was within this environment of homage to the Dutch school that the Canadian Art Club sought to challenge the earlier "salon" style of Canadian landscape painting, little knowing that the most extraordinary revolution in art history would before long lie in the global triumph of the Impressionists.

When A.Y. Jackson demanded in 1920 that Canadians reject the "Dutch cow," then, he was not only challenging the time-honoured Canadian habit of importing European landscape techniques but impugning the influence of the Hague school in particular in late nineteenth and early twentieth-century Canadian painting. This critique — and, indeed, the powerful myth that Tom Thomson and the Group of Seven invented a style uniquely suited to the Canadian wilderness — has produced one of the most tenacious elements in the mystique, namely that the Group represented a radical break from the past. In truth, the Canadian Art Club provided a solid creative and institutional foundation for the launching of the Group. As young men, Lawren Harris and A.Y. Jackson, both of whom had trained in Europe, naturally sought out and admired the work of the CAC and other Canadian painters. Even to the casual observer there are unmistakable stylistic traces of turn-of-the-century Morrice and Suzor-Côté in their "mature" Group of Seven styles, to say nothing of the obvious "Dutch" derivations in Tom Thomson's work as late as 1912.[24] Equally important was the patronage cultivated by the CAC and later enjoyed by Thomson and the Group, most notably in the person of Dr. James MacCallum, the Toronto ophthalmologist and friend of Curtis Williamson, whose early financial and moral support of Thomson and the Group has itself become legendary. In short, they may have seen themselves as renegades in 1920, but prior to the Great

War the men who would unite as the Group of Seven were openly—and appropriately—enamoured of their Canadian forebears.[25]

The seminal event in the formation of the Group of Seven not only predated their inaugural show by almost a decade but came at the high-water mark of the Canadian Art Club. In 1911 Lawren Harris met J.E.H. MacDonald at Toronto's Arts & Letters Club, where the two immediately struck up a friendship based on their mutual desire to explore new approaches to Canadian landscape painting. With the help of Dr. MacCallum, Harris—who was himself independently wealthy owing to his membership in one of the families that had built the Massey-Harris farm machinery empire—persuaded MacDonald to quit his job as a commercial designer in order to paint full time. The two artists spent the summer and fall of 1912 at MacCallum's Georgian Bay cottage sketching, still very much in the "Dutch" manner of the CAC. In January 1913, Harris and MacDonald ventured to Buffalo, New York, where they saw for the first time the work of several Scandinavian painters, including Gustaf Fjaestad and Otto Hesselbom of Sweden, and Harald Sohlberg of Norway. The show struck both painters as nothing less than an epiphany. MacDonald later described the impact of Fjaestad's work in particular as a "revelation," exclaiming, "Except in minor points, the pictures might all have been Canadian, and we felt 'This is what we want to do with Canada.'"[26] With these Swedish and Norwegian canvasses fresh in their minds, Harris and MacDonald returned to Toronto. Together with the newly transplanted Montrealer A.Y. Jackson and a number of MacDonald's friends at Grip Limited—the Canadians Tom Thomson, Frank Carmichael and Frank Johnston, and the Englishmen Arthur Lismer and Fred Varley—they immediately set about to consolidate a new movement in Canadian painting. With MacCallum's backing, they built themselves a studio complex in prestigious Rosedale and were quickly dubbed the Algonquin group.[27]

The new group was not especially subtle in its appropriation of northern European styles. In 1984 the Art Gallery of Ontario presented an exhibition called *The Mystic North*, a show that brought together a large number of turn-of-the-century Canadian, Scandinavian, Swiss and

Dutch paintings. In his foreword to the promotional literature that accompanied this exhibition, David Wistow diplomatically confirmed what the paintings themselves showed rather starkly: "By placing the Group of Seven in the broad context of a late nineteenth and early twentieth-century international landscape tradition, *The Mystic North* reveals striking parallels of subject matter and style between the Group's paintings and those of their northern European counterparts."[28] Striking parallels indeed. The similarity of Lawren Harris's *Snow II* (1916), for example, to Fjaestad's *Winter Moonlight* (1895) is nothing short of uncanny. Equally striking is the likeness of Harris's mature landscape style, denoted by the simplified, almost geometrical austerity of works such as *Lake Superior* (1924) and *Mount Lefroy* (1930), to the scenes painted by the Dane Jens Ferdinand Willumsen at the turn of the century, most notably *Mountains Under the Southern Sky* (1902). J.E.H. MacDonald's style was also transformed under the influence of the Scandinavians, most strikingly — and by no means inconsequentially — in the diminution and ultimately the removal of human subjects from many of his landscapes. As Dennis Reid notes, even the work of A.Y. Jackson — who had not been to the Buffalo exhibition — immediately reflected, in its "symmetry and symbolic suggestiveness... his response to the enthusiastic reports of the Scandinavian show." Clearly Harris's and MacDonald's epiphany had become infectious; even the unpredictable Varley, less than two years out of his native Yorkshire, could not contain his enthusiasm for "nature... in all its greatness."[29]

The extraordinary impact of the northern Europeans upon the Algonquin group was not merely stylistic. Most of the artists whose work the group admired had themselves been caught up in the highly charged creative and political cross-currents of their times, and especially in the flourishing of new, openly nationalist loyalties. The Scandinavians seen by Harris and MacDonald, for example, had studied with the Impressionists in Paris in the 1880s, but by the 1890s had returned to their homelands, adopting a Symbolist concern with "feeling and mood" and even "dream and imagination" in their exploration of their own indigenous landscapes. They used the term *patriotism* to describe their passion for the wilderness settings that had been all but ignored by their precursors, "monumentalizing" their landscapes and implying "the existence of unseen meanings behind the appearances of the wilderness subject matter."[30] Reflecting on the Scandinavians' profound desire to fuse form and content in this powerful *northern* visual and emotional experience, Wistow observed:

> Crucial to this new development were the vast tracts of wilderness to which these northern artists turned for spiritual purification — in much the same way Gauguin sought a southern paradise when he departed for Tahiti in 1891.... This search for transcendental experiences in the sublime grandeur of primeval nature led the artists to their essential motifs — virgin forests, crashing waterfalls, and broad uncharted vistas devoid of human presence.[31]

As extraordinary as their colours and brushwork were, the Scandinavians' true gift to the Algonquin painters lay in their full blown aesthetic, ideological and even spiritual conceptualization of *the North* — an idea that evoked not only the mystical but the literal oneness of the land and its people. Little wonder that Harris and MacDonald were awe-struck in Buffalo, and little wonder that they returned to Toronto in the hope of becoming, if not the Canadian Fjaestad and Hesselbom, then at least their transatlantic messengers. As Roald Nasgaard concludes bluntly, "[a]ny discussion of the history of the Group of Seven inevitably centres on the contradiction between fact and fiction, between its members' claim to a kind of primitivistic originality and the reality that they were working in an artistic and philosophical framework with a demonstrable European pedigree." For Nasgaard, the case is unambiguous: in 1913 the Algonquin painters literally "resuscitated the tradition of Scandinavian Symbolist landscape painting" in their search for an artistic approach suitable for Canada, and thereafter they allowed themselves to be seduced by their nationalist vision into a "dogmatic isolationism."[32] Even their most ardent contemporary apologists quietly acknowledged that much of their work was "derivative of these Scandinavians."[33]

That this generation of Canadian landscape painters should have adopted a northern European, Impressionist-influenced sensibility is, at one level, far from surprising. Like their debt to the Canadian Art Club, the inspiration they derived from the Scandinavians' work was the natural consequence of the cultural environment in which they lived and worked. Trained in Europe and accustomed to thinking of the *avant-garde* as the preserve of the European capitals, the young Lawren Harris and A.Y. Jackson—and through them the other Canadian members of the group—would as a matter of course have conceived their own artistic ambitions with an eye to what they saw happening abroad. For serious painters, whatever their nationality, anything less would have been thought parochial or, worse yet, *colonial*—an epithet to which even the most nationalist English Canadians were acutely sensitive. However passionate they might have been about forging a new Canadian landscape idiom, it is unthinkable that they should have done so without reference to the European landscape tradition, or without consideration of their place in it. The question that remains, then, is not so much whether the work of the Algonquin group was derivative, but rather why these artists and their devotees went to such great lengths in the 1920s and beyond to obscure their debts to Canadian and European painters. For Nasgaard, there is but one explanation: the presumption of such influences "interfered with the most fundamental conception of the new painting, namely that it grew out of an unprecedented, original and immediate response to the uniqueness of the Canadian landscape."[34]

However much they may have later "obfuscated" their stylistic origins, to borrow Nasgaard's term, in their formative years at least the Algonquin painters seem to have been highly attuned to the contradictions implied by their cosmopolitan aspirations, on the one hand, and their nationalist vision, on the other. They were at pains to be viewed as innovators, hence their disdain for those who obligingly mimicked "tasteful" European styles, yet they were equally loathe at this early stage to retreat into any sort of primitivism. It would appear, in fact, that the challenge of navigating between these contradictory impulses provided much of the group's creative dynamic at the outset. A.Y. Jackson was invited to join the Algonquin group in 1913, for example, precisely because his reputation as a Paris-trained professional would provide counterweight to the "amateurs" recruited from Grip. Tom Thomson was the most amateur of all, it would seem, for Jackson spent much of his first winter in Toronto correcting the flaws in Thomson's technique. And yet, in less than a year it was Thomson who seemed to Jackson and the others to have achieved the most compelling synthesis of these conflicting impulses; as Dennis Reid observes, they came to see his work as "the direct response of untutored genius to the inspiration of the North."[35] This claim resonated powerfully throughout the twentieth century, the myth of the "untutored genius" inviting even the most ordinary of Canadians to see themselves and their native land reflected in Thomson's life and work. As Arthur Lismer later said of Thomson, "the rest of us were painting pictures; he was expressing moods. He was simply a part of nature."[36]

The twenty months that spanned the Buffalo exhibition and the outbreak of war must have been heady ones indeed for the fledgling group. Armed with the stylistic and thematic inspiration of the Scandinavians, the creative and institutional legacy of the Canadian Art Club, the generous patronage of Dr. MacCallum, and their own energetic group dynamic, it is clear that the Algonquin artists had consolidated in little more than a year all of the main planks in what would become the Group of Seven platform. The *modus operandi* for which the Group of Seven would become renowned—lengthy sketching trips over the summer and fall, followed by work on full-sized canvases over the winter—was by 1914 well established. Moreover, the group had by this time won the favour of Eric Brown, the director of the National Gallery in Ottawa, and National Gallery trustee Sir Edmund Walker, both of whom supported "the young artists in the most tangible way by insisting that the Gallery purchase major works by Thomson, Lismer, Harris, MacDonald and Jackson."[37] Thanks to Walker, in fact, who was head of the selection committee for the 1913 exhibition of the Ontario Society of Artists, Tom

Thomson not only entered a canvas, *Northern Lake*, but took first prize and made his first sale. In short, from its personnel and its patrons, to its mission and even its techniques, the Group of Seven had coalesced by 1914 in all but name. Had the group *not* been so well consolidated, it is entirely likely that the disruptions of the Great War, and especially Thomson's accidental death in 1917, would have destroyed it. But for its powerful vision and solidarity, the Algonquin group might easily have been relegated to history as one of many Edwardian relics that had become, like the Canadian Art Club, anachronistic and irrelevant in the postwar world.

DISTINCTLY A CANADIAN PHENOMENON

As it happened, of course, this band of painters, now calling themselves the Group of Seven, re-emerged in the 1920s to not only dominate Canadian landscape painting but to spearhead the "new" Canadian nationalism—a triumph that testifies as much to the cultural continuity of the Great War era as to its better known ruptures.[38] As harbingers of social and cultural change, the Group of Seven proved to be prescient in at least one crucial respect: they were in the vanguard of a recognizably modern nationalist movement that would in the 1920s achieve critical mass and begin to revolutionize Canadians' sense of themselves. This was a nationalist impulse unlike any that had preceded it in Canada. For one thing, it did not hearken back to the theme of empire as had the nationalist dreams of G.M. Grant and others at the turn of the century.[39] After the butchery and sacrifice of the Great War, which Canada had entered as a subordinate "Dominion," even some of the most stalwart Canadian Tories agreed that the time had come to redefine the imperial relationship.[40] The new nationalism was *un*-imperial as well in the sense that it sought to heal the myriad schisms the war effort had caused within Canada, particularly the breach between English and French Canadians caused by conscription. Secondly and more importantly, the nationalists of the 1920s added a potent new cultural component to the post-Confederation economic and political project of "nation-building." As historian Mary Vipond has shown, they perceived a new, highly insidious threat to the Canadian "identity," namely the "'invasion' of Canada by American ideas and values via the mass media." In French Canada, as in English Canada, there emerged a widespread and sometimes hysterical fear in the 1920s that American magazines, radio and especially cinema were carrying "the aggressively material and secular values" of the United States into the homes and the hearts of Canadians.[41] In the absence of a strong imperial tie, fear of American cultural dominance quickly emerged as the defining characteristic of an insular and identity-obsessed strain of modern Canadian nationalism, one that would persist throughout the twentieth century.

As prophets of the new nationalism, the Group of Seven may have exuded all of the superficial optimism of the dawning modern age but, in retrospect, it is clear that they also spoke to some of its more deeply rooted fears and anxieties. At the most obvious level, the Group's celebrated repudiation of European academic traditions accorded perfectly with war-weary Canadians' psychological withdrawal from the realpolitik of the Old World, while their powerful evocation of a vast, virgin wilderness, unsullied by human hands, came as a welcome salve after the claustrophobic barbarity of the trenches. More subtly, but with equally profound implications for Canadians' sense of themselves, the Group of Seven and especially their supporters proclaimed a rugged new, distinctively northern Canadian identity, one that melded aspects of the Norwegians' highly romantic idea of *the North* with Canadians' own historic experience of *the wilderness*. In their evocation of the mystical and spiritual qualities of the northern landscape, they set about to reinterpret the land itself—not merely as a source of creative inspiration but as the well-spring of Canadian youthfulness, strength and virtue in an increasingly commercialized, sickly and effete modern world. As J.E.H. MacDonald suggested in 1919,

> The Canadian spirit in art is just entering on the possession of
> its heritage. It is opening a new world and the Canadian artists
> respond with a spirit that is very good. This world has not the

picture-dealers' tone nor the connoisseurs' atmosphere but it has character attractive to the artists.... The Canadian spirit in art prefers the raw youthful homeliness of Canada to the overblown beauty of the recognized art countries. It aims to fill its landscape with the clear Canadian sunshine and the open air....[42]

It was the responsibility of the artist, said Arthur Lismer, to make Canadians

nationally conscious with our environment, setting the stage for true nationality.... [The] virility and emphatic form of [the land] is reflected in the appearance, speech, action and thought of our people. It is the setting for our development, firing the imagination, establishing our boundaries. It is home land, stirring the soul to aspiration and creation.[43]

Lawren Harris was even more visionary. Comparing Canada to the United States in 1926, he asserted:

We in Canada are in different circumstances.... Our population is sparse, the psychic atmosphere is comparatively clean, whereas the States fill up and the masses crowd a heavy psychic blanket over nearly all the land. We are on the fringe of the great North and its living wilderness, its call and answer—its cleansing rhythms. It seems that the top of the continent is a source of spiritual flow that will ever shed its clarity into the growing race of America, and we Canadians being closest to this source seem destined to produce an art somewhat different from our Southern fellows—an art more spacious, of a greater living quiet, perhaps of a more certain conviction of eternal values.[44]

Here, in this heady mix of myth and history, lay the promise of a modern Canadian nation whose northern virtuosity would transcend both the corrupt decadence of Europe and the crass materialism of the United

States. Here, in a conception of the North that embraced the nation's "two founding races" equally, lay the promise of Wilfrid Laurier's famous dictum that the twentieth century would belong to Canada.

The definitive expression of this extraordinary nationalist vision came from F.B. Housser, self-styled "journalist, art enthusiast and outdoorsman," and author of *A Canadian Art Movement: The Story of the Group of Seven*. First published in 1926 as a popular introduction to the work of Tom Thomson and the Group of Seven, this monograph was reissued in 1974, ostensibly as "a classic in the history of the development of Canadian art."[45] In the decades since its first appearance, Canadian school children have probably put *A Canadian Art Movement* to better use in their projects and essays than any other single book on the subject of art. It is ubiquitous in public and school libraries; and with its highly imaginative, Kiplingesque narrative style, it remains, even now, a remarkably engaging text.

Housser did not mince words: he claimed that nothing of value had been painted by a Canadian before 1910. The dominance of British and European traditions in Canadian painting he called "a millstone about our neck," one that had driven generations of Canada's artists into "voluntary mediocrity." Although Cornelius Kreighoff had shown some promise, according to Housser, Paul Kane's work was merely "historical" and "archaeological," while J.W. Morrice's was "rich in colour, rather sad, moody and poetic; the expression of a man buried in a world of 'art for art's sake.'" Canadian art "authorities" were largely to blame for Canada's dismal artistic past, for they had insisted that "pine trees were unpaintable" while encouraging the public taste for "the softer, mistier and tamer landscapes of the old world." Miraculously, according to Housser, there arose in 1910 a truly Canadian art movement, one that was inaugurated "not by professional painters, but by amateurs who fell in love with the spirit and scenery of our Ontario Northland." They painted without "the mental paraphernalia of academics and without any sense of the solemnity and importance of rules or methods, in pure holiday spirit." These painters, who would go on to form the Group of Seven, were "distinctly a Canadian phenomenon, drawing [their] inspiration from the backwoods" and their influences from the "Aztec and Iroquois rather than [the] Scandinavian or Oriental." As for their aspirations:

> The idea [of painting the Canadian North] was a joint one, nor had it any ulterior motive to promote it other than a wish to make Canada's spiritual life richer. There was naught to be gained either of fame or of money by going to the backwoods and painting in a manner which they knew would be disliked by those who judged their work; nor by launching into an adventure in which they have to this day persisted through ridicule and even slander. They set their conviction against the entire press of the country and the opinion of those whose word was accepted as authoritative in Canada on questions of art. They have encouraged competitors and have consistently refused to be drawn into quarrels.[46]

Although Housser allowed himself a good deal of latitude in interpreting the historical evidence, his fanciful characterization of the Group of Seven is not easily dismissed. Toward the end of *A Canadian Art Movement*, in a tone of uncharacteristic understatement, Housser struck at what was for him the heart of the matter: "I am trying to show that in treatment and technique, the Northern Ontario canvasses by the Group of Seven were dictated by the country itself." Here is nothing less than the essence of the Group of Seven mystique, for even the most restrained Canadian art critics have frequently concurred in Housser's judgement that the finest work of Thomson and the Group evinces "the union of man and place."[47] But Housser went much further, waxing poetic on the North, the wilderness, and the vast potential of what he called the Canadian "race":

> The so-called northern wilderness of Canada has made a fringe of civilization across a continent.... This North is a magnetic land, able to get hold of men.... [T]his land... constitutes by far

the greater portion of the total area of Canada. It is the race's inescapable environment.

"The message that the Group of Seven gives to this age," he continued, "is the message that here in the North has arisen a young nation with faith in its own creative genius." For Housser, the task of painting the Canadian North demanded nothing less than

> a new type of artist; one who divests himself of the velvet coat and flowing tie of his caste, puts on the outfit of the bushwhacker and prospector; closes with his environment; paddles, portages and makes camp.... In Europe the racial spirit clings like pollen to rural-peasant pasture lands and ancient cities. In Canada the race's mood still hovers in space over the natural forms of the wilderness and is 'a thing in itself.' [48]

What makes *A Canadian Art Movement* a truly remarkable text in the annals of Canadian nationalist myth-making is that, for all of its blatant boosterism and chauvinistic excess, its author was, in fact, resigned to the likelihood that his vision of a "distinctly northern" Canada was implausible given the urbanizing and industrializing trends of the modern age. As a conservationist, Housser feared for the very survival of the wilderness in the face of industrial Canada's voracious appetite for raw materials; in this context, his description of the paintings of the Group of Seven assumed a decidedly wistful tone:

> One does not have to throw imagination far into the future to realize that ere long much of what we Canadians now call wilderness will be as myth.... The wilderness is being reclaimed and the forest is making its last stand.... While these pictures live we can never forget our cradle-environment.

At his most pessimistic, Housser saw the paintings of Tom Thomson and the Group of Seven as Canada's "last stand" against modernity itself:

"Their movement is to-day about the only activity in Canada providing encouragement to those who would desire to see our people liberated from the hypnotic trance of a purely industrial and commercial ideal."[49]

Like all informed Canadians, Housser undoubtedly knew that the year 1921 had marked a watershed for Canadian society. In that year the census showed for the first time that a majority of Canadians were urban dwellers. The lives and lifestyles of the urban Canadian middle classes were becoming indistinguishable from those of other North American urbanites; indeed, many of the patterns that characterize urban Canadian life today had, in fact, by this time become well established. Thirty per cent of the Canadian gross national product in 1921, for example, was derived from manufacturing and construction—a proportion that remained more or less constant throughout the twentieth century. For the first time, the number of Canadians employed in the service sector equalled the number in the primary (resource) sector. Fuelled by massive foreign investment, many Canadian-based businesses had by the 1920s consolidated into large corporations whose white-collar employees lived in affluent urban and even suburban neighbourhoods, most notably in Toronto and Montreal. So dramatic was this urbanizing trend—which included the massive migration of wealth as well as people to the cities—that civic officials openly worried in the 1920s about "rural depopulation" and other "rural problems." As for the "wilderness," as Housser well knew, it had long since been integrated as a resource-rich hinterland into the metropolitan centres of Canadian industrial capitalism, complete with the marginalization of aboriginal peoples, the sometimes wholesale destruction of the environment, and the proletarianization of the workforce employed to "extract" and transport its mineral and timber wealth.[50]

For the labourers and farmers who still lived and worked on the land, the North continued to resemble the "malevolent force" that had threatened the very survival of their pioneer forebears. But for the urban middle and upper classes that comprised Canada's primary art market in the 1920s, the Canadian "wilderness" had been transformed into a "playland" of cottages, resorts, children's camps, scenic highways, conservation areas, provincial parks and wildlife preserves. As historian Gerald Killan has shown, urban Ontarians had, in fact, begun as early as the 1880s to recast "nature" as "a place of health and refuge, a sanctuary from urban pressures and ennui." When Algonquin Park was created in 1893, for example, provision was explicitly made for the private cottages and lodges of the Toronto business and professional élite. Similarly, the Forestry Reserve Act of 1898 set aside huge tracts of land in the Temagami, Algoma and Nipigon regions of Ontario, most of which were accessible by train and quickly came to be viewed by wealthy pleasure-seekers as "parklands in all but name." In the 1920s, with the proliferation of automobiles among the Canadian middle class, what had been a trickle of recreational traffic to Ontario's "cottage country" became a torrent. Island and shoreline properties within driving distance of Toronto were gobbled up at such a fierce rate that the Ontario government hastily designated several new provincial parks for public use, including Presqu'ile, Severn River and Franklin Island on Georgian Bay. By 1923, the provincial parks system had become the central component in the government's "tourist development strategy" and an impetus to what Killan describes as "the resort boom of the 1920s." As provincial Lands and Forests minister, James Lyons, noted in 1925, the strategy was a huge success: "[T]he wild life of the parks... their scenic beauty, preserved in its natural state, and varied allurements are being given steady publicity through the press and radio by those who have come and have seen and have conquered."[51]

F.B. Housser and the Group of Seven were themselves part of this new urban recreational class. Their vision of the North may have drawn upon mystical notions of the primeval forest and the lore of wilderness survival, but they experienced the North as tourists. City-born and bred, professionally trained commercial designers, cosmopolitan intellectuals, members of the Arts & Letters Club—the artists who came together in the Group of Seven encountered the Canadian North, not as pioneers, but as "adventurers." Like their bourgeois patrons, including Housser and Dr. MacCallum, they "escaped" Toronto by train and automobile for seasonal sojourns at the cottages, parks and forest reserves of the near-

North, some of them expanding their purview in the late 1920s to include the West and the far North. As so many weekend cottagers, campers and canoe-trippers have done since, they revelled in the romantic fantasy that they "could understand something of the feeling of the early explorers."[52] What is more, despite the oft-repeated claim that the Group of Seven were, in Housser's words, "inspired as the result of a direct contact with Nature herself," it is clear that there was nothing particularly spontaneous or intuitive in their reactions to the North—at least not before they had seen the Scandinavians' work. Writing to his mother in 1910 from Georgian Bay, for example, A.Y. Jackson admitted that he found no inspiration whatsoever in the local scenery: "It is a great country to have a holiday in… but it's nothing but little islands covered with scrub and pine trees, and not quite paintable."[53] In short, for the likes of Jackson, Lawren Harris and J.E.H. MacDonald, the "wilderness" they came to love so dearly was—as it is for so many modern Canadians—a highly idyllic extension of an essentially urban, cosmopolitan experience.[54]

MONUMENTALIZING WILDERNESS

Placing the Group of Seven in the context of evolving ideas about the Canadian wilderness is admittedly a theoretical Pandora's box, given that the metropolis-hinterland relationship has been nothing less than a modern Canadian preoccupation. Scholars, First Nations people, novelists, naturalists, photographers, musicians, politicians and, of course, artists have at one time or another applied themselves to this enormously complex relationship, as they do still. At the heart of this pursuit, it would seem, lies an essential, discomfiting question, not only about the Canadian "identity" but, indeed, about Canadians' "humanity." Historian and environmentalist John Wadland has succinctly framed the question this way:

> Although modern Canadians tend to consider wilderness and culture antithetical notions, as consumers they unite in identifying both with their leisure time—with their recreation…. The linear

historical imagination to which we are heirs has also established and reinforced this assumption that the metropolis spawns and contains our realities. In this context, the wilderness is regarded as an ambiguous, detached, and ultimately romantic space to which we "escape" from the metropolitan reality.... The issue, then, becomes one of ascertaining whether culture can exist solely within extensions of the metropolitan order and as a parasite on wilderness, or whether wilderness, protesting its own diminishment by limiting our material culture, is demanding a voice which we ignore at our peril.[55]

For Wadland and for many other environmentally conscious observers, an essential element of the modern Canadian project of self-definition lies in reconciling, theoretically and if possible politically, Canadians' seemingly incongruous ideas about their relationship to (or within) nature—nature as wilderness, as hinterland, as aboriginal homeland, as cottage playland, nature as something to be commercialized, exploited and ravaged but also preserved, managed and revered. "The *sine qua non* of what we have chosen to identify as Canadian culture," Wadland concludes, "is the wilderness. And on a symbolic level wilderness is the closest we shall ever come to absolute nature."[56]

As Canada's best known and even archetypal visual interpreters of the country's "symbolic wilderness," the Group of Seven tapped directly and powerfully into what had become by the 1920s Canadians' enormous psychic investment in this idea of "absolute nature." Although this investment has since become a more or less permanent feature of the modern Canadian "identity," it is clear that its origins were historically specific. At the risk of distilling a great deal of Canadian art history into a single generalization, it seems obvious in retrospect—strikingly so, in fact—that the Group of Seven monumentalized the rugged beauty of the northern wilderness at precisely the moment when the reality of the wilderness had ceased to be central to the Canadian experience. In marked contrast with the work of their "salon," "Dutch" and even Canadian Art Club predecessors—painters for whom nature was most often a hostile and alien force, something to be tamed and civilized under human occupation—the work of the Group of Seven virtually eradicated the human presence in nature, thus announcing symbolically the end of the historic condition of having to prevail against it. If "nineteenth century" artists like Homer Watson and Horatio Walker had humanized a hostile and violent pre-industrial wilderness by softening it, the Group of Seven idealized the newly pacified modern wilderness by attributing to it a raw, pristine power it had largely ceased to command.

Of the many writers whose thoughts have turned to the paintings of the Group of Seven, two in particular seem to me to have provocatively exposed some of these fundamental tensions. Neither, interestingly, is primarily an art historian or critic. In an extremely dense semiotic analysis of *The Jack Pine*, philosopher and environmental activist Jonathan Bordo has argued that "the key to understanding the new wilderness ethos" that made its first appearance in the work of Tom Thomson and the Group of Seven is "the deliberate and systematic absenting of human presence itself." The paintings lack not only visible human figures but even the "traces" of human presence—the shelters, paths, fences, haystacks and ruins typical of the Western European landscape tradition. In their place we see instead, in works like *The Jack Pine* and *The West Wind*, a rich "symbolic deposit," namely a highly anthropomorphic and even "humanoid" tree figure. What is more, Bordo suggests, the quasi-abstracted, Impressionist-influenced techniques of Tom Thomson and the Group reveal, not an objective pictorial representation of a specific place, but rather a highly subjective record of "the artist's *contact* with the place." Thus, in contrast with the popular notion that Tom Thomson "captured the true likeness of Algonquin [Park] in early autumn," the reverse is true: "Painting surfaces invented Algonquin [Park].... The mimesis is not natural; it is political and social." For Bordo, the social and political price Canadians have paid for this iconography can be seen in the contemporary "piety" of wilderness protocol—"Act in the wilderness as if you were not there"—and, far more tragically, in the "marginalization of aboriginal presence from the land and the disappearance of aboriginal presence from [artistic] representation."[57]

More accessible perhaps but no less critical has been Margaret Atwood's career-long observation of Canadians' encounter with the wilderness, not only in the her epochal *Survival* but in novels such as *Surfacing* and *Cat's Eye* and in short story anthologies such as *Wilderness Tips*. Atwood has a keen and often unforgiving eye for the contradictions of modern Canadian life, and a gift for subverting romantic wilderness myths.[18] In "Death by Landscape," a short story centring on the mysterious disappearance of an adolescent girl while on an overnight canoe trip, Atwood explicitly rejects the conventional, nostalgic view of the work of the Group of Seven in favour of something far more macabre. The story opens with the banality of life at a girls' summer camp, circa 1950. Lucy, the victim, was one of many girls who were "routinely packed off" to "Camp Manitou," one of several "generic" camps in northern Ontario that "favoured Indian names and had hearty, energetic leaders, who were called Cappie or Skip or Scottie." Like the noisy meals, silly nicknames and mock-Indian talk of the camp, the canoe trip on which she vanished was to have been just another routine outing, part of a thoroughly domesticated wilderness experience to which middle class Toronto girls had been subjected for generations. But the disappearance—the arbitrary, merciless and ultimately unfathomable "absenting" of the child, to borrow Bordo's term—disclosed a powerful and ferocious wilderness to which the campers and their leaders had never been exposed and which was, consequently, incomprehensible to them. The child's closest friend at camp, Lois, who had been the last to see her alive, was for the rest of her life both immobilized and obsessed by the seeming irreconcilability of these two wilderness experiences. Incapable of ever returning to the North, even as an adult, she instead filled her Toronto condominium with original paintings by Tom Thomson and the Group of Seven. Atwood writes:

> She wanted something that was in [the paintings].... It was not peace: she does not find them peaceful in the least. Looking at them fills her with a wordless unease. Despite the fact that there are no people in them or even animals, it's as if there is

something, or someone, looking back out…. She looks at the paintings, she looks into them. Every one of them is a picture of Lucy. You can't see her exactly, but she's there, in behind the pink stone island or the one behind that.[59]

On the surface, it would seem that Atwood is here offering the paintings of the Group of Seven as an antidote to the conquered, sanitized and ultimately anthropomorphic experience of wilderness described by Jonathan Bordo. But, of course, the potential of "the wild" to arbitrarily kill and maim has itself been fully integrated into modern Canadian wilderness mythology, most obviously in the form of folklore but also as a key element in Canadians' recreational fantasies. However rarely, people do drown, freeze to death and disappear in the Canadian North; they are occasionally mauled by bears and cougars; and their planes, boats and even snowmobiles do go down in icy waters. This is the stuff, not only of search-and-rescue headlines, but of modern "outdoorsmanship." In white-water rafting, kayak and canoe tripping, mountain climbing, dogsled racing, the tracking and killing of animals (particularly by such "traditional" means as the crossbow) and various other recreational pursuits, pitting oneself *against* nature would appear to be of the essence. As "adventurers" like F.B. Housser have boasted since the late nineteenth century, it is the element of risk that makes the wilderness experience so compelling — even within the relatively tame context of a summer camp. The disappearance of a camper on a canoe trip is itself a clichéd element in a modern urban mythology — it is a time-honoured campfire tale, in fact — and as such, as Atwood well knew when she wrote "Death by Landscape," it is a symptom of the modern condition of wilderness rather than an alternative to it. Such clichés cast wilderness as an adversary — patient, cunning, even vindictive — and hence as an extension of the "protocol" identified by Jonathan Bordo: "Act in the wilderness as if it does not *want* you there." In this context, it is hardly surprising that the "mystery" of Tom Thomson's own "death by landscape" in 1917 has itself become an enduring staple of Canadian folklore.[60]

As F.B. Housser and other supporters of the Group of Seven well knew in the 1920s, the credibility of the "new generation" of Canadian painters—not only as artists but as point men for the new nationalism—would ultimately hinge on the authenticity of their encounter with the wilderness. It would not do, therefore, to simply say that the Group was composed of well-meaning urban romantics in search of adventure, nor would the task of building a new, virile "northern" nation be achieved by any idealistic reworking of Symbolist wilderness mythology. The sheer weight of their nationalist vision demanded something far more powerful and dynamic, something that would truly authenticate the mystical union of the Canadian North and its people. It demanded, in short, not just a new mythology but a mystique. Thus began the posthumous conversion of their modest, soft-spoken friend, Tom Thomson, into one of Canada's most celebrated folk heroes—the "Canadian Paul Bunyan who had," in the words of Robert McMichael, "traded in his axe for a paint brush" and "chopped and carved his paint into wood panels with an intensity and sureness which has no parallel in Canadian art."[61] And thus began the monumentalization of the canvasses of Thomson and the Group of Seven as the essential pictorial representation of the modern Canadian nation.

EPILOGUE

In art as in politics, nationalism can breed orthodoxy. As early as the 1920s, the Group of Seven mystique had become an artistic straightjacket in Canada, its styles and ideology dominating not only the Group's formal successor, the Canadian Group of Painters, but many professional and amateur imitators, and even the work of Emily Carr—the only Canadian landscape artist whose mass popularity in the twentieth century was even remotely comparable to the Group's. Canada's first abstract painter, Bertram Brooker, was rejected in the 1920s by the Toronto art establishment on the grounds that—as the *Canadian Forum* put it—"abstraction is not a natural form of art expression in Canada."[62] Other contemporaries of the Group of Seven, most notably the Montreal native John Lyman, spent their careers reacting against what they perceived as the Group's self-righteous hegemony in Canadian painting, arguing that "the real trail must be blazed towards a perception of the universal relations that are present in every parcel of creation, not towards the Arctic Circle."[63]

The predominant status of the Group of Seven in modern Canadian art history was cemented institutionally in the 1960s, when Robert and Signe McMichael converted their private collection of Thomson and Group of Seven canvasses into the public McMichael Canadian Collection. Like F.B. Housser before them, the McMichaels have not only been single-mindedly devoted to the works of Tom Thomson and the Group of Seven, but insistent that all acquisitions sponsored by themselves (and even their successors) be judged against the nationalist agenda entrenched by these artists. In a striking passage from his memoirs, for example, Robert McMichael has recounted how he and his wife ultimately rejected Colonel R.S. McLaughlin's gift of the famed canvas *After the Bath*, painted in 1890 in Paris by the London, Ontario, native Paul Peel:

> Yet could this painting by a Canadian artist be considered in the *oeuvre* of the artists of our "national school"? Signe and I had always insisted the Collection be dedicated to the pioneers or our artistic nationalism and we, and the government [of Ontario], had agreed it would be confined to their art. The fame and captivating qualities of this unique painting gave us pause and tested our commitment.... We were almost overpoweringly tempted to take the famous and enchanting *After the Bath* into the Collection, but our decision was never really in doubt. We knew in our hearts that accepting it would change the Collection forever. It would no longer be a memorial to our truly national art.[64]

Beginning in the early 1980s, when Robert McMichael gave up active directorship of the Collection (to become Director Emeritus), the gallery endured several highly publicized and rather nasty legal wrangles over the question of its mandate, its leadership and, above all, the right of the McMichaels to continue to determine the suitability of the gallery's acquisitions. In every case, the McMichaels were pitted personally against the Collection's board of trustees (and the Government of Ontario, under whose auspices it operates). In the fall of 1996, the septuagenarian McMichaels took the Province to court alleging that the gallery's trustees had violated the original *raison d'être* of the Collection (as defined by the original 1965 agreement they had concluded with then-premier John Robarts). Judge Peter Grossi ruled in favour of the McMichaels, invoking the full-blown Group of Seven mystique in his judgement: "In my view, the meaning of 'Canadian art' is defined by the context of the Group of Seven and their contemporaries and the indigenous peoples of Canada, in particular the colours, the relationship to nature, to energy and to uncontrollable forces to reflect the expansiveness of their wide horizons."[65] One year later, after a lengthy public relations battle—in which even ordinary Canadians were enlisted by the gallery board in its fight for the principle of unhindered control of the Collection—the Ontario Court of Appeal overturned Grossi's decision, much to the relief of gallery officials and others who had feared that his decision would have established a dangerous precedent allowing donors to meddle in the policies of public institutions.

On 11 June 1998, the Supreme Court of Canada turned down the McMichaels' petition to have their case against the gallery heard, thus ending the couple's twenty-year legal struggle and, with it, the hegemony of the nationalist vision that has been their lives' work.

NOTES

1. Cited in Robert McMichael, *One Man's Obsession* (Toronto: Prentice-Hall, 1986), pp. 151, 160.

2. *McMichael Canadian Art Collection* (http://www.mcmichael.com, March 2003). The Art Gallery of Ontario (Toronto) and the National Gallery (Ottawa) also maintain large Tom Thomson and Group of Seven collections.

3. As art historian Joyce Zemans has shown, the proliferation of inexpensive Thomson/Group of Seven reproductions in the nation's libraries, banks, doctors' offices and especially its classrooms began in the 1920s with a poster project sponsored by the National Gallery of Canada. During World War II, with the endorsement not only of the Gallery but the Department of National Defence, this officially sanctioned campaign to disseminate the work of the Group entered an even more explicitly patriotic phase with the inauguration of what has become known as the Sampson-Matthews silkscreen project. See "Establishing the Canon: Nationhood, Identity and the National Gallery's First Reproduction Program of Canadian Art," *Journal of Canadian Art History* 16:2 (1995), pp. 6–39.

4. John Berger, *Ways of Seeing* (London: Penguin, 1972), pp. 11–16, 135.

5. Scott Watson, "Disfigured Nature: The Origins of Modern Canadian Landscape," in Daina Augaitis, ed., *Eye of Nature* (Banff: Walter Phillips Gallery, 1991), pp. 103–112.

6. Zemans, p. 11.

7. Dennis Reid, *A Concise History of Canadian Painting*, second edition (Toronto: Oxford University Press, 1988), p. 138.

8. Watson writes sardonically: "However much Group of Seven images oppressed school children and government workers, the Group members acted as individual touchstones to the fount of Canadian modernism, as living contacts to the country's unhappy marriage to the twentieth century. Futurism, cubism, constructivism and Dada flourished in Europe amidst modernity's crisis, while Canadians thought modernity was a picture of Algonquin Park." See "Disfigured Nature," p. 108.

9. Cited in John Herd Thompson with Allen Seager, *Canada 1922–1939: Decades of Discord* (Toronto: McClelland and Stewart, 1985), p. 162.

10. Cited in Reid, p. 149; Thompson, p. 162.

11. McMichael, p. 325.

12. Again, Scott Watson: "In an odd way, [the Group] seemed to reckon that the moment the evidence (that is, their inspirational motif) was gone, the paintings would come into their own." See "Disfigured Nature," p. 104.

13. Ibid., p. 102.

14. Cited in Thompson, p. 158.

15. Ibid., p. 158.

16. McMichael, p. 58.

17. Reid, pp. 106–123.

18. Ibid., ch. 9.

19. Ibid., p. 125.

20. Ibid., p. 137.

21. H.H. Arnason, *History of Modern Art,* second edition (New York: Prentice-Hall, 1977), p. 27.

22. Ibid., p. 28.

23. Reid, p. 120.

24. See, for example, Cullen's *Logging in Winter, Beaupré* (1896), or Suzor-Côté's *Settlement on the Hillside* (1909). Thomson's *Sunset Over Hills* (c. 1912), for example, with its dark, well blended tones, its concern with visual depth and, indeed, its overall romantic feel, seems to me quite obviously derivative of the "European" styles decried by the Group.

25. Reid, p. 138.

26. Cited in David Wistow, *The Mystic North* (Toronto: Art Gallery of Ontario, 1983), p. 1.

27. It is clear that the myriad socio-economic advantages enjoyed by the Algonquin Group—education, wealth, prestige, connections, influence—were critical to the postwar success of the Group of Seven. On its own initiative and largely at its own expense, the Group organized over forty exhibitions throughout Canada in the early 1920s, including their famed inaugural show in Toronto; and with the help of their influential friends at the National Gallery, they insinuated themselves into the British Empire Exhibition at Wembley in 1924, where they won the acclaim of the European critics and cemented their stature as a "serious" painting movement.

28. Wistow, p. 1.

29. Reid, pp. 142, 144. In the 1950s, Arthur Lismer confided to Robert McMichael that Varley was never "really attracted to the wild, untamed country which so fascinated the other members of the Group." See McMichael, p. 68.

30. Roald Nasgaard, *The Mystic North: Symbolist Landscape Painting in Northern Europe and North America 1890–1940* (Toronto: University of Toronto Press, 1984), p. 3. For a detailed analysis of the linkages between Symbolism, Impressionism and Post-Impressionism, see ch. 1. Nasgaard interprets the Group's attraction, not to contemporary Scandinavian painters but to an older generation of artists, as indicative of its essential conservatism.

31. Wistow, p. 2.

32. Nasgaard, pp. 4, 165–7, 169.

33. F.B. Housser, *A Canadian Art Movement: The Story of the Group of Seven* (Toronto: Macmillan, 1926), p. 65.

34. Nasgaard, p. 159.

35. Reid, p. 144.

36. Cited in McMichael, p. 100.

37. McMichael, p. 318. See also Zemans, pp. 7–14.

38. Even in 1920 there was nothing inevitable in their rise to pre-eminence in the Canadian art world. The Canadian "Dutchmen," as A.Y. Jackson sardonically called many of his conservative contemporaries, continued to exhibit in Toronto after the war, even as Jackson, Harris and the other Group members continued to pursue their own "revolutionary" agenda.

39. See Carl Berger, *The Sense of Power: Studies in the Ideas of Canadian Imperialism 1867–1914* (Toronto: University of Toronto Press, 1970).

40. In a series of imperial conferences in the 1920s culminating in the passage of the Statue of Westminster in 1931, the global empire Britannia was recast as a "commonwealth of self-governing nations."

41. Mary Vipond, *The Mass Media in Canada*, revised edition (Toronto: Lorimer, 1992), p. 24.

42. Cited in Housser, p. 145.

43. Cited in Nasgaard, p. 166.

44. Cited in ibid., p. 167.

45. Housser, cover jacket.

46. Ibid., pp. 11, 20–4, 146, 210.

47. Reid, p. 145.

48. Housser, pp. 14–15.

49. Ibid., pp. 155–6.

50. Alvin Finkel et al. *History of the Canadian Peoples: 1867 to the Present* (Toronto: Copp Clark Pitman, 1993), pp. 184–205. Called the "New Ontario" by its corporate and political boosters, and aided by what Finkel et al., call an "orgy" of spending on railway branch lines, the area between Sudbury and Hudson Bay saw a four-fold increase in mining operations between 1900 and 1910, and another doubling in the following decade.

51. Gerald Killan, *Protected Places: A History of Ontario's Provincial Parks System* (Toronto: Dundurn, 1993), pp. 10, 20, 30.

52. J.E.H. MacDonald, cited in Nasgaard, p. 163.

53. Cited in ibid., p. 164.

54. The Group's complex role in the articulation and promotion of the "New Ontario" is examined at length in Paul H. Walton, "The Group of Seven and Northern Development," in *RACAR: Revue d'art canadien/Canadian Art Review* 17:2 (1990), pp. 171–9. See also Douglas Cole, "Artists, Patrons and Public: An Inquiry into the Success of the Group of Seven," *Journal of Canadian Studies* 13 (1974), pp. 69–78.

55. John Wadland, "Wilderness and Culture," in Bruce Hodgins and Margaret Hobbs, eds., *Nastawgan: The Canadian North by Canoe and Snowshoe* (Toronto: Betelgeuse, 1985), pp. 223–4.

56. Wadland, p. 226. At Trent University, where I have taught for many years and where John Wadland has spent his teaching career, it would be no exaggeration to say that the exploration of this question, in its myriad political, historical and theoretical permutations, has been the defining characteristic not only of the disciplines of Canadian Studies and Native Studies but of much of the History and Cultural Studies that are taught there.

57. Jonathan Bordo, "*Jack Pine*: Wilderness Sublime or the Erasure of the Aboriginal Presence from the Landscape," *Journal of Canadian Studies* 27: 4 (Winter 1992–3), pp. 98–128. See also Mathew Teitelbaum, "Sighting the Single Tree, Sighting the New Found Land" in Daina Augaitis, ed., *Eye of Nature* (Banff: Walter Phillips Gallery, 1991), pp. 71–88.

58. In "Wilderness Tips," for example, Atwood places a group of trendy contemporary Torontonians at a century-old lodge in northern Ontario. For one of the protagonists, George, the lodge is "a little slice" of an "alien past," thus he treats it "with a tenderness, a reverence, that would baffle those who know him only in the city." Prue, "who in the city is the first with trends," wants "everything in this peninsula to stay exactly the way it has always been," and although she herself "drives like a maniac" she thinks "all those motorboat people should be taken out and shot." See *Wilderness Tips* (Toronto: Bantam, 1996), pp. 183–7.

59. Margaret Atwood, "Death by Landscape," in *Wilderness Tips*, pp. 100–118.

60. Joyce Zemans notes that "the decision to focus upon Thomson [in the National Gallery's first program of reproduction] was clearly a calculated one, likely based on Thomson's already legendary stature as an artist and a folk hero as well as on the popularity of his work." See "Establishing the Canon," pp. 14–15.

61. McMichael, p. 100.

62. Cited in Reid, p. 189. Abstract painting would not rear its head again in Toronto until the 1950s.

63. Cited in ibid., p. 203.

64. McMichael, pp. 245–6.

65. Cited in Aaron Milrad, "What Does the McMichael Collection Do Now?" *Globe and Mail* (26 November 1996), p. A19; and in Thomas Claridge, "McMichael Agreement in Force" *Globe and Mail* (16 November 1996), p. A3.

CHAPTER TWO

DREAM, COMFORT, MEMORY, DESPAIR

CANADIAN MUSICIANS AND
THE DILEMMA OF NATIONALISM

If landscape painting provided the first pretext for aggressive
cultural nationalism in modern English Canada, then pop music provided
the last. State support in the realm of culture prior to World War II did
not extend much beyond the funding of modest archives, museums and
art galleries; thus, as suggested in Chapter One, the cultivation of "the
Canadian spirit in art" tended to rest largely on the largesse of private
patrons and on the enthusiasm of voluntarist, often amateur, arts organizations.[1] Not until the era of the Massey Commission, which released its
ground-breaking *Report* in 1951, did the state begin to engage seriously
in the support and subsidization of Canadian culture. And in surprisingly short order, the creative crucible facilitated by this engagement
began to yield internationally recognized theatre, scholarship, television
programming and journalism. Yet as late as 1970 *Rolling Stone* magazine
observed that, with respect to popular music, Canada was "notorious for
virtual non-support of its own talent."[2] The exodus of Canadian performers to the United States after World War II came to be seen as a great
national loss; critics cited the careers of Guy Lombardo, Percy Faith, the
Diamonds, and especially Paul Anka as evidence of Canada's prolonged
indifference toward popular music. Only in the late 1960s did it become
acceptable, or profitable, for a Toronto folk-singer to write a "Canadian
Railroad Trilogy" or for a Winnipeg rock band to make a hit single out
of "Running Back to Saskatoon." Canadians who came of age in this era
recall with great pride how a soft-spoken teacher from Nova Scotia began
a career of superstardom with a song written in a Prince Edward Island

farmhouse, and how "Four Strong Winds" blew across *their* prairies.[3] They remember that two of the anthems of the "Sixties generation" in North America—"Woodstock" and "Ohio"—were written by introspective folk singers raised in small Canadian towns.

The aim of this chapter is to explore the dynamics of national self-consciousness in English-Canadian popular music during this "golden age," 1968 to 1972. Of special concern is the tension that grew out of the connection of Canadians to the American musical mainstream on the one hand and the mounting pressure Canadian musicians and songwriters faced from the cultural nationalists of the Centennial era on the other. Much of the music written by Canadians in this period seemed to celebrate life in the Dominion and, as is so often the case in periods of intense Canadian nationalism, it criticized the United States. Not far beneath this facile exterior, however, lurked a haunting anxiety about what it meant to be nationalistic. The commercial imperative of the English-language pop music industry was, and remains, a profoundly homogenizing force: even among Canadian musicians who did not relocate to New York or Los Angeles, there was an implicit recognition that success meant cracking the American market. Canadian musicians traveled widely in the United States and recognized that there were a good many Americans unhappy with the social and political *status quo*; they recognized as well that Canada was not without problems of its own. Underscoring this ambivalence, above all, was the pervasive influence upon their music of what were quintessentially American musical styles and lyrical themes. I argue that the emergence of mature, politically sensitive and broadly accessible Canadian popular music in this era had less to do with homage to Canadian geographical and historical landmarks than with the extent to which it had co-opted and preserved an earlier American folk-protest tradition.

GETTING INTO THE PATRIOTISM BAG

In the mid-1950s, when most learned Canadians believed the only music worthy of study was "serious" or "high brow," choral leader Leslie Bell observed that "the endless 'pop' tunes that are born and buried each month play a vital part in Canada's life and, despite their frequent lack of musical worth, offer a valuable index to her habits, customs and ways of thinking." Although unimpressed by the continental phenomenon by then known as the "Hit Parade," mainly because it tended to have an homogenizing effect on youth in all North American urban centres, Bell revered the rural Canadian folk traditions in which one could find "a truly independent national taste." Don Messer in Prince Edward Island, "singing cowboys" like Wilf Carter and Hank Snow, square dances on the prairies, and the traditionally isolated folk traditions of Quebec and Newfoundland—these were the last bastions of musical distinctiveness in Canada. But even these, Bell despaired, echoing the Massey Commission, were "losing ground against the onslaught of American radio."[4]

For the most part, of course, "American radio" was also homogenizing whatever American regional traditions had persisted into the age of the electric guitar. The Jeremiahs of the rock-and-roll age in the United States were themselves busy lashing out against pop music's "lack of musical worth" as well as against Elvis Presley's lasciviousness. Canadian and American suspicions of this new music differed, however, on at least one level. For some Canadians there was something additionally troubling about the fact that the sound, the styles, and the records themselves were American. Here was further evidence, in this era of accelerated continental integration, of Canada's incapacity to resist the mass culture of the United States. A recent textbook on post-war Canada has made the sardonic but not altogether misguided point that some Canadians breathed a sigh of relief when Paul Anka's "Diana" proved that "they could do it too."[5] In such differing responses the first stirrings of the ambivalence that would later permeate the Canadian popular music industry can be seen; however, as the authors of this text were quick to add, in Canada "no one cared very much." Voices like Leslie Bell's cried in the wilderness.

The year 1967 was Canada's Centennial and, just as Confederation had been consolidated in part out of antipathy for the "noisy" republic to the south, Canadians expressed their celebration of this anniversary in terms of the relief they felt at not being part of the United States. Canadians recoiled when ghettos in Newark and Detroit exploded into violence that summer, when the Tet Offensive of February 1968 revealed the futility of the Vietnam War, and when Robert F. Kennedy and Martin Luther King, Jr. were gunned down the following spring. Lyndon B. Johnson's popularity as president slipped to an all-time low just as, on a wave of jubilant nationalism, Pierre Trudeau was elected Prime Minister. Even the youth of America looked to Trudeau's Canada to harbour draft evaders and lead the crusade to liberalize marijuana laws. Canadian journalist Alexander Ross exclaimed that "[h]undreds of young Americans, not all draft-dodgers by any means, are pouring across the border in search of a simpler, cleaner alternative to The American Way. The word is out that a country that can produce a poet as great as Leonard Cohen and a politician as groovy as Pierre Trudeau must know something Americans don't."[6] That the border was indeed open to what one Canadian writer has called "American refugees from militarism"[7] helped to entrench the notion that Canada was pacifistic. Thoughtful Canadians recognized that, in truth, their government had done nothing to curb Canadian participation in the production of arms destined for South-East Asia and that its selective admission of fleeing Americans mimicked the class inequalities of the draft.[8] Nonetheless, Vietnam was not their war. Hawks were few in Canada and, in the liberal press, the war in Indochina served as a useful measure of the distance toward self-serving unilateralism the United States had traveled in the postwar era. Some outspoken Canadian critics of "American imperialism" openly associated the plight of the Vietnamese with their own struggle against economic and cultural domination by the United States.

The nationalist surge in both English Canada and Quebec in the late 1960s was the beginning of the end of Canadian indifference toward popular music. Along with the Liberal government's attempted crackdown on foreign ownership in Canada came the imposition by the Canadian Radio-Television Commission (CRTC) of a quota system for radio broadcasting. Commencing in January 1971, the CRTC ruled, 30 per cent of the radio programming in Canada must qualify as "Canadian content" (or "Cancon"), that is, it must be written, performed or produced in Canada. This policy opened the recording industry to Canadian talent as nothing had done previously, and a great scramble to build record companies and to sign artists followed. Many musicians who came to be identified with the nationalism of this era—Bruce Cockburn and Murray McLaughlin, for example—owed the relative ease with which they broke into the industry to this regulation. The Juno Awards, named after CRTC president Pierre Juneau and based upon equally strict Canadian-content criteria, were also founded at this time.

Paradoxically, the CRTC's Cancon regulations were something of a mixed blessing for Canadian performers. Perhaps unexpectedly, Canadian content quotas fostered a keen awareness in the Canadian pop music industry of the limitations of nationalism, one that would, as I shall argue in the next chapter, have decisive implications for the evolution of the recording industry in this country. Most obviously, Canadian artists did not want their success to appear to be due solely to the meddling of the government. Musicians of every stripe attempted to dispel the perception that they had a nationalist axe to grind or, worse, that their work was somehow officially sanctioned. It was widely known, for example, that prior to 1970 Anne Murray had identified very closely with her maritime Canadian roots. As Jon Ruddy of *Maclean's* pointed out, only this could explain why she had "languished" for several years in the chorus of CBC's "Singalong Jubilee."[9] It was Gene McClellan's "Snowbird" (1970) that made Murray the favoured child of Canadian pop music critics, for unlike Joni Mitchell and Neil Young, they said, she had not forgotten the way back home from the United States. Laudatory articles like John Macfarlane's "What If Anne Murray Were an American?" abounded.[10] Only two years later, however, by which time she had moved to an exclusive Toronto suburb and had begun to savour enormous success in the American market, Murray reflected: "I don't like being used by journalists. You know, as some kind of a national symbol. I'm an entertainer. I just want to share some joy with other people. That's all."[11]

Gordon Lightfoot's cool attitude toward Canadian-content rules was no secret in the burgeoning Canadian record industry. In 1971, he told

Robert Markle: "Well, the CRTC did absolutely nothing for me, I didn't want it, I didn't need it, absolutely nothing… and I don't like it. They can ruin you, man. Canadian content is fine if you're not doing well. But I'm in the music business and I have a huge American audience. I'm going to do Carnegie Hall for the second time. I like to record down there, but I like to live up here. I really dig [Canada], but I'm not going to bring out any flags."[12] Nevertheless, the fact remained that Lightfoot was a pioneer in the Canadian popular music industry and a hero to cultural nationalists precisely because he wrote affectionately about his homeland and did not take up residence in the United States. In a calmer moment that same year he admitted: "I guess there was a Canadian flavour, a Canadian feeling to my music. And the 'Canadian Railroad Trilogy' exemplified it."[13] *Maclean's* correspondent Courtney Tower concurred, noting that nationalism seemed by 1970 to be a defining aspect of the burgeoning Canadian music scene: "Canadian pop songs, contrary to the notions of most adults, don't deal exclusively with sex, drugs and the hassles of adolescent love. Many recent lyrics are, in the words of Ian Tyson of Ian and Sylvia 'getting into the patriotism bag.' Increasingly, composer-performers such as Tyson, Gordon Lightfoot, Neil Young (of Crosby, Stills, Nash and Young) and Robbie Robertson (of The Band) are producing songs that celebrate a fresh awareness of Canada."[14]

One of the few Canadian artists to admit openly that he had benefited from Canadian content quotas (and that he had received a Canada Council grant) was Bruce Cockburn. Even so, he felt compelled, like the others, to put as much distance as possible between his music and overt political nationalism. Cockburn's debut album was the inaugural release of Bernie Finkelstein's True North Records, a production company established to promote Canadian talent under the CRTC umbrella. It earned such dubious compliments as Toronto music pundit Peter Goddard's observation that "radio's new appetite for Canadian music has created for Bruce Cockburn an audience that it took Gordon Lightfoot years to gather."[15] In 1971 Cockburn told journalist Ritchie York: "I'm a Canadian, true, but in a sense it's more or less by default. Canada is the country I dislike the least at the moment. But I'm not really into nationalism—I prefer to think of myself as being a member of the world.... The Canadian music scene is not yet as rotten as the US scene. But it's showing signs of catching up."[16]

It is apparent in retrospect that Canadian musicians were attempting to distance themselves not only from the protective shield of government regulations but also from the intensely nationalist music media in Canada. Critics like William Westfall of *Canadian Forum* and Jack Batten and John Ruddy, both of *Maclean's*, had been adamant in 1968 and 1969 about the need to check "derivativeness" in Canadian pop music. They argued that everything about Canadian music, from rock festivals to programming at CHUM in Toronto, was a shallow, predictable imitation of American sources.[17] Typical of this hostility was a November 1969 article by Ruddy entitled "How To Become A Rock Star Without Really Trying." Its subtitle read, "Your First Move? Get With The 'Canadian' Music Scene: It's as Yankee as Dylan and Drive-ins."[18] Having lobbied for federal legislation to bolster the demand for Canadian pop music, the critics were euphoric about the CRTC's Canadian-content regulations. They did not fancy themselves "protectionists" but they had come to realize that subtle persuasion and even threats of regulation were having no impact on Canadian broadcasters.[19]

As the critics well knew, the government had intervened in Canadian music at precisely the moment young Canadian songwriters had begun to respond lyrically to the political crises that were arising in the United States. No sooner had Pierre Juneau been made the Canadian recording industry's man of the year for 1970 than a song by a Canadian rock band made *Billboard*'s Number One position for the first time. The song was the Guess Who's "American Woman" and it featured the ostensibly anti-American refrain:

American woman, stay away from me
American woman, let me be
I don't need your war machines
I don't need your ghetto scenes.[20]

Life in this instance appeared to copy art.

THE AMERICAN FOLK-PROTEST TRADITION

In the 1950s and even the early 1960s Canadian musicians knew that they had no chance of breaking into the Top 40 in the American-controlled music industry with songs that challenged the social and political *status quo*. Any doubt about the importance of conformity and the need to avoid controversy, especially in the form of criticizing the capitalist ethos that ruled the pop music business, was put to rest in 1963 when the American television network ABC blacklisted veteran folk-singer Pete Seeger from its national music show.[21] "Protest" singers who could fill university coffee houses night after night had trouble getting recording contracts and, in any case, they were simply not welcome on the tightly controlled playlists of AM radio stations. Canadians, like aspiring American and British performers, quickly learned the lesson that kept rock-and-roll free of disruptive folk influences: Top 40 pop stars did not bite the hand that fed them. As critic John Orman has suggested, rock-and-roll served to "maintain the status quo by diverting people from serious political thought."[22] How, then, did Canadians come to be writing hit songs like "American Woman" less than a decade later?

Even though protest musicians had faced extraordinary pressures from the recording industry, their music was sufficiently powerful and popular to chip away at the hegemony of the repetitive, conformist pop music of the Hit Parade. Led by Seeger and especially Woody Guthrie, a handful of left-leaning American folk singers persevered courageously through the barren years of McCarthyism and emerged in the late 1950s as heroes to a generation of North American youth that challenged post-war conformity in all of its manifestations. American music critics agree that the origins of the politically inspired music of the Vietnam era in the United States lay squarely in the Seeger/Guthrie tradition.[23] Much in the Canadian folk movement of the 1960s can also be traced to this source as well. Resurgent interest in the protest songs of the 1950s prompted the release of several commercial recordings beginning in 1958 — *Pete Seeger* (1958), *Ballads of Sacco and Vanzetti* (1960), *Dustbound Ballads* (1964) — to which Canadians had relatively easy access. Asked in 1971 what his formative musical influences had been, Gordon Lightfoot recalled listening to "folk music, things by Pete Seeger and Bob Gibson," after studying music in California in the late 1950s.[24]

Like most of the American "folkies" of the 1960s, however, Canadian singer-songwriters were heirs to the Guthrie/Seeger tradition through a crucial conduit, Bob Dylan. From an adolescence of Top 40 rock-and-roll, writes folk music historian Jerome L. Rodnitzky, Dylan "picked up the mantle of Woody Guthrie and carried protest songs to new heights of popularity and power."[25] More than this, adds John Orman, he "liberated the lyrics of rock music."[26] Dylan's influence on American folk, rock and pop music in the mid-1960s was nothing less than revolutionary, for, in contrast to Seeger's experience, his favoured place in the recording industry gave him access to an enormous audience. In Canada, where there had been no indigenous tradition of politically motivated folk music, his influence was nothing short of formative. Neil Young recalls trading in his Gretsch electric guitar for a twelve-string acoustic in the summer of 1965 under the sway of Dylan and others who had turned to folk, and virtually all other Canadian "folkies" spoke of similar experiences.[27] Always eloquent, Bruce Cockburn described his perception of the impact that the American folk tradition had upon Canada:

> When you're young, you tend to act out roles with a passion and our role in Ottawa in the 1960s was to be folkies and to sing mostly the folksongs of other countries. The problem with Canadian songs is that they borrowed so heavily from other traditions; for instance logging songs set to English ballads. Sure, this happened in the States, too, but they went on to develop the borrowings with the vigour and violence of their experience. They "exploded" the traditions and we never did. So, if you examine traditional Canadian songs, you won't find anything applicable to today.... [B]ecause social developments in the States always happened a generation before they did in Canada, we soon began borrowing the social commentary and the songs that went with it.[28]

Since the 1960s, scholars and lay critics of popular music have debated the relationship between "folk" and "rock" music. This distinction is crucial to understanding the development of Canadian popular music in the Centennial era. For Rodnitzky, a Guthrie/Seeger purist, Dylan's significance as a "folk" singer was on the wane by 1963 precisely because he had electrified folk music and forced its accommodation to the commercial standards of AM rock radio. When folk music became "folk-rock," argues Rodnitzky, "mood replaced message" and eventually the explicit social or political meaning of the folk tradition was lost to a feeling of "general alienation and a hazy, nonconformist aura." The "assimilation" of protest music into rock was all the more "sad" because it had been "gradual and practically unnoticed."[29] Orman is not as pessimistic about the superficiality of rock music in the mid- and late 1960s, seeing in much of the politically inspired music of performers like the Jefferson Airplane, Jimi Hendrix and Janis Joplin the social awareness of the earlier folk movement.[30] In any case, both Rodnitzky and Orman would agree with Carl Beltz that, by the "troubled period" of 1969 to 1971, popular music in America had become "disillusioned, directionless [and] plagued by uncertainty about its own identity."[31]

The superficial integration of protest themes in rock music is nowhere more obvious than in the Guess Who's "American Woman." Ritchie York may have been correct when he wrote in 1971 that the Guess Who had done more for Canadian music than anything in history.[32] But the truth was, as *Rolling Stone* continually reminded its readers, they had done so at the expense of originality.[33] Burton Cummings, the lead singer and primary songwriter of the Winnipeg band, recognized that there was nothing "intrinsically Canadian" in its music: "We weren't influenced by anything except a rehash of North Dakota AM radio."[34] "American Woman" was not conceived as a political statement in the Seeger/Dylan folk style; it arose spontaneously during a jam session, a product of Cummings's "[b]ubblegum instinct for the quick, ordinary, foolishly memorable phrase."[35] Any doubt about the ephemerality of the song was put to rest in the summer of 1970 when the Guess Who accepted an invitation to play at the White House, agreeing to omit

"American Woman" from the performance. Bassist Jim Kale later explained: "We're not American, so we don't get involved in American politics.... We're anti-war, of course, but the Vietnam War isn't Richard Nixon's war. He didn't start it. He simply inherited it." Kale added, "Neil Young told me we shouldn't play [the White House] at all." [36]

Jerome Rodnitzky has dissected the protest music of Woody Guthrie and concluded that he was "essentially a piece of rural Americana reacting to the Depression." The social issues in his music were clear and simple, and the protest it expressed was always explicit. That rurality and directness were the defining features of this folk music seems indisputable, he argues, since the predominantly urban Sixties generation found it "corny, simplistic and irrelevant." [37] The increasingly anachronistic character of the Guthrie tradition helps to explain why folk artists like Phil Ochs, who refused to follow Dylan's shift toward amplified, commercial music and "hazy" lyrics, failed to maintain popularity through the 1960s. The youth of an increasingly complex and urban United States gravitated toward commercial musical forms because commerciality characterized the world in which they lived.

By and large, this characterization of the folk/rock dichotomy has held sway in popular music criticism, though most scholars are less likely than Rodnitzky to see the two camps as wholly separate. Myrna Kostash has applied the same typology to the Canadian context: "Folk music, by definition, is rooted in particularity, in locales and events and personalities which are historically specific and are *named*, and the singer-songwriter was valued precisely for the individuality and personality s/he brought to the corpus of the tradition.... But rock music was part of a continental culture produced by and distributed from the commercial and political centres of North America (that is, the United States) which, because of their metropolitan and corporate character, were deemed to be of universal significance and value." [38] Admittedly very much a product herself of the Sixties generation in Canada, about which she is both critical and nostalgic, Kostash is vigilant in her differentiation of Canadian "folk singers" — Ian and Sylvia, Gordon Lightfoot, Buffy Sainte-Marie — from pop and rock music. The evidence suggests, however, that any hard definition of the distinction between folk and pop music obscures more than it illuminates about Canadian music in the late 1960s and early 1970s.

Rurality, directness and simplicity were, indeed, the cornerstones of Canadian folk music; but these qualities were also evident in much of the pop and rock music written by Canadians who had crossed over from folk in the late 1960s. Even *Rolling Stone* observed in 1968 that a common feature of Canadian rock bands was that they "have their country roots showing."[39] Canadian musicians seem not to have abandoned the folk themes they had co-opted from Woody Guthrie and Bob Dylan, even when Guthrie had become old-fashioned and Dylan had strapped on an electric guitar. For musicians like Gordon Lightfoot, Bruce Cockburn, Neil Young and Joni Mitchell, folk was a medium perfectly suited to express what they, as Canadians, were seeing in the world around them. Cockburn attempted to articulate this impulse in 1972:

> I think a lot of the songs that are being written are distinctively, if not obviously, Canadian. Playing something close to American music but not of it. I think it has something to do with the space that isn't in American music. Buffalo Springfield had it. Space may be a misleading word because it is so vague in relation to music, but maybe it has to do with Canadians being more involved with the space around them rather than trying to fill it up as Americans do. I mean physical space and how it makes you feel about yourself. Media clutter may follow. All of it a kind of greed. The more Canadians fill up their space the more they will be like Americans. Perhaps because our urban landscapes are not yet deadly, and because they seem accidental to the whole expanse of the land.[40]

Writing in the mid-1970s, Myrna Kostash was suspicious of the "back to the land" movement that characterized the Sixties counterculture, calling it "essentially nostalgic" and even "American."[41] But, in truth, Canadian musicians betrayed a deeply rooted reverence for rural life and for natural ecology at this time, so much so that these values were commonly identified as "Canadian" and juxtaposed with "urban" America (a term that had not yet come to be synonymous with "Black"). This attitude was not mere romanticism; it was based on experience. Gordon Lightfoot, for example, grew up in Orillia, Ontario and identified himself throughout the 1960s with small-town simplicity in songs like "Did She Mention My Name" and "Pussywillows, Cat-Tails." Although Lightfoot was reputed to have selected folk music for mercenary rather than artistic reasons, the fact remains that his music drew heavily on the explicitness of the folk-protest tradition and even, occasionally, on the "confessional" singer-songwriter tradition. In 1968, for example, he wrote a personal musical memoir describing his increasing alienation as he traveled from Toronto via Albany to New York City. "Cold Hands From New York" documented the myriad social problems of large urban centres in the United States—poverty, isolation, street violence; it also featured one of the first references in Canadian music to the Vietnam War:

> There were men who lived in style
> And others who had died
> Where no one knew them
> 'Cause they couldn't win.[42]

Like many young Canadians, Lightfoot had gone to New York "to find what I'd been missin'" and found it instead "unreal."

Bruce Cockburn's music was rooted in a profound love of the Canadian wilderness. Though raised in an Ottawa suburb, Cockburn's childhood fondness for his grandfather's farm and his far-reaching tours of rural Canada as a young man solidified his affinity for nature. "I prefer the country to the city," he remarked in 1972, "because I feel better there and I like myself better there."[43] Cockburn abandoned an early career in rock music and some dabbling in jazz for introspective folk music, making a name for himself by performing the soundtrack to the acclaimed Canadian film *Going Down the Road* and by writing songs like "Going to the Country." Like Lightfoot, Cockburn's experiences of urban America had been troubling. During a year at Boston's Berklee School of Music, he claimed to have developed an intense distrust of America and a "sensitivity to the atmospheric tension so that he could tell, even in his sleep, when his bus had crossed the border to the States."[44] The Canadian musicians who had moved to the United States and "forgotten the way home" expressed similar sentiments. Neil Young was raised in Omemee, a rural village outside Peterborough, Ontario, and as a high school student aspired to attend the agricultural college at Guelph and become a farmer.[45] He left Canada to pursue a career in music because he was "fed up with the Canadian scene" in the late 1960s, but by all accounts he was never comfortable—as a young man at least—with life in America. Young's second solo album, *Everybody Knows this is Nowhere* (1969), was "about the need for and the impossibility of escape from Los Angeles."[46] Escape, for Young, meant Canada. In 1970, at the height of his "rock" success with the supergroup Crosby, Stills, Nash and Young, he retreated to rural Ontario to contemplate his recent divorce. There he wrote one of his most plaintive country-folk songs, "Helpless," about a town where

> There's dream, comfort, memory, despair
> And in my mind I still need a place to go.... [47]

Though not identified as explicitly with rural life *per se*, Joni Mitchell's concern for environmental issues in songs like "Big Yellow Taxi" (1970) established her reputation as a singer of unusual "innocence."[48] It was rumoured in late 1969 that Mitchell had become so deeply alienated by the American music industry that she was retiring to her home town, Saskatoon, to paint and write poetry.[49] Earlier that year she described her attitude toward life in the United States: "It's good to be exposed to politics and what's going [on] down here, but it does damage to me. Too much of it can cripple me. And if I really let myself think about it—the violence, the sickness, of it all—I think I'd flip out."[50]

This reverence for "space" and the need to be able to escape from the "crippling" effects of life in urban America did not, however, find expression as simplistic anti-Americanism in the music of these young Canadians. For all that they disliked and feared in the United States of the turbulent 1960s, they recognized that there were many Americans—not all of them members of the Counterculture—who shared their estrangement. They also knew that Canada was no Utopia, that it was naive to look to life in Canada, or to any rural myth, as a panacea for the ills of the United States. These conflicting impulses produced a remarkable ambivalence in the protest music Canadians wrote: they were able to judge life in America from the vantage point of the outsider and the insider simultaneously, blending toughness and sympathy in a way that was unique to the American music scene.

In 1968, the same year that he wrote "Cold Hands From New York," Gordon Lightfoot wrote and recorded what was, in retrospect, the best song about the Detroit race riots of 1967. "Black Day in July" was a song of explicit social criticism in the tradition of Pete Seeger, expressing Lightfoot's sympathy for American Blacks driven out of desperation to violence. With his usual flair for history, he recognized that the origins of the trouble lay in the distant past:

> Black day in July
> And the soul of Motor City is bared across the land
> And the book of law and order is taken in the hands
> Of the sons of the fathers who were carried to this land.

Though explicit lyrically, this song betrays none of the superficial self-righteousness of "American Woman." Lightfoot indicted those who believed they could remain aloof to the crisis, adding the verse:

> The printing press is turning and the news is quickly flashed
> And you read your morning paper and you sip your cup of tea
> And you wonder just in passing, is it him or is it me?[51]

"Black Day in July" was, predictably, ignored by AM radio in the United States but "underground" FM stations gave it wide coverage and American music critics cited it as an important contribution to the American protest tradition.[52]

The best-known protest song of Bruce Cockburn's early career was, ironically enough, produced in a pop, rather than folk, style. "It's Going Down Slow" (1971) opened with a graphically anti-war verse, about the loss of Asian "pawns," set to a bouncy piano rhythm. But for the closing refrain, Cockburn slowed the song down to an almost hymnal pace, a powerful expression of his Christian-pacifist conviction that corruption and warfare were not unique to the United States but common to humanity:

God damn the hands of glory that hold the bloody firebrand high…
Let the world retain in memory that mighty tongues tell mighty lies
And if mankind must have an enemy let it be his warlike pride.[53]

Perhaps the most poignant example of a Canadian's capacity to write with ambivalence about American society in the Vietnam era is to be found in Joni Mitchell's "The Fiddle and the Drum" (1969). Though not a "hit," this song expressed the pathos and the confusion felt by those who believed they were seeing the "good" in the United States turn inexplicably to aggression. Typically, Mitchell's poetic lyrics spoke volumes:

Oh, my friend, how did you come to trade the fiddle for the drum?
… we can remember all the good things you are
And so we ask you, please, Can we help you find the peace and the star?[54]

Of the many protest songs of the Vietnam era, no doubt Neil Young's "Ohio" was, and remains, the best known. On 4 May 1970, Ohio National Guardsmen killed four students at Kent State University during a rally to protest president Nixon's decision to invade Cambodia. Though remarkably passive in interviews, Young must have been enraged. Although he had no history of writing protest music, by 21 May Crosby, Stills, Nash and Young were in the studio recording "Ohio":

Tin soldiers and Nixon's coming...
This summer I hear the drumming
Four dead in Ohio.[55]

Although it was banned on many radio stations, "Ohio" had instant appeal among American youth, stirring Vice President Spiro Agnew to a speech denouncing rock music.[56] Asked about the genesis of the song a month after its release, David Crosby chided, "Neil surprised everybody. It wasn't like he set out to write a protest song. It's just what came out of having Huntley-Brinkley for breakfast."[57] Young himself was just as vague: "I don't know; I never wrote anything like this before but there it is...."[58]

In the end, it was the natural affinity of Canadians for the American folk tradition and their uniquely ambivalent perception of American society, not anti-Americanism, that accounted for their remarkable ascendance as heroes of the Counterculture. Canadians did not simply offer a foreigner's critique of American society — this kind of parochialism would only have alienated them from their American audience. Rather, they had preserved in their music the explicitness, sensitivity and vitality of a protest tradition that was, in its essence, American.

CONCLUSION

In the half-decade after Canada's Centennial year, Canadian popular musicians were at odds with the concept of "cultural nationalism." Some left the country — "fled" was the term most often used in the nationalist Canadian music press — and were, therefore, spared much of the sentimental praise that accrued to those who stayed. For the likes of Anne Murray, Gordon Lightfoot and Bruce Cockburn, the pressure to be "Canadian" was unceasing and often stultifying. More than most Canadians listening to their music perhaps, these artists had become, by virtue of the music business itself, "members of the world." However grateful they may have been for Cancon regulations that allowed them a greater opportunity of success in the music business, they were frustrated by the tensions inherent in being national symbols as well as artists; and however proud they may have been to be Canadian, intimate contact with the United States and the world at large had sharpened their awareness of the limitations of nationalism.

With the notable exception of Bruce Cockburn, Canadian musicians by 1972 had followed the American lead and abandoned political and social themes altogether. Joni Mitchell, Gordon Lightfoot and Anne Murray integrated thoroughly into mainstream American pop, producing no fewer than ten hits each in the following decade-and-a-half, no mean feat in an industry renowned for producing "one hit wonders."[59] Of these three, Mitchell proved to be by far the most musically innovative, stretching herself to incorporate traditional jazz in the 1970s and even synth-pop in the 1980s. Neil Young's career eclipsed for a time after his resounding success as a solo artist in the early 1970s, but after some dabbling in electronic and even rock-a-billy styles, he returned in the mid-1980s to his country roots and in the early 1990s inspired a new generation of "grunge" rockers led by Nirvana. As the CRTC and others had hoped, Canadian-content rules opened the doors of the music industry to many Canadians in the 1970s and beyond. From Bachman-Turner Overdrive and Bryan Adams to Céline Dion and Shania Twain, however, this legacy has been largely one of conformity to American pop standards.

In light of the homogenizing power of the North American popular music business, Bruce Cockburn's ceaseless dedication to social action in the years since "It's Going Down Slow" is truly remarkable. His inimitable acoustic sound has been broadened to include searing electric guitars and tough percussive rhythms, and Cockburn himself has made the transition from the country to the "inner city front" and back again. Yet, if anything, his life and his music have become not less but more political. His travels in the 1980s included a lengthy stay at a refugee camp on the Honduran border of Nicaragua, on which he based much of his *Stealing Fire* album, and concerts in British Columbia in aid of Haida land claims in the Queen Charlotte Islands. In the turbulent 1990s, Cockburn sponsored innumerable social causes in Canada and played a leading role in the Canadian campaign to ban landmines. Although he still lives in Canada and frequently lashes out at what he perceives as inhumane American policies, his accusation that neo-conservative Canada is "open for business like a cheap bordello" suggests that he is no more likely than in 1970 to embrace narrow political nationalism.[60]

Following the lead of the British pop music industry and the inspiration of Bob Geldof in particular, Canadian musicians assembled in Toronto in February 1986 to perform "Tears Are Not Enough" in aid of African famine relief. With uncharacteristic sentimentality and patriotism, Canadians beamed when their old favourites, led by Gordon Lightfoot, collaborated on the opening verse. This was more than a charitable gathering; it was, as the CBC's commercially-released film production of the session evinced, a celebration of the Canadian pop music tradition, and a triumph of nationalism. Canadians may have known that several of the "Northern Lights" were American citizens and that David Foster had, in fact, written the tune for "Tears Are Not Enough" originally to be used as a love theme in an American movie. But no one let on. Like the music media that had criticized the Canadian performers who left the country in the late 1960s and deified those who remained, Canadians rallied momentarily around a mythic nationalism, a sentiment of such power that it could, even in the cynical, selfish 1980s, suspend disbelief. The significance of the closing sequence in the CBC film was not that beleaguered Ethiopia was receiving lifesaving wheat but that the wheat was Canadian. Perhaps this is why Bruce Cockburn, still as sensitive to political opportunism in Canada as he was during the "golden age" of Canadian pop music, chose to stay in Europe over the winter of 1986.

NOTES

1. See Maria Tippett, *Making Culture: English-Canadian Institutions and the Arts before the Massey Commission* (Toronto: University of Toronto Press, 1990).

2. Juan Rodriguez, "Jesse Winchester's Trip to Canada," *Rolling Stone* (19 March 1970).

3. Myrna Kostash reminisces about Ian Tyson's "Four Strong Winds" in *Long Way from Home: The Story of the Sixties Generation in Canada* (Toronto: Lorimer, 1980), p. 138.

4. Leslie Bell, "Popular Music," Ernest MacMillan, ed., *Music in Canada* (Toronto: University of Toronto Press, 1955).

5. Robert Bothwell, Ian Drummond and John English, *Canada Since 1945: Power, Politics and Provincialism* (Toronto: University of Toronto Press, 1981), p. 174.

6. Alexander Ross, "Colour Them Big Pink," *Maclean's* (February 1969), p. 57. See also Ritchie York, "I'd Rather Be Burned in Canada," *Rolling Stone* (13 December 1969).

7. Renee G. Kasinsky, *Refugees from Militarism: Draft-Age Americans in Canada* (New Brunswick: Transaction Books, 1976).

8. See, for example, "What American Involvement in Vietnam is Doing to Canadian Business," *Financial Post* (14 October 1967); Ian Adams, Lamar Carson and Goffredo Parise, "Our War," *Maclean's* (February 1968); and Walter Stewart, "Proudly We Stand the 'Butcher's Helper' in Southeast Asia," *Maclean's* (May 1970).

9. Jon Ruddy, "The Pit and the Star," *Maclean's* (November 1970), p. 43.

10. John Macfarlane, "What If Anne Murray Were an American?" *Maclean's* (May 1971).

11. Anne Murray, cited in Bill Howell, "Upper Canada Romantic," *Maclean's* (May 1972). "Snowbird" reached the Number Eight position on the Billboard chart in 1970.

12. Gordon Lightfoot, cited in Robert Markle, "Early Morning Afterthoughts," *Maclean's* (December 1971).

13. Gordon Lightfoot, cited in Ritchie York, *Axes, Chops and Hot Licks* (Edmonton: Hurtig, 1971), p. 81.

14. Courtney Tower, "The Heartening Surge of a New Canadian Nationalism," *Maclean's* (February 1970).

15. Peter Goddard, "A Maple Leaf on Every Turntable Means Made-In-Canada Pop Stars," *Maclean's* (November 1970).

16. Bruce Cockburn, cited in York, *Axes, Chops and Hot Licks*, p. 56.

17. See, for example, Jack Batten, "Canada's Rock Scene: Going, Going…," *Maclean's* (February 1968); William Westfall, "Pop Counter-Revolution?" *Canadian Forum* (August 1969); and Jon Ruddy, "How to Become a Rock Star Without Really Trying," *Maclean's* (November 1969).

18. Ruddy, "How to Become a Rock Star."

19. Ritchie York was especially critical of Canadian broadcasters. See *Axes, Chops and Hot Licks*, p. 11. Curiously, in the foreword to this book Pierre Juneau included broadcasters among those who had helped the Canadian music industry.

20. The Guess Who, "American Woman" (Cirrus Music, 1970).

21. Jerome L. Rodnitzky, *Minstrels of the Dawn: The Folk-Protest Singer as a Cultural Hero* (Chicago: Nelson-Hall, 1976), p. 14. See also Tony Palmer, *All You Need is Love: The Story of Popular Music* (New York, London: Penguin, 1977), pp. 206-7.

22. John Orman, *The Politics of Rock Music* (Chicago: Nelson-Hall, 1984), p. xi.

23. Rodnitzky, Orman and Palmer subscribe to this view, as does Carl Belz, *The Story of Rock* (New York: Oxford, 1972).

24. Gordon Lightfoot, cited in York, *Axes, Chops and Hot Licks*, p. 80.

25. Rodnitzky, p. 20; see also Palmer, p. 208.

26. Orman, p. 51.

27. Scott Young, *Neil and Me* (Toronto: McClelland and Stewart, 1984), p. 59.

28. Bruce Cockburn, cited in Myrna Kostash, "The Pure, Uncluttered Spaces of Bruce Cockburn," *Saturday Night* (June 1972), p. 22.

29. Rodnitzky, pp. 20-21, 137.

30. Orman, ch. 1.

31. Belz, ch. 5.

32. York, *Axes, Chops and Hot Licks*, p. 13.

33. See, for example, Nancy Edmunds' review of *Wheatfield Soul* in *Rolling Stone* (14 June 1969); Lester Bangs' review of *Canned Heat* in *Rolling Stone* (7 February 1970); and Craig Modderno, "Guess Who: Good Business Partners," *Rolling Stone* (7 January 1971).

34. Burton Cummings, cited in York, *Axes, Chops and Hot Licks*, p. 24. "Signs," by Canada's Five Man Electrical Band, was another pop song to appeal to protest lyrics in vogue at this time. It reached Number Three on the *Billboard* chart in 1970.

35. Jack Batten, "The Guess Who," *Maclean's* (June 1971). Batten was critical of musicians who casually politicized their lyrics after seeing an arena full of Guess Who fans shaking their fists during "American Woman."

36. Jim Kale, cited in Modderno, "Guess Who: Good Business Partners."

37. Rodnitzky, ch. 8.

38. Kostash, *Long Way from Home*, pp. 137-38.

39. n.a., Review of Buffalo Springfield, *Last Time Around* in *Rolling Stone* (24 August 1968).

40. Bruce Cockburn, cited in Kostash, "Pure, Uncluttered Spaces," p. 21.

41. Kostash, *Long Way from Home*, p. 140.

42. Gordon Lightfoot, "Cold Hands from New York" (Warner Brothers, 1968).

43. Bruce Cockburn, cited in Kostash, "Pure, Uncluttered Spaces," p. 21.

44. Bruce Cockburn, cited in ibid., p. 22.

45. Young, *Neil and Me*, p. 42.

46. n.a., *Rolling Stone* (9 August 1969).

47. Neil Young, "Helpless" (Broken Arrow-Cotillion Publishing, 1970).

48. n.a., "Joni Mitchell" *Rolling Stone* (17 May 1969). "Big Yellow Taxi" made *Billboard's* chart twice: in 1970 the studio version reached Number 67, and in 1974 the live performance climbed to Number 24.

49. n.a., "Joni Mitchell Hangs It Up," *Rolling Stone* (13 December 1969).

50. n.a., "Joni Mitchell."

51. Gordon Lightfoot, "Black Day in July" (Warner Brothers, 1968).

52. Lightfoot did not get his first "pop" hit, "If You Could Read My Mind," until 1970, and of the fourteen AM hits he subsequently wrote, none had a political theme.

53. Bruce Cockburn, "It's Going Down Slow" (Golden Mountain Music Corporation, 1970).

54. Joni Mitchell, "The Fiddle and the Drum" (Siquomb Publishing Corporation, 1969).

55. Neil Young, "Ohio" (Broken Arrow-Cotillion Publishing, 1970).

56. Young, *Neil and Me*, p. 110.

57. David Crosby, cited in n.a., "Tin Soldiers and Nixon's Coming," *Rolling Stone* (25 June 1970).

58. Neil Young, cited in ibid.

59. See Joel Whitburn, ed., *Top Pop, 1955–1982* (Wisconsin: Record Research, 1983).

60. Bruce Cockburn, "Call It Democracy" (Golden Mountain Music Corporation, 1985).

CHAPTER THREE

GIMME SHELTER

CULTURAL PROTECTIONISM AND
THE CANADIAN RECORDING INDUSTRY

"[S]tay away from the Canadian music business. It's full of
politics and bureaucracy. It's trouble. Don't sign to a Canadian
company. Don't sign to a Canadian publisher. Go south
of the border. You'll get a better deal."

BRYAN ADAMS (1992)[1]

"For all I know, Canadian content may become the last bastion
for Canadian culture on radio after all the stations get bought
up by American media groups and are programmed out of
Dallas or somewhere...."

BRYAN ADAMS (2000)[2]

"Tears Are Not Enough," Canada's contribution to the
1986 campaign for Ethiopian famine relief, was notable not only for its
saccharine sentimentality but also for demonstrating rather starkly that
"Canadian-content" regulations had largely failed to deliver the musical
"uniqueness" imagined by its pioneers. There was something unnerv-
ing about the pairing of ground-breaking veterans like Joni Mitchell,
Neil Young and Geddy Lee with the lightweight "hair bands" of the
era—Platinum Blonde, Honeymoon Suite and Corey Hart, for example.[3]
The depth and the breadth of the talent of the generation that had risen
to international prominence just prior to the introduction of Cancon was
in particularly sharp relief, even if this was not immediately obvious

to some of the participants. As Geoff Pevere and Greig Dymond have observed, during the "Tears Are Not Enough" recording session Young suffered the "ultimate indignity" of "being told he was singing off-key by blow-dried yuppie-pup producer David Foster." To this affront Young offered his now famous reply: "That's my sound, man."[4]

In 1992, having been denied Cancon status for his hit "(Everything I Do) I Do It For You," Bryan Adams angrily stated what many Canadian music fans had long since come to believe: Canadian content breeds mediocrity. Adams advised Canada's aspiring artists to pursue their careers "south of the border"; and as Canadians had done as a matter of course since the 1930s, many did. In the 1990s, some of Canada's most innovative musicians and producers—Daniel Lanois, the post-Band Robbie Robertson and the re-born Alanis Morissette, most notably—achieved massive critical and commercial success largely without reference to Cancon.[5] Yet at the end of the decade, by which time even beloved Canadian artists like Céline Dion had ceased to satisfy the criteria for Canadian content, the CRTC "arbitrarily" raised the Cancon quota for commercial radio from 30 per cent to 35.[6] The argument is now frequently heard that the success of "great" Canadian artists like the Tragically Hip, the Barenaked Ladies and Sarah McLachlan demonstrate that the original logic of Cancon was sound, at least in the sense that it gives Canadian acts a leg up in the domestic market at the start of careers that may become runaway successes. Yet the doubts expressed by Gordon Lightfoot and others in the 1960s and 1970s remain: if Canadian music is truly "world class," why are Canadian-content quotas necessary at all?

This chapter has two related objectives. Firstly, I would like to undertake a brief review of Canadian policy initiatives in the areas of music broadcasting and sound recording as they took formative shape in the 1970s and became entrenched the 1980s. In particular, I shall focus on the legacy of discord that such initiatives—most notably those having to do with Cancon—seem to have left as a more or less perennial feature of these industries. Secondly, and more importantly, I would like to explore the question of what Canadian musicians, labels and music consumers might reasonably have expected from such a strategy of "official" cultural protectionism. I argue that the principal objective of Canadian-content legislation and of state involvement in the recording sector in Canada—the development of a strong indigenous recording industry—was a reasonable one given the structure of the music business internationally, but that it was undermined by the very policies which were implemented to bring it about.

CANADIAN CONTENT

Concern for the survival of "Canadian culture," particularly in relation to American mass culture, has been a central feature of national life in Canada since Confederation (1867) at least. As noted in Chapter One, various forms of cultural protectionism—ranging from tariffs against imported cultural goods to the patronage and later the subsidization of the arts—were a mainstay of Canadian public policy throughout much of the twentieth century. In contrast with the "high" arts and even with the broadcasting, magazine and book-publishing industries, however, all of which were thought to be directly threatened by increasing American competition, sound recording remained of little concern to cultural nationalists and hence to the state. The Canadian cultural élite in the era of the Massey Commission, for example, thought the music business both commercially marginal and culturally insignificant; indeed, "American" popular music was one of the very homogenizing cultural forces from which the Commission itself believed Canadian culture needed defending.[7] (This élitist bias seems somewhat puzzling in retrospect, given that cultural nationalists and the Canadian state had made an extremely high priority of public broadcasting in the 1920s and of regulating private radio broadcasting in the national interest the following decade.) The question of ownership and control of the recording industry in Canada did not become a matter of public discussion until the Centennial era, when a nationalist outcry on the part of journalists and industry pioneers like Walt Grealis compelled federal policy-makers to direct their attention towards it.[8] As noted in Chapter Two, this nationalist upsurge coincided with the coming-of-age of the baby boom generation and with it, the musical and lyrical "maturation" of rock-and-roll and its myriad blues, pop, folk and "protest music" hybrids.

The music business in Canada has been dominated throughout most of its history by a handful of foreign (multinational) "major labels," companies which have themselves been integrated, vertically and horizontally, into global entertainment empires. The Canadian role in this transnational record industry—one that is typical of all "small market" countries in the industrialized West[9]—has been to serve as a market for mostly non-Canadian recordings of non-Canadian musical performances. In part as a result of Canada's historically high tariff on imported recordings, all of the multinational "majors" had established subsidiary operations in Canada by 1920, where they came to dominate the domestic market (and where they continue to account for approximately 85 per cent of industry revenues).[10] These "branch plants" have been concentrated in Toronto, with a limited number of adjunct offices in other Canadian cities, where they have mainly been in the business of pressing records, tapes and CDs for domestic consumption, using foreign (usually American or British) master tapes. The Canadian subsidiaries operate with limited autonomy, signing and promoting some local talent, but this is a relatively recent development and one that is itself arguably a byproduct of Cancon regulations. The subsidiaries' sometimes distant relationship with their parent companies has, in fact, proven to be something of a mixed blessing for Canadian recording artists. For the most part, Canadian artists from Hank Snow in the 1930s to Neil Young in the 1960s recognized that they had little choice but to leave Canada if they hoped to have a musical career that included a record contract.

As noted in the last chapter, the project of mobilizing Canadian policy-makers in support of an indigenous recording industry was shaped in the late 1960s by a growing public taste for music about Canada—most notably for the music of Gordon Lightfoot—and, indeed, by a growing unease about the fact that Canadian recording artists had had to exile themselves to pursue their craft. Private radio broadcasters were singled out as having collaborated in the colonization of the Canadian recording industry, on the grounds that they had refused to sacrifice audience share (and hence advertising revenues) in order to promote Canadian artists. Responding to this growing public concern, the Trudeau Liberals implemented "Canadian-content" rules for commercial radio broadcasters under the terms of the Broadcasting Act, to be administered by the newly designated Canadian Radio-Television and Telecommunications Commission (CRTC). Starting in January 1971, AM radio stations in Canada were required to play a minimum of 30 per cent Cancon as a condition of the renewal of their broadcasting licenses. Musical selections considered Canadian content under the new legislation were those which met two of the following four criteria: (a) the instrumentation or lyrics were principally performed by a Canadian; (b) the music was performed by a Canadian; (c) the lyrics were written by a Canadian; (d) the live performance was wholly recorded in Canada. After Bryan Adams' 1992 hit "(Everything I Do) I Do It For You" failed to qualify as Canadian content, setting in motion an extraordinarily acrimonious public debate about state regulation of popular music in Canada, the rules were loosened so as to award Cancon status to "special cases" like Adams'. Henceforth, "in addition to meeting the criterion for either artist or production, a Canadian who has collaborated with a non-Canadian receives at least half of the credit for both music and lyrics" and is therefore considered Cancon."

It was not until the early 1980s that the Canadian government arranged for the provision of direct subsidies to the sound-recording industry, several years after it had initiated financial support for the book-publishing and film industries. The institutional structure through which this support was channelled took the form of an ostensibly "private sector" agency, the Foundation to Assist Canadian Talent on Record. FACTOR was created in 1982 by several Canadian-owned private broadcasting corporations, the Canadian Independent Record Producers Association (CIRPA) and the Canadian Music Publishers Association (CMPA). It was designed to "stimulate the growth and development of the independent sector of the Canadian recording industry" by making grants and interest-free loans available to Canadian acts on a competitive basis for the production of demos and video clips and for the organization of international tours.[12] Publicly, broadcasters expressed their desire to support the Canadian recording industry in self-less, often nationalist terms, while simultaneously reasoning that if they failed to cooperate they might run the risk of having too little Canadian "product" for their playlists. Under the terms of the Liberals' Cancon legislation, however, private broadcasters were required not only to play Canadian music but to actively promote Canadian talent off-air (although the CRTC never specified the proportion of profit each station was expected to spend on this promotion). To be sure, membership in FACTOR has not gone unnoticed by the CRTC in its consideration of broadcast license renewal applications.

With FACTOR in place but woefully underfunded—its first annual budget was $200,000, too little to capitalize the production of more than two record albums—the federal government announced the creation in 1986 of a Sound Recording Development Program (SRDP) which would pump $25 million into the Canadian recording industry over five years. The SRDP included three major components—production support ($18 million), promotion, touring and marketing support ($4.5 million), and business development ($2.5 million). FACTOR and its French-language counterpart, *Musicaction*, which was founded in 1985, received $2.2 million annually from SRDP funds. This amount, along with an increased commitment from the private sector, brought FACTOR's annual operating budget to roughly $4 million in 1990. The rationale for government involvement in the FACTOR program, as expressed in *Vital Links*, an influential booklet published by the Department of Communications in 1987, was that the "recent serious decline in the number of Canadian-content recordings—especially the precipitous 45 per cent drop in French-language production since 1978—had created problems for Canada's radio broadcasters, who were finding it difficult to obtain an adequate supply of new releases."[13] Partisan support for the indigenous recording industry continued to make good nationalist fodder, even fifteen years after the introduction of Canadian-content rules. At the press conference announcing the creation of the SRDP, held at a Montreal disco, Tory Communications Minister Marcel Massé was quoted as saying that "the sorry state of Canada's recording industry is due to the viselike control exercised by multinational companies over the distribution of records in Canada."[14] In November 1991, at the end of SRDP's first five years of operation, the federal government announced that it would become a permanent program, with an annual budget of $5 million. In 1999–2000 the SRDP's annual budget was $9.45 million; in 2002, FACTOR's annual budget stood at $11 million, of which $8.1 million was provided by the Department of Heritage.[15]

THE TROUBLE WITH NORMAL

From their inception, Canadian-content quotas, and to a lesser extent FACTOR, were contentious within the recording and broadcasting sectors, as well as among policy-makers and outside observers. Within the industries themselves, support for Cancon tended to coalesce around the Canadian Independent Record Producers Association (CIRPA), while opposition emanated most noticeably from the Canadian Association of Broadcasters (CAB).

CIRPA was founded in 1975 as a voluntary association for Canada's independent record industry, assuming the crucial role of watchdog and lobbyist. CIRPA's position on Canadian content was unequivocal: it saw the very survival of the Canadian recording industry as hinging on radio exposure for Canadian acts. Thus, the Association lobbied in the late 1970s and the 1980s not only for increased Canadian-content requirements for FM radio—which, it argued, would represent simply a return to the "status quo ante of 1971, when AM was the band of choice"—but for a much more strenuous monitoring policy that would prevent broadcasters from playing their requisite Canadian content in non-peak periods.[16] CIRPA's position was supported in these years by the influential Canadian record industry trade paper *The Record* and explicitly by many of the country's most influential rock music critics, most notably Chris Dafoe of the *Toronto Star*. Notable for its relative silence in the debate over Cancon was the Canadian Recording Industry Association (CRIA), which represented the major label subsidiaries in Canada and for which, therefore, the country of origin of recorded "product" was of far less importance than its overall sales in the Canadian market.

The position of the CAB, the association that has represented private broadcasters in Canada since 1926, was explicitly opposed to that of CIRPA. Given that the CAB has always spoken exclusively for the interests of private-sector capital, it is not easy to distil its specific objections to Cancon from the Association's generalized resentment of regulation of its industry. The broad outlines of its case are, however, clear. A CAB survey of FM-radio programmers conducted in 1990 revealed that very few broadcasters believed there was "enough Canadian music to sustain a higher quota." Radio entrepreneur Bill Gilliland—with the sponsorship of "concerned music industryites"—articulated in *The Record* what was undoubtedly a widely held view of the Canadian record industry among broadcasters:

> Throughout the '60s and '70s and '80s, radio programmers across Canada busted their buns devising creative and effective ways to present the nation's music artists to listeners. Beginning in the mid-'80s, music video programmers added their very, very substantial support to the record industry by imaginatively presenting the nation's music artists to viewers. Radio and video support continues in the '90s. Why, then, aren't the made-in-Canada recording artists as successful as many critics think they should be? Is the market for domestic recording artists grossly overestimated?[17]

Clearly implicit in Gilliland's observations was the suggestion that some radio programmers in Canada had reservations, not only about the quantity of Canadian musical recordings, but about their quality as well.

At the level of policy analysis, traditionally the domain of economists and academic observers, the debate over Canadian content as it evolved in the 1980s tended to centre on the more generalized question of its value (utility) for Canadians and for "Canadian culture." Unlike the debate between independent recording companies and radio interests, this was a debate about first principles. For Paul Audley, one of several independent policy analysts whose writing echoed the official governmental line about Cancon, any discussion of the subject had to begin with the premise that "Canadians who are involved in the creation and performance of music ought to have a fair chance to have their music recorded and played on radio stations in Canada."[18] This position was restated in November 1990 by CRTC policy analyst John Feihl, who urged Canadians to "change [their] perspective" on the Cancon issue by asking not whether 30 per cent Cancon is too much, but whether 70 per cent non-Canadian content is too little.[19]

The widespread consensus in favour of Canadian-content regulations, outside of certain narrowly partisan circles, was evident in the low number of policy analysts who criticized the assumptions upon which it rested. I am aware of only one scholarly work from this period, William Watson's *National Pastimes: The Economics of Canadian Leisure* (1988), that came out squarely in favour of dismantling Canadian-content policy as it then existed, and the evidence suggests that because this work was published by the neo-conservative Fraser Institute, it was largely ignored within policy-making circles. Watson's methodology was simple, perhaps deceptively so: as an economist, he wanted to ask whether Canadians were getting their money's worth, quite literally, from Canadian-content regulations. Most of the leisure goods consumed within Canada, he observed, were not subsidized, while most of those that were eligible for designation as Canadian-content received some form of subsidy. Watson asked whether a performer or a recording may be said to have provided benefits to the people who had paid for it via their taxes, but who had not seen or heard it because it was of too little value to them to do so. With regard to sound recordings, Watson argued that, at most, the state ought to be subsidizing activities that teach Canadians about each other, and that the pertinent criterion for Cancon eligibility should therefore be the "Canadianness" of a recording's subject matter rather than of its production. He asked: "Should the state really have a position on where the generic rock music Canadians listen to is produced?" The answer: "[S]ound-alike recordings by such people as Corey Hart, Bryan Adams and Luba, [which are] destined for the US market have no claim to public support."[20]

Regardless of one's ideological proximity to Watson, his insistence that Canadian consumers be brought into the Cancon debate represented a challenge that had been simmering since the 1960s — one which would later burst upon the broadcasting and recording industries during the Adams controversy. Taken alongside data published by the Canadian Association of Broadcasters which revealed that domestic radio audience share decreased in direct proportion to the amount of Canadian content broadcast, there was a certain force to the argument that so-called ordinary Canadians were casting their votes on Canadian content with their ears, that is, with their radio tuners and record-buying dollars.

If *laissez faire* critics of Cancon like William Watson and the CAB had been alone in advancing the argument that the consumption of recorded music ought to be driven by "market forces," the suggestion that Canadians vote with their ears might be easily dismissed. The truth of the matter is that even ardent Cancon supporters acknowledged in the 1980s that the main preoccupation of the Canadian music industry — and therefore of the CRTC and FACTOR — was not that of protecting or enhancing Canadian culture so much as it was that of finding and developing international markets. And herein lay the rub: the path to success in New York and Stockholm and Tokyo lay in developing the generic sounds of the increasingly globalized corporate "playlist," which actually meant *reducing* the "Canadianness" of Canadian recorded product.

WILL IT PLAY IN BOISE?

Canadian-content requirements, as originally envisaged by the CRTC, were driven by two main goals: the development of a Canadian recording industry and the nurture and support of Canadian musical talent. However compatible these objectives might have seemed as matters of policy, in practice they have proven to be at odds. Because of the dominant position of the major multinational labels both domestically and internationally, Canadian recording artists have always recognized that their greatest success was likely to come in the form of an international record contract. This is as true for post-Cancon artists as it was for the pioneers of the 1930s: the top-selling Canadian acts have always been those that produce records for major foreign record companies. In 1984, a celebrated but by no means exceptional year, the top-selling Canadian rock acts—Bryan Adams, Helix, Platinum Blonde, Corey Hart and Honeymoon Suite—were all signed to major multinational record deals and actually broke first in the United States.[21] Today the same general rule applies. In 1991, Shania Twain was "discovered" at a Huntsville, Ontario, resort but signed her first record deal with Mercury Nashville. In a slight variation on the same theme, Alanis Morissette abandoned the Canadian music scene altogether in 1993 after two albums with MCA Canada, obliterating her dance-pop past and signing with Madonna's Maverick Records label.

What is more, the success—and arguably even the survival—of independent Canadian record companies has been tempered since the 1970s by their ability to expand into markets beyond Canada. The reason for this, simply stated, is that the Canadian market for records is too small in all but a handful of cases to recover the costs of production: an album has to go Gold (50,000 copies in Canada) before the costs of bringing a new act onstream—including recording, marketing, touring and videos—are likely to be recovered. Thus, the most successful Canadian independent labels (those unaffiliated with transnational firms) have been: those which distribute foreign product in Canada—as in the case of Attic Records; those which have managed to crack international markets with Canadian product—notably Nettwerk and True North; or, most ironically of all, those which have managed to break non-Canadian performers in international markets—Stony Plain, for example.[22]

Thus, to be a successful Canadian recording artist or Canadian record company is, paradoxically, to have broken into international markets. Consequently, the most successful Canadian musicians and record companies are those that fit most readily into the larger world of Anglo-American popular music. This has long been the rule of thumb for musicians and record executives in Canada; in the 1980s it also became the guiding principle of Ottawa's policy on the subsidization of the recording industry. As *Vital Links* put it, "In most cases, export sales are... essential if Canadian-owned companies are to turn a profit on a recording project. Efforts must be made, therefore, to tour the artist internationally and to license Canadian products to recording and music-publishing companies in other countries."[23] To this end, it was decided in October 1990 that FACTOR funding for Canadian recording projects would be "earmarked for fewer artists in order to deliver product better suited for the international market," with the result that "individual labels would of necessity be eligible for fewer projects."[24] CIRPA followed suit in 1990, presenting a report to the Ontario Ministry of Culture and Communications requesting $5 million annually for, among other things, "assistance in expanding foreign markets."[25]

Since the objectives of the CRTC included strengthening the recording industry in Canada and supporting Canadian acts, the success of Canadian-content legislation was gauged in part in terms of its success in carrying Canadian musicians and Canadian product into foreign markets. When so judged, as virtually everyone in the broadcasting and recording industries agreed, Cancon was found wanting. As one Canadian record executive stated bluntly in 1980: "So much garbage was being recorded just to help fill the airways that a lot of third-rate stuff was called a hit. What was worse came when you took a good record that was a Canadian hit to the States. They wouldn't listen. To them, a Canadian hit meant second-rate."[26]

It was not only performers signed to independent Canadian labels who suffered this fate. On the contrary, as Toronto singer/songwriter Andrew Cash noted in 1986, the multinationals had even grown suspicious of the judgements of their Canadian branch offices: "Most Canadian record companies are US-owned subsidiaries and many of the local acts they've signed... haven't been picked up in the US. What's the point in pinning your hopes on a big contract and allowing yourself to be moulded and processed if you end up getting dropped after one or two records, just because the US parent company wasn't interested...?"[27] Rather than stimulating exposure for Canadian product in non-

Canadian markets, Cancon contributed to the perception in this period that this product was inferior. As veteran Canadian rock critic Peter Goddard suggested in 1980: "Ironically, the legislated Canadian-content regulations... undermined [the] international impact [of Canadian acts]. Soon enough, artists who had the clout... signed with either British or American companies; hits outside Canada were the name of the game."[28] Fellow critic Craig MacInnis called this "the sure-it's-a-gold-record-in-Canada-but-will-it-play-in-Boise syndrome."[29]

The central paradox of cultural protectionism in the recording industry—and this applied to both Cancon legislation and direct subsidization of sound recordings—was thus that the criterion by which Canadian acts qualified for support was their appeal in international markets. "Distinctive" Canadian recordings did not necessarily qualify since they were unlikely to make the tight playlists of commercial radio and were unlikely to sell well internationally. Thus, to echo William Watson, the argument can be made that Canadian-content legislation and government subsidization of the recording industry, rather than preserving whatever was distinctive about Canadian culture or teaching Canadians about each other, were effectively homogenizing Canadian musical culture along lines dictated by the multinational Anglo-American recording industry. As Goddard put it, "No one at the centres of pop power in New York or Los Angeles gives a gilt-edged hoot about regional sound or style unless it can move 50,000 units a day."[30]

Nowhere was this paradox more strikingly evident than in the designation of Canadian-content recordings for radio airplay. As they had since 1971, non-Canadian acts covering domestic copyrights qualified as Cancon. Notable examples of this phenomenon in the 1980s included the Neville Brothers' cover of Leonard Cohen's "Bird On A Wire" and Aerosmith's "The Other Side," which was produced by Canadian Bruce Fairbairn (and recorded in Vancouver). As Laura Bartlett, Promotion Vice-President of Virgin Canada, noted in July 1990: "A situation such as Aerosmith is completely absurd. If I phone my Los Angeles office and tell them that Colin James (lacking in sufficient Cancon points) is not Canadian content but Aerosmith is, they'll think I lost my mind."[31]

Moreover, a Canadian artist living in Canada (and paying taxes here) who had gone to the United States and recorded an American song—as was the case, for example, of material from Colin James, k. d. lang, Lori Yates and others in the 1980s—failed to qualify for Cancon certification. Since it was axiomatic that private broadcasters would play only the minimum level of Canadian content to meet their quota obligations, Canadians' failure to meet Cancon regulations had the effect of actually shutting them out of their home market. The situation got so bad that BMG Canada adopted a policy of re-recording non-Cancon tracks by Canadian artists in Canada so as to meet the terms of Canadian-content eligibility. Michelle Wright and Jeff Healey were two artists distributed by BMG who re-recorded tracks in Canada using Canadian personnel. As CBS national-promotion director Shan Kelly stated bluntly in 1990: "[O]verall, I believe that Cancon ghettoizes Canadian music."[32]

CONCLUSION

The question of whether there is anything worth preserving in Canadian musical culture seems to me to be less salient than the more pragmatic question of what, in the last analysis, Canadians might reasonably have expected from a policy of cultural protectionism. Since for the most part Canadian-content legislation and direct subsidization of the record industry neither produced a competitive recording industry nor significantly affected musicians' aspirations, it seems fair to ask whether the nationalist vision that informed such policies—to produce made-in-Canada stars who achieved international success while remaining on a Canadian label—were ever viable. I would argue not only that these twin objectives were untenable but that, in truth, the pragmatic business of accommodating to the dominant agenda of the multinational music industry has always worked against such a vision.

Cancon regulations and the subsidization of the recording industry could never have produced a competitive Canadian recording industry because at a practical level these mechanisms evolved into means of improving Canadian musicians' chances in a global industry dominated by the multinationals. Cultural protectionism may have allowed—or forced—Canadians to hear more music by Canadian artists on the radio, and it may well have stimulated a taste for this recorded product nationally. However, by definition no interventionist policy was ever likely to enable Canadian record companies to compete with the multinationals internationally. On the contrary, there is strong evidence to suggest that official protectionism has limited the ability of indigenous companies and artists to compete outside Canada, while stigmatizing them to some extent within.

My argument is not that these protectionist policies were poorly conceived or even that they have failed in practice, but rather that they were inadequate when measured against the nationalist agenda out of which they arose in the 1970s and against which they were measured in the first two decades of mandatory Canadian-content quotas. Cancon legislation failed for the most part to serve as a launching pad from which Canadian performers could attain international stardom, and this failure was inevitable. The most Canadians might have asked of it is that it help local artists to a portion of the domestic market. The worst we might have feared is that it would ghettoize such acts and so reduce their chances of international success. Geoff Pevere and Greig Dymond expressed this ambivalence brilliantly in *Mondo Canuck*: "Sure, there was a fair amount of dreck (Terry Jacks, Paul Anka's midlife crisis), but the first half of the seventies was a great time to be an impressionable young radio addict: CanCon made it easy to believe that, as far as pop music was concerned, Canucks took care of business every bit as fiercely as anybody else in the world."[33]

Similarly, the most that Canadians might have asked from programs like FACTOR and the SRDP is that these programs foster independent record production in Canada. The key term here is not *Canada*, however, but *independent*, for it is the nature of independent labels—whether in Canada or elsewhere—to play an adjunct role in a world dominated by the majors. Independent labels have always borne the lion's share of responsibility for seeking out and nurturing new talent, knowing full well that, once discovered, this talent (or the label itself) is likely to be appropriated by a major. There are, in fact, few clearer examples of the monopolistic logic of global capitalism. As Jackie Luffman of Statistics Canada noted bluntly in 1999, "Canadian-controlled recording companies are holding their own in the marketplace but the marketplace is anything but stable. There have been several mergers involving companies which were already among the largest, and thus the industry is becoming even more concentrated and the big companies are becoming even bigger."[34] Official cultural protectionism could never have been expected to dramatically increase the Canadian indies' share of the international market, but what it has done over the years—and this point should be underscored—is to broaden dramatically the volume and range of Canadian recorded product available to Canadian consumers. If all that such institutions as FACTOR ever accomplish is keeping Canadian indies afloat—as a source of Canadian music for Canadian consumers, but also as a source of a new talent for world markets—they will have succeeded admirably.

As for Canadian artists, most appear to be ambivalent still. Bryan Adams' mixed views of Canadian-content regulations and the domestic recording industry—captured in the epigraph above—suggest strongly that the long shadow cast in Canada by the US recording and broadcasting industries continues to be the mixed blessing it was in the heyday of Cancon. The "American media groups" Adams felt free to disparage in 2000, at the twilight of his career as a pop star, were, of course, precisely those that had made him rich and famous in the 1980s. If there is an act that appears to demonstrate the triumph of the original logic of Canadian content, it is the Tragically Hip—homegrown heroes and nationalist standard-bearers for literally millions of Canadian music fans. Yet even here there is more than a little ambiguity. As journalist Joshua Ostroff has suggested, the Hip's elevation to "Canadian rock icon" is attributable at least in part to the awkward truth that, despite the band's many salvos at the American market, "[t]heir fans treat the band's lack of success in the U.S. as a badge of honor."[35] In any case, the Kingston quintet may well prove to be the exception that proves the historic rule, ending up as the first and only band to achieve true "superstardom" in

Canada but nowhere else. Far more typical of "Canadian" musical success stories in the globalized world of twenty-first century pop are those squarely in the triumph-through-exile tradition—campus favourites the Barenaked Ladies, alt-rocker Alanis Morissette and chart-topping country-pop diva Shania Twain. One-time Quebec child-star (and French-language chanteuse) Céline Dion has travelled even further down the road of global superstardom, announcing recently that she has become a permanent fixture at Caesar's Palace in Las Vegas, where her nightly show is sponsored by Chrysler.[36]

Meanwhile, in the spring of 2003, Canadian broadcasters were facing the prospect of yet another increase in the CRTC's Cancon quota for commercial radio, from 35 per cent to 40 per cent. This upward revision was not entirely unexpected. During the regulator's 1998 review of "radio policy," certain "industry players" had argued that "a 40% Canadian-content level should be attainable across the board within five years." Once again, broadcasters and record labels girded for battle, resurrecting all of the old arguments. Rael Merson, president of Rogers Broadcasting, was quoted as saying that "there is not enough product in many genres to justify a playlist that is 40% Canadian" and, hence, that "a 40% Canadian-content rule would 'dilute' Canadian radio stations, causing them to lose listeners to U.S. stations whose signals come across the border."[37] Whether this argument will carry sway at the next round of CRTC hearings is doubtful, since Canadian FM stations have recorded average revenue growth of 31.4% since 1998, apparently reversing the inverse relationship between Canadian content and profitability. A sign of the times is that Standard Broadcasting Corporation, which owns 51 radio outlets nationwide, now "volunteers" a 40 per cent Cancon minimum when it goes before the CRTC for a new license—most recently in its successful launch of an urban music station in Calgary. But some things never change. Said one unnamed "radio executive" who resents the idea that Cancon quotas should be raised yet again: "You can only play so much Gordon Lightfoot."[38]

NOTES

1. Bryan Adams, cited in Geoff Pevere and Greig Dymond, *Mondo Canuck: A Canadian Pop Culture Odyssey* (Toronto: Prentice Hall, 1996), p. 2.

2. Bryan Adams, cited in Stephen Cooke, "Adams Makes the Best of It," *The Halifax Herald* (4 January 2000).

3. See Michael Barclay, Ian A.D. Jack and Jason Schneider, *Have Not Been the Same: The CanRock Renaissance, 1985–1995* (Toronto: ECW Press, 2001).

4. Pevere and Dymond, *Mondo Canuck*, p. 171.

5. The subtext of Paul Cantin's biography of Alanis Morissette is that the artist was utterly dismissed in Canada in the period between her dance-pop career and her re-birth as the confessional rocker who penned *Jagged Little Pill*. This indifference was, arguably, a function of Cancon, though Cantin does not press the point. See *Alanis Morissette: You Oughta Know* (Toronto: Stoddart, 1997).

6. Céline Dion's album *Let's Talk about Love* did not qualify as Canadian under CRTC rules. See Canadian Association of Broadcasters, "CRTC's Arbitrary Decision to Hike Canadian Content Hurts Listeners and Broadcasters Alike" (Press Release 30 April 1998).

7. See Paul Litt, *The Muses, the Masses and the Massey Commission* (Toronto: University of Toronto Press, 1992).

8. Walt Grealis was publisher of the music-industry trade magazine *RPM* which, in the early and late 1960s, was a leading nationalist voice calling for government protection of the domestic recording industry.

9. This pattern is described in Roger Wallis and Krister Malm, *Big Sounds from Small People: The Music Industry in Small Countries* (New York: Pendragon, 1984).

10. Jackie Luffman, "Variations on a Theme: The Changing Music Scene," *Quarterly Bulletin from the Culture Statistics Program* (Statistics Canada) 11:4 (Winter 1999), p. 2.

11. "Canadian Content" (Toronto: CIRPA, 2000).

12. FACTOR [The Foundation to Assist Canadian Talent on Record], untitled pamphlet (no date).

13. *Vital Links: Canadian Cultural Industries* (Ottawa: Government of Canada, Department of Communications, 1987), p. 54.

14. "Ottawa To Help Record Industry Change Its Tune," *Globe and Mail* (10 May 1986).

15. *Evaluation of the Sound Recording Development Program* (Department of Canadian Heritage, Corporate Review Branch, April 2000).

16. "Executive Directors' Report," *CIRPA Newsletter* (August 1990), p. 1. See also David Farrell, "FM Regs Help Promote Fool's Gold," *The Record* (6 August 1990).

17. Bill Gilliland, cited in "Gilliland Proposes 30% Music Content for Daily Newspapers and Consumer Magazines," *The Record* (13 August 1990).

18. Paul Audley, *Canada's Cultural Industries: Broadcasting, Publishing, Records and Film* (Toronto: Lorimer, 1983), p. 139.

19. John Feihl, "The Impact of the Canadian Content Regulations on the Canadian Recording Industry," *Association of Canadian Studies Newsletter* 12:3 (Fall, 1990), p. 32.

20. William Watson, *National Pastimes: The Economics of Canadian Leisure* (Vancouver: The Fraser Institute, 1988), p. 112.

21. Greg Quill, "Record Industry Needs New Deal," *Toronto Star* (1 December 1984).

22. See Liam Lacey, "Little Labels Can Make a Big Mark," *Globe and Mail* (4 April 1986).

23. *Vital Links*, p. 53.

24. Jeff Bateman, "FACTOR Vetting Quality over Quantity," *The Record* (8 October 1990).

25. "CIRPA Study Recommends Ontario Support Program," *The Record* (15 October 1990).

26. Cited in Peter Goddard, "Pop Record Makers Ignore Borders," *Toronto Star* (15 November 1980).

27. Andrew Cash, cited in Greg Quill, "What Do Most Indies Want?" *Toronto Star* (21 February 1986).

28. Goddard, "Pop Record Makers Ignore Borders."

29. Craig MacInnis, "High Price of Selling Rock," *Toronto Star* (29 December 1987).

30. Ibid.

31. Laura Bartlett, cited in "Cancon Reg Has Industry Seeing Red," *The Record* (23 July 1990).

32. Shan Kelly, cited in "Canadian Artists Resort to Re-Recording Songs," *The Record* (23 July 1990).

33. Pevere and Dymond, *Mondo Canuck*, p. 168.

34. Luffman, "Variations on a Theme," pp. 5–6.

35. Joshua Ostroff, "A Hip Homecoming," *Ottawa Sun* (4 July 1998).

36. "Chrysler Sponsors Céline Dion in Las Vegas," (Chrysler Corporation news release) 16 January 2003. In the 1990s Twain, Morissette and Dion together sold 155 million albums worldwide, 95 per cent of which were outside Canada. See Luffman, "Variations on a Theme," p. 1.

37. Rael Merson, cited in Barbara Shecter, "Radio Fears Canadian Content Boost," *Financial Post* (4 April 2003).

38. Cited in ibid.

CHAPTER FOUR

HISTORICAL UNDERDOSING

POP DEMOGRAPHY AND THE CRISIS IN CANADIAN HISTORY

> Historical Underdosing: To live in a period of time when nothing
> seems to happen. Major symptoms include addiction to news-
> papers, magazines, and TV news broadcasts.
>
> DOUGLAS COUPLAND, *GENERATION X*

Who can doubt that Canadian history is in some kind of crisis? J.L. Granatstein sounded the alarm in *Who Killed Canadian History?* (1998), a scathing exposé of the educational bureaucrats, university administrators, scholars, journalists and politicians thought to have conspired "to eliminate Canada's past"; and judging from the public response to his call to arms, in which he has been joined by other self-styled "national" historians, including David Bercuson, Robert Bothwell and Desmond Morton, the crisis is real.[1] Organizations recently launched in the cause of "promoting greater interest in Canadian history" include Canada's National Historical Society (founded in 1993), the McGill Institute for the Study of Canada (founded in 1994), the Dominion Institute (founded in 1997), and the Citizenship Education Resource Network (founded in 1998). In 1997 and again in 1998 Canadians' "shocking" lack of historical knowledge formed the backdrop for the House of Commons debate over Bill C-279 — "an act to promote the observance of two minutes of silence on Remembrance Day."[2] Even Prime Minister Jean Chrétien has lamented in the House that "young Canadians [know] too little about each other and what we have done together."[3] As if to confirm that the struggle for Canadian history had reached truly Granatsteinian proportions, in late January 1999 McGill University hosted "the largest history conference ever staged in Canada," in which 800 educators, filmmakers, publishers and writers met to deliberate the question: "Why has Canadian history vanished from classrooms in half the provinces of Canada? Is it dead — or merely buried by school boards and education departments frightened by hard choices and new ideas?"[4]

This chapter seeks to illuminate the crisis in Canadian history by appeal to three related arguments. The first is that history has largely ceased to inform Canadians' lives, not because of the failure of institutions, but because of the cultural transformation of their understanding of the past occasioned by new media and especially by new ideas about how the past is organized. My second claim is that, along with free markets and small government, so-called neo-conservative ideologues in Canada have sought, deliberately if not systematically, to appropriate Canadian history and to deploy it in support of their contemporary political agenda. My third argument is that this neo-conservative recasting of Canadians' sense of their own history has been abetted by a powerful new literature I call *pop demographics*, which banishes older notions of the historical past as a coherent, life-informing narrative in favour of a new, market-based interpretation in which the essential component is the *generational cohort* and the essential historical dynamic is *generational competition*. Although I am mainly interested in these phenomena as they apply to English Canada, there is evidence to suggest that they extend as well into Quebec; indeed, as I shall demonstrate, these trends are part of a discursive revolution that is at least continental in scope and anchored in the far broader globalization discourses that are the hallmark of our times.

COLLECTIVE AMNESIA

J.L. Granatstein may view the crisis in Canadian history as one of "political correctness," multicultural "airbrushing" and bureaucratic bungling, but in my view these phenomena — if they exist at all — are symptoms of a far deeper, essentially cultural dislocation: history has become largely irrelevant to the lives of ordinary Canadians. If, as Granatstein and others have claimed, history has declined as a core subject area in Canadian high schools, for example, surely this is merely a reflection of the current reality, namely that one can get along very nicely in contemporary Canadian society without knowing history and, indeed, without feeling as though one's lack of knowledge is any kind of hindrance. Did not both Prime Minister Jean Chrétien and Quebec Premier Lucien Bouchard confirm in October 1999 that one could quite easily rise to the highest political offices in the land without knowing so much as the date of Confederation?⁵ Can high school students, or even their teachers, be expected to rise to a higher standard? I take the view that if Canadians actually still lived within an historical paradigm — that is, if history actually provided the social, cultural, economic and political architecture within which they contextualized their lived experience — then surely high school history would be, *a priori*, the robust and exciting program that Granatstein imagines it ought to be. One may agree entirely, as I do, with Granatstein's contention that "[h]istory is important... because it is the way a nation, a people, and an individual learn who they are." But "who we are" and how "we" understand ourselves as social and political actors is determined not merely by teachers, textbooks and bureaucrats but by far more pervasive (and powerful) discourses about the way the world is organized and how "we" fit into it. Relevance is socially constructed; it precedes intellectual curiosity, not vice versa.

It is worth recalling that much of Granatstein's critique of the state of Canadian history had been put forward by historian Michael Bliss in his controversial 1991 Creighton Centennial Lecture. Reviewing the entire panorama of postwar English-Canadian historiography, Bliss argued that by the 1970s the project of writing "national" history had passed from professional historians to a group of "Via Rail nationalists" who "identified Canada and things Canadian with... the age of big government, universal social welfare programs, and subsidized culture." This new nationalist interpretation of Canada, he suggested, one which had become identified politically with the policies of the Trudeau Liberals, had by the 1980s become "increasingly unpopular in the minds of a rest-less electorate, a restless business community, and restless provinces"; and yet there were no new "national symbols or national-isms" in the Mulroney era to take their place. Bliss concluded bluntly that the "torch had passed from Creighton to the Grants, Bertons, Atwoods, and Gordons, and in their hands it had gone out."[6]

Bliss's indictment not only of recent historiography but of "progres-sive" education came at a time when right-wing demands for sweeping social reforms in Canada were gaining momentum. By the mid-1990s, for example, the Reform-allied *Alberta Report* had put the decline of Canadian history at the centre of a campaign to do away with what it called "political correctness." Editor Ted Byfield wrote in 1995 that Canadian and American books on World War II in particular had become "a mere propaganda exercise in currently fashionable causes," including women in the work force, the internment of the Japanese, the Holocaust, the American decision to use the bomb, and the allied bombing of Dresden. Concluded Byfield: "Of the immense sacrifices of white American males, who did nearly all the fighting and dying, there was simply nothing at all."[7] When *Who Killed Canadian History?* was published, complete with a chapter on Canadians' apparent indifference towards World War II, Byfield cited it as clear evidence of his own genius. Granatstein had affirmed that Canada was mired in an official misinformation conspiracy on an Orwellian scale: "[A] servile state school system brainwashes the populace, and a slave media, assiduously parroting the party line, pounces on all non-conformity."[8]

The definitive linking of this historiographical counter-revolution and what was by the mid-1990s openly being called a "neo-conserva-tive" political agenda came in David Frum's *What's Right: The New Conservatism and What it Means for Canada*. Like Bliss and Byfield, Frum struck at the very heart of what he called the "liberal" nationalist mythology, accusing its leading proponents of an absurd, self-serving historical revisionism, one that systematically recast an essentially conservative Canadian history and culture in the image of 1960s coun-tercultural idealism and 1970s welfare-statism:

Is it not bizarre to convene symposia on the national identity while systematically wiping away all traces of the past from the nation's currency, its post office boxes, even its flagpoles? Our liberal nationalists celebrated a Canada that never existed. The Canada that sang "The Maple Leaf Forever," that hanged Louis Riel, that listened to black-clad priests denounce the theory of evolution, that erected statues to Queen Victoria, that volunteered for the trenches, that shunned the New Deal reforms of Franklin Delano Roosevelt, that made a hero out of Soviet defector Igor Gouzenko — *that* Canada, historical Canada, was erased from our textbooks, its monuments destroyed, its achievements disparaged. Instead of taking pride in the construction of a vast, rich, and free nation, we were instead — as Margaret Atwood argued in a hugely influential 1972 book — humbly to think of ourselves as "survivors."

For Frum, the Canadian question was (and presumably remains) a simple one: "To be a patriot, do I really have to be such a sucker?" Of course not!

Like a nervous middle-aged man in a James Thurber story, official Canada has rounded a corner, only to bump into the actual Canada heading in the opposite direction.... Perhaps the best way to understand the politics of our country today is to think of them not as some radical transformation of Canada, but as a simple rediscovery of a country that was there all along.

The evidence for this "rediscovery" was everywhere to see in contemporary politics, said Frum — in the passage of Free Trade, the defeat of the Charlottetown Accord, the demise of the Conservatives and their replacement with the Reform Party, and Canadians' overwhelming support for provincial governments promising to balance their budgets.[9]

These (and other) elements of the neo-conservative agenda, so artfully cultivated in commerce, in the mass media, and especially in the corridors of political power in Canada, are arguably part of a far larger and far more profound discursive dislocation in contemporary Canadian life. Writing specifically of the demise of the "left-nationalist project" to which he has dedicated his adult life, Canadian philosopher Ian Angus has recently put the case this way:

> [In Canada] we are pressured by forces of globalization that are primarily driven by corporate economic power. These forces are the basis for the pervasiveness of the language of fate in contemporary life. We are repeatedly told that we must adjust to this or that tendency, that we must scramble in order not to lose out and resign ourselves to fit the imperatives of the new world system.... Independent decision making within the system shrinks to marginal spaces without resources and isolated, private consumer choices.... It is not a felicitous era in which to speak of political vision and common goals, even less of a philosophy oriented to the destiny of a people.[10]

Surely history, the very catalogue of Canadians' accumulated "political vision[s] and common goals," could not be expected to withstand such a profound and broadly based onslaught.

Michael Bliss was correct to note that the task of interpreting Canada's "public community" had passed in the Trudeau years from the Creightons to the Atwoods, but his claims of its death in the Mulroney era turned out to be greatly exaggerated. By the 1990s, the torch had passed to the nation's neo-conservative think tanks, pundits and lobbyists (the Fraser Institute and the C.D. Howe Institute, most notably), who claimed, along with Byfield and Frum, to have "restored" Canadian public life to its founding principles. Acrimonious public policy debates (free trade, deficit reduction, "workfare") marked the "common sense" revolution in politics, but it was in the realm of *discourse* that Canadians were slowly, almost imperceptibly weaned off their earlier ideas of "social citizenship." This discursive revolution—a trend that has preoccupied many Canadian popular writers in the mid-1990s—was no less dramatic for having been so subtle, as Canadians increasingly identified their "quality of life," not with the common good but with the performance of their mutual funds, and learned to demonize unions, "welfare moms" and "subsidy-receiving pornographers" even as they lionized bank presidents and cyber-billionaires.[11] Whereas citizenship was once understood largely within social and political discourses, it has been transformed by the discourses of the free market and especially by its ideological vanguard, advertising. Once understood as social and political actors with legitimate claims on public life, Canadians have in the last decade been reconstituted as essentially commercial actors—"viewers" to be targeted, "consumers" to be courted, rich "cohorts" promising vast profits to the pollsters and pop demographers who can crack their enigmatic cultural codes. This is especially true of Canadian youth—those singled out by Granatstein and others for their ignorance. To judge from the likes of *Maclean's*, the most authoritative voices on young people today are not social workers or teachers or even parents, but pollsters and "youth-marketing research companies."[12] As they themselves well know, young people today are "sold" virtually everything, from baggy pants and piercings to fashionable opinions and even university degrees; and in the marketplace, if almost nowhere else, they command respect.[13]

I would argue that the irrelevance of history—the condition of collective amnesia in which Canadians (and others) increasingly seem to find themselves—is nothing less than an essential component of this new socio-economic order and especially of the popular discourses that sustain it. The evidence for this claim is ubiquitous in contemporary Canadian society and may be briefly summarized. Firstly, to cite what has by now become a millennial cliché, we are said to live in a revolutionary age in which social, political, economic and especially technological change orients our thinking towards a "postmodern" future that will be radically different from anything we have known in the past. The "master narrative," we are told, is dead; we have reached (or achieved) "the end of history." Secondly—and this would seem to apply most readily to the young people whose ignorance Granatstein and others find so insufferable—we are informed that we live in a high-tech "information age" (or "knowledge-based economy") in which "new," highly technical sorts of information are privileged, not only in the workplace but in the schools and in the seemingly endless leisure pursuits now available to us. Thirdly, we hear often that historical differences are today diminishing, as the world embraces globalization and rushes headlong into a transnational monoculture dominated by free markets, the English language, Big Macs and Britney Spears. Where historical differences do remain—or where they are "worsening," as in the former Soviet Union or Rwanda or the Middle East—they are highly suspect; to paraphrase Mackenzie King, some parts of the world just seem to have *too much history*. Fourthly, the cohorts for whom historical discourses may actually be relevant are ageing and, in any case, their experiences, though perhaps quaint, have no real bearing on the globalized, postmodern world described above. Lastly, to all of this we may add what is perhaps the most compelling case of all, namely the continuing displacement of history books by televisual, entertainment-oriented mass media driven almost exclusively by advertising profits. This profound cultural shift, heralded so dramatically in the 1980s by the likes of Alan Bloom and Neil Postman, has proceeded apace in the 1990s, to the point where historians now spend a good deal of their classroom time de-programming not only the patriotic nostalgia of the *History Channel* but the pseudo-historical fictions of Hollywood.[14] (As one teacher has so memorably put the case recently, the pedagogical goal when teaching Henry James' *The Wings of the Dove* these days is simply to prevent "an examination of prewar European class structure" from degenerating into "an acrimonious debate over whether or not the decorseted Helena Bonham Carter was 'babe-a-licious'" in the movie version.)[15]

TWO-THIRDS OF EVERYTHING

At the heart of this discursive revolution, starting in the 1980s, has been *pop demography*, a relatively new, extraordinarily influential body of writing which was once published under the decidedly un-scholarly rubric of "futurism."[16] With its origins in the rather fantastic—and also fantastically popular—writings of the likes of Daniel Bell and Alvin Toffler in the 1960s and the 1970s, pop demography is now a vast and varied body of writing that seeks to explain the past, the present and especially the future with reference to inter-generational dynamics. As Harvard demographer Nathan Keyfitz reminds us, true demography—the academic study of "population variables"—dates from the eighteenth century and is a *bona fide* scholarly pursuit, complete with its own journals, associations and, most importantly, methodological standards.[17] Pop demography, by contrast, is a heterogeneous, highly speculative and methodologically undisciplined literature written for a popular readership. It is also, today, a cornerstone of North American publishing.[18] Pop demographers, pollsters, "cool hunters" and other "trend-watchers" now have their own specialized periodical literature (*American Demographics, Futurist*); they enjoy a commanding presence in marketing and sales magazines (*Marketing, Adweek, MediaWeek, Marketing News*), in the business press generally (*Forbes, Money, Report on Business*), and even in general interest periodicals (*Maclean's, Time, Newsweek*). In Canada, as elsewhere, pollsters, including Angus Reid, Allan Gregg and Michael Adams, are today celebrities, staples of talk television and radio, and even best-selling authors.[19] Canadian pop demographers and so-called cyber-gurus, most notably David K. Foot and Don Tapscott, have achieved even greater, international levels of fame and fortune.

Foot, a University of Toronto economist, has, in fact, been at the cutting edge of pop demography since the 1980s. With first edition sales of 600,000 and a second "millennial" edition now in print, Foot's *Boom, Bust and Echo: How to Profit from the Coming Demographic Shift* (1996) is the best selling Canadian non-fiction book in history—emerging, even to the author's surprise, as a pivotal text in the discursive revolution of our times. Never one for understatement, Foot claims in the introduction to this book that demography is "the most powerful—and most underutilized—tool we have to understand the past and to foretell the future" and that, in fact, it "can explain about two-thirds of everything." As the book's subtitle suggests bluntly—and this should come as no surprise from an author whose credentials include a Harvard Ph.D., seats on various corporate boards and a thriving sideline as a consultant to North American corporations—"[d]emographics are critically important for business." Foot boasts that the real "power" of demography is its ability to plot "long-term trends" and that the "further ahead in the future you are looking, the more relevant demographics will be to you." The therapeutic, self-help quality of pop demography—undoubtedly one of the reasons why Foot's work seems to have resonated with so many ordinary people—is pervasive: "For your own peace of mind, you need to understand that what you have experienced may relate more to demographics than to any personal failings. The more knowledge you have about those demographic realties, the better prepared you are to cope with them—and perhaps find a way to turn them to your own advantage." So, too, is its "obvious" applicability, as Foot puts it, to social phenomena: "Who is more likely to join a gang that 'swarms' people and steals their baseball jackets, a senior citizen or a teenager? Who is more likely to attend a chamber music concert, an eleven-year-old or a fifty-one-year old?"[20]

Boom, Bust and Echo divides the Canadian population into various cohorts, the labels for which have by now become commonplace. "Depression kids" have lived "a life of incredible good fortune," since they missed World War II and never had to worry about finding jobs or being promoted; "boomers" have dominated the postwar demographic landscape by virtue of their numbers alone; "Generation X," a term first coined by novelist Douglas Coupland in 1991, is comprised of "late boomers," those born between 1960 and 1966; the "echo" generation is comprised of the children of the boomers, born between 1980 and 1995 ("part of a large cohort and that's always bad news"); and "millennium kids," born between 1995 and 2010, are the children of the baby-buster women, part of a small cohort and therefore a privileged one. The essential social dynamic described in *Boom, Bust and Echo*—and by Foot in his innumerable radio and television appearances—is that of generational competition, in which each cohort, by virtue of its demographic profile alone, occupies a distinct social, cultural and especially economic space that must be continually staked out and defended in relation to the others. To cite only the most dramatic of these supposed rivalries:

> One of the worst things that Gen-Xers have to cope with is their parents—the Depression generation. These are the 55- to 60-year-olds sitting at the top of the corporate ladder, approaching the end of very successful careers, and unable to fathom why their 30-year-old offspring are living at home. Tension is tremendous in these families. Often the father [*sic*] is certain that his own success is based solely on his own merit, while he sees his sons' [*sic*] failure as a lack of drive and ambition.[21]

The current debate about the "ability" of "future generations" to cover the costs of the baby boomers' claims on health care and the Canada Pension Plan is but the most obvious evidence of the impact of the pop demography paradigm on Canadian public policy. In the world according to David K. Foot, generational conflict displaces all other forms of social struggle, pitting fathers against sons, mothers against daughters, middle-aged boomers against *both* the elderly and the young, even the living against the unborn. In this brave new world, Canadians have vested interests rather than traditions, and far from having anything of value to teach each other, each cohort lives in a world of its own making, deeply suspicious of the others and concerned only to prevail in a world of shrinking resources and growing demand for them. Surely this is the death of history.

There are many elements in *Boom, Bust and Echo* worthy of serious critique but I shall limit myself, for the purpose of a brief illustration, to the book's treatment of education in Canada. Foot characterizes the state of the Canadian educational system, circa 1996, in the language of the marketplace, citing data from the OECD: Canada's "spending on education, at more than 7 per cent of gross national product, is the highest per capita among the G-7 leading industrialized countries.... We are spending more on education than other countries and getting less in return. In a world economy in which success is based more on knowledge than on natural resources, Canada's relatively poor performance in education threatens our international competitiveness. *Our social cohesion is also at risk*" (emphasis added). Foot's recommendation for Canada's politicians and educational bureaucrats is, predictably, to improve the "efficiency" of the schools and thereby to increase their output. He subscribes unequivocally to the notion that the demands of the Canadian economy—and the anticipated needs of the labour force in particular—should drive all educational decision-making. Questions of pedagogy and especially curriculum are secondary, as in, for example, his insistence that colleges and universities be integrated: "An ageing population will create more demand for practical courses, of the kind offered by colleges, than for theoretical courses that are the specialty of the universities." The *laissez faire* assumptions behind Foot's analysis of postsecondary education are blunt: "Rather than sit back and wait for customers, colleges and universities should build their businesses aggressively." Universities "can no longer afford to be ivory towers." Unhurried intellectual reflection—arguably the hallmark of a liberal education—will increasingly be offered only to a constituency which is older, not in need of job training and sufficiently leisured and monied to pursue academic study as a lifestyle choice. Not only will seniors "pay for the chance to work all day looking for dinosaur bones" but it is also true that the "60-year-old who has a good time on a dinosaur dig with an expert from the department of archaeology or who benefits from a college course on home renovation may be favourably disposed when she [*sic*] makes out her will."[22] Whatever Foot might like to claim about the applicability of population analysis to educational reform—or, for that matter, to any aspect of public policy—in *Boom, Bust and Echo* he deploys pop demography in the service of a revolutionary shift in government priorities, towards the marketplace and away from anything resembling a traditional, liberal arts notion of the public good.[23] For Foot, the dictates of the marketplace and the public good are synonymous.

NOTHING IN COMMON

David K. Foot's role in popularizing the application of ostensibly demographic analysis to Canadian social life can hardly be overestimated. Michael Adams' *Sex in the Snow: Canadian Social Values at the End of the*

Millennium (1997) is a dramatic example of this trend—and more generally of the tyranny now exerted by pop demography over supposedly serious social commentary in this country. Adams is a veteran pollster at Environics and, like Foot, a recognizable television personality. *Sex in the Snow* is centred on the claim, interestingly, that "[m]ore and more Canadians refuse to be constrained by the specifics of their demographics; instead they are determined to be the authors of their own identities and destinies." Adams elaborates this thesis along what might be called extreme liberal-technological lines, arguing that "the media-rich environment in which we live is making it easier for people to construct for themselves sets of values that are not limited by personal demographic characteristics." Canadians are free to not only "invent" themselves but, as he puts it, to "reinvent" themselves: "[N]ew interactive information technology allows Canadians to explore and express different facets of their own personalities, unburdened by such demographic characteristics as sex, race or religion. It allows for the personality equivalent of digital compression." For Adams, since the biological, historical and especially material conditions of Canadians' lives (class, gender, ethnicity, religion) are not particularly important in the new age of Net-based technologies, they are simply no longer consequential to Canadians' lived experience. Cyberspace, he enthuses, is creating a global culture in which the realities of people's lives (conceived as limits to individual choice) matter much less than the fictions that they can imaginatively ascribe to themselves.[24]

Like *Boom, Bust and Echo*, *Sex in the Snow* breaks contemporary Canadian society into labelled cohorts, which Adams calls "values tribes." The methodology ostensibly used, firstly to demonstrate that Canadians have fragmented into tribes, and secondly to describe the values content of those tribes, Adams calls "cluster analysis" or "sophisticated multivariate computer analysis." (Such jargon itself enhances the mystique of pop demographics.) Of Adams' twelve tribes, three are comprised of Canadians 50 years of age or older, four of baby boomers, and five of "post-boomers." Of the latter, the most socially and culturally significant is the group the author labels "Aimless Dependants," the largest of the five youth tribes, comprising 1.9 million Canadians (fully

8 per cent of the total population) in 1995. The content and especially the tone of Adams' treatment of this group — which is often flippant, occasionally grave and always condescending — hinges on his observation that its members tend to "approach life in a somewhat unemotional way, scoring low on values measuring an adventurous, open attitude towards life." The most significant attribute of this tribe is its anxiety and rage — symptoms, says Adams, of "a very weak sense of being in control of their lives." Although he does nothing whatsoever to contextualize the socio-economic plight of these young Canadians, he observes that "their anxiety is expressed through an obsession with job security" and concludes that "they have found *nothing satisfactory to replace tradition* and as a result are 'slackers without a cause'" (emphasis added). They are, says Adams, "people who have allowed their fears — and sometimes their laziness or inertia — to shut them off from much of what the world has to offer in terms of social, spiritual and material pleasures.... Aimless Dependants are poor navigators in the consumer marketplace and in life in general."[25] Thus does he dispose of the 1.9 million Canadian young people whose life circumstances — family life, social class, ethnicity, education, language skills, cultural capital, etc. — have relegated them to the margins of society.[26]

Robert Collins' *You Had to Be There: An Intimate Portrait of the Generation that Survived the Depression, Won the War and Re-Invented Canada* is another significant text in the pop demography *oeuvre*. The book is the outgrowth of a 1995 commemorative article on World War II commissioned by *Maclean's*, in which the author interviewed 181 men and women who shared with him "their memories and opinions." Instead of "sharing" their experiences in any informative, historical sense, however, in *You Had to Be There* Collins' interviewees are deployed in a relentless defence of the proposition that "[t]he views and perhaps the values of my generation are seriously out of synch with those of most younger Canadians today." Says Collins of his cohort, "We like music with lyrics we can understand.... We wonder how girls with rings in their lips and studs in their tongues can eat without slobbering. We don't understand how guys can blow their noses with rings in them. We wonder why pre-teens' hands never extend from the sleeves of their jackets." Privileging technology and especially superficial stylistic fads over the crucial political, social and economic interests which Canadians most certainly do have in common, he concludes, "we differ vastly from our children and grandchildren...." (That Collins does not explore in detail the extraordinary similarity of the economic plight of Depression-era youth and the downward mobility of youth today seems to me particularly unfortunate.) If Collins does actually speak for an entire cohort, which is his explicit claim, it is one that now believes itself to be under siege. In response to "the occasional querulous twenty-something" who has "cited our free postwar education as yet another example of our alleged joy ride through life," Collins retorts defiantly, "this is absurd.... We earned it!"[27]

To the extent that *You Had to Be There* provides any historical analysis of the formative experiences of "Generation M[ature]," class, gender, ethnic, regional and especially ideological differences are collapsed in favour of a consensus approach centred, predictably, on its members' common age. There is, for example, no analysis of the Canadian economy in the 1930s. The only claim the book makes in this respect — although it is muted by Collins' somewhat nostalgic description of respectable men who were merely "down on their luck" — is that Canadians were stigmatized for taking relief. There is no analysis of the politicization of the young men in the relief camps, nor of the efforts of Canadians on the political left to confront what they saw as the crisis of capitalism. The CCF is mentioned, but only on the context of its attempt to aid Depression-era farmers doubly hurt by drought and the collapse of grain prices; the radical left is not mentioned at all. Far from seeing common themes in Canadians' episodic struggles in hard times, Collins criticizes baby boomers and their children for their abuses of the welfare system his generation built from scratch (even as he claims that "the Depression left us with an abiding sympathy for people in need"). He might, one presumes, have indulged what has become a popular distinction between the "deserving poor" of the Depression era and the alleged "welfare fraud" perpetrators of our own time, but he does not.

Collins' concluding chapter, "The Way We Are," evinces most strikingly the defensive and sometimes apologetic tone that pervades the book, starting with the extremely important observation that contemporary Canada is characterized by "ageism."[28] Collins states bluntly that younger Canadians now openly "vent their wrath" on seniors, often stereotyping them as casino addicts and opportunists who expect younger tax-payers to subsidize their affluent retirements. He is quite correct to reject insulting contemporary stereotypes about the elderly, including their presumed technophobia. (He notes that many of his generation have been technophiles throughout their lives, and he explicitly condemns David K. Foot for his condescending suggestion that Collins' generation probably does not like to use bank machines.) Occasionally, Collins appeals to inter-generational sensitivity but not unambiguously: "We are not without pity for young Canadians in the current merciless job market. Over and over, my age group has expressed genuine sympathy for today's young job-hunters. But all their mewling and snivelling gets under our skin." The book ends with an allusion to the common experience of his generation and young people in the 1990s, at least insofar as "[b]oth groups are facing a profound biological change" and both are "distrusted or disliked by other generations." Collins opines: "I doubt we could penetrate the teenager's private domain of self-absorption, but pre-teens might be receptive. Already, they've been exposed to more information than our parents ingested in a lifetime. Yet perhaps there is something they can learn from us about touch and caring, manners and civility, friendship and humanity." Regrettably, nothing in the text itself seems to support such an optimistic and important claim.[29]

Growing up Digital: The Rise of the Net Generation by Canadian Internet booster Don Tapscott is a leading text in the burgeoning field of cyber-prophecy and another excellent example of the discursive revolution spearheaded by the likes of David K. Foot. Building explicitly on Foot's ostensibly demographic model, Tapscott warns gravely that the maturation of the "Net Generation" (North Americans who were between the ages of 2 and 22 in 1998) is likely to be accompanied by a full-scale inter-generational war: "Unless the boomers have a change of heart about youth, their culture and their media, the two biggest generations in history may be on a collision course—a battle of the generational titans.... The writing is on the wall for the techno-phobic, old-style-thinking boomers. Unless they throw out years of conditioning, they will be washed away by the N-Gen tsunami." Other than a couple of anecdotes about children being able to program their parents' VCRs, Tapscott provides no evidence whatsoever for the utterly dubious claim that baby boomers are technophobic and resistant to change; yet *Growing Up Digital* hinges entirely on the twin propositions that, in marked contrast with their elders, N-Geners experience Net-based technologies as "transparent" and that this experience, especially as it applies to the world of work, is itself revolutionary: "Increasingly, N-Geners don't see the technology at all. They see the people, information, games, applications, services, friends, and protagonists at the other end. They don't see a computer screen, they see their friends' messages, their 'zines, their fanclubs, their chat groups, Crash, Bandicoot, the Sistine Chapel, the Mayan ruins, and Our Lady Peace." Technology is only *technology*, claims Tapscott, for the people who were born before it was invented (a myth now also widely promulgated within the computer industry, most notably in the advertising of corporate giants like IBM, Microsoft and Cisco). Like many of the children whose online habits he is already celebrating, Tapscott seems incapable of distinguishing between the real world and cyberspace. (Does he really believe that anonymous exchanges of personal data constitutes friendship, or that a computer graphic is somehow the equivalent of the Sistine Chapel ceiling?) As for critics of this brave new world, including parents and others who worry that too much time spent in front of the computer is stifling children's social maturation, Tapscott simply dismisses them as cowards: "It is not the N-Gen children who are being robbed of social development, it is those adults who, through fear or ignorance, deny themselves the experience of participating in the great revolution of our times."[30]

The confusion of the real world and cyberspace is, of course, simply confusion, not transparency. But it is, without question, confusion of the most profitable kind—something Tapscott well knows, since his musings never stray far from the agenda of his primary audience, business: "Digital kids are learning precisely the social skills which will be required for effective interaction in the digital economy. They are learning about peer relationships, about teamwork, about being critical...." N-Geners, Tapscott reassures his presumably corporate readership, are hard-working, ambitious and above all optimistic about their place in the private sector economy: "Companies want a flexible workforce and they have also found that this is a way to reduce costs by paying workers less and by using people only when necessary. We can anticipate that many N-Geners will actually prefer such arrangements, providing improved work variety and opportunity for skill enhancement and lifelong learning." (He does not explain why an entrepreneurial and highly independent generation would "prefer" a system of constantly shifting, insecure, low-wage jobs.) Relatedly, Tapscott embraces the collapsing boundary between education and commerce.[31] In the cyber-classroom, he enthuses, children will teach each other and teachers will be re-cast as "facilitators," standing by as the kids create web pages of their own design. As one of his cyber-teachers reports enthusiastically: "The kids not only learned about the new media and developed language and presentation skills, they learned about how to interact with clients and meet deadlines...."[32] Surely, this is the death of history.

Like Michael Adams and other pollsters-for-hire, who, it is worth recalling, are primarily in the business of asking people for their opinions, Tapscott presumes that what 2- to 22-year-olds "think" has some bearing on the kind of world they inhabit. Giving credence to young Canadians' speculations on their adult careers, for example, or on future labour force conditions (something even economists cannot predict accurately) seems absurd; and yet it is precisely this sort of opinion-survey methodology, deployed so relentlessly by business in its pursuit of new markets, that gives young people the impression that what they "think" matters greatly—far more than, say, the social, political or material conditions of their lives, conditions over which they enjoy virtually no control and in which, as J.L. Granatstein and others attest, they show little interest.[33] If, as I would argue, history (and, indeed, the other humanities and social sciences) have as their *raison d'être* the study of people's lived experience within the context of their life circumstances, then this kind of methodology, and especially the discourses it informs, constitutes nothing less than a full-blown intellectual revolt.

Doug Owram's *Born at the Right Time: A History of the Baby Boom Generation* shows how far in the direction of pop demography at least one professional historian has travelled in the last decade. Owram argues that "[f]rom the time the baby boom was born, it was extraordinarily powerful and from a young age, it thought of itself as a group distinct from previous generations." (Can generations "think"?) Taking a page from David K. Foot, he notes explicitly in his preface that his "Generation X" undergraduates in the 1990s have shown an "unremittingly hostile" attitude towards baby boomers, even suggesting that the "intergenerational warfare" of our times itself legitimizes a generational approach to historical research.[34]

Owram is at pains to delimit the precise composition of the generation under study in *Born at the Right Time*, a tortured intellectual exercise that illustrates, paradoxically, the substantial limitations of this approach:

> In what follows, I attempt to re-create some of the primary interests of baby boomers without pretending that everyone in the generation can be captured in such a story. Practicality required that I concentrate on the mainstream of the generation rather than the margins.... The very poor, the very remote, certain ethnic communities had a very different experience and, just as they did not fully participate in the generational sense of self, so they are not fully part of this story. Nor, for that matter, are the very rich, or those who, for whatever reason, did not become tied into the broad youth world of the postwar years.

Having defined "the mainstream of the generation" so exclusively, Owram proceeds to correlate it explicitly to the youth counterculture of the 1960s and to speak, not of a generation *per se* but of a "shock wave effect," a "shared historical moment," a certain "outlook and experience":

As shock wave or a shared historical experience, the baby boom does not run from 1946 to 1962. Those on the sharp upward curve of births created the shock wave effect. Those who were children in the 1950s and grew through teenage years to adulthood in the 1960s and early 1970s can lay some claim to the shared historical moment. Those who came later shared neither in the shock wave effect nor in the cultural influence of the baby boom period.

By means of such rationalization, Owram backs well away from the generational analysis promised in his subtitle, locating the cultural and historical essence of the "baby boom generation" in an overwhelmingly urban, middle-class, English-Canadian youth *counterculture*, one whose defining experience was that of adolescence and young adulthood in the late 1960s. And as one might expect, even this assertion demands extensive qualification:

> Only a small percentage of young people in the 1960s were political radicals, but a much greater number, especially in the universities, grew up in an age in which youth and radicalism were connected. New ideas swarmed over the generation. Though some of these ideas would fade, the radicalism of the sixties shaped the ethics of a generation and defined the political agenda for the next decades.

(Can a generation have "ethics"?) Having generalized about the baby boom generation from an admittedly small number of youth radicals—a generalization that ignores those young Canadians, possibly the majority, who did not challenge the socio-economic status quo even in the 1960s—Owram is also forced to concede that many of the "new" ideas that were "swarming" around were, in fact, inherited from older Canadians (most notably George Grant) and from thinkers from the even more distant past (including Marx, the social gospellers, the Transcendentalists, Gandhi, and the Existentialists). By the time he has finished whittling the baby boom "generation" down, little remains of it.[35]

However much he might like to valorize (or even nostalgize) the "power" of his own generation, I would argue that nothing in Doug Owram's characterization of the baby boom rescues it from the claim now commonly made in studies of the 1950s "teenager," namely that the social construction of this enormously profitable cohort derived, not from what Owram calls its "generational sense of self," but from the advertisers, marketers and promoters who "discovered" it.[36] Owram's claim that the baby boom generation underwent a "shared historical experience" may well be true. But he has not, in my view, demonstrated in *Born at the Right Time* that this experience originated from within the cohort itself; indeed, the bulk of his book locates the experiences of the baby boom generation well within a conventional historical framework of continuity and change, emphasizing the dominant role of socio-economic conditions over which the cohort had virtually no control (including, for example, the extraordinary growth of the Canadian economy in the postwar period, changing child-rearing practises, the rise of the suburbs, educational reform and the massive growth of the universities, the rise of the civil rights movement and of feminism, and especially the emergence of television, rock music and other highly profitable cohort-specific mass media). In the end, I would argue, Owram's claim that a "generational history" is possible or even desirable runs headlong into his own overwhelming evidence to the contrary.

CONCLUSION: ALONE TOGETHER

A discourse is, at bottom, a way of talking about something. Discourses are always socially constructed and anchored in power relationships, however socially or politically neutral they might appear; and however permanent or intractable they seem, they are always fluid rather than static, products of shifting patterns of social consensus and struggle, of compromise and refusal. When discourses achieve hegemony, they are invisible; they become naturalized. We lose sight of them precisely because they so effectively seem to represent the world as we experience it. A triumphant discourse is, in the words of French economist Jacques Attali, a "monologue of power."[37]

Pop demography, as I have tried to sketch it here, is a discourse whose time has come. It constitutes a radical new conception of the relationship of Canadians to each other and to their past, one which reduces social conflict—if not social experience—to competition between generational cohorts. In so doing it challenges all competing discourses, particularly those centring on seemingly out-of-date notions like tradition, custom, continuity, narrative and history. Pop demography is a paradoxical discourse in so far as it simultaneously cuts us off from each other—driving deep wedges into our most immediate sources of identity, community and tradition (the family, the school, the workplace)—even as it seems to collectivize our experience of the world. It simultaneously accounts for our sometimes overwhelming experience of personal isolation and alienation, even as it reassures us that we share this experience with others. In the world of pop demography, we are alone together. The therapeutic quality of the *genre*—epitomized in David Foot's explicit presumption that his readers are experiencing a sense of "personal fail[ure]" and are, therefore, in search of "peace of mind"—derives from the idea that we are part of a larger group whose experience of the world is more or less exactly like ours. It makes appeal, in short, to the same collectivist impulses that have traditionally grounded our sense of identity (class, ethnicity, gender, religion, ideology), even as it sunders the linkages between our actual traditions and our lived experience.

Pop demography is a paradigm whose time has come precisely because it privileges the social categories that have risen to hegemony under neo-conservatism and the economics of globalization. In the most superficial texts of the *genre*—Adams' *Sex in the Snow*, for example—the essential similarity of people within a cohort (or a "values tribe") derives entirely from their lifestyle choices and especially their patterns of consumption. Such a claim might well be laughable in an era of relative socio-economic stability, but it is extremely powerful in our own times because it accords perfectly with our anxious, fragmented experience of the world. We are encouraged to think of ourselves, at least in the public sphere, as consumers above all—not only as consumers of products and services but of government programs. Certainly we have come to expect that the advertisers, marketing analysts, music and movie promoters, and sloganeers who today dominate public life situate us subjectively as members of "niche" markets designated according to ostensibly demographic criteria. We are acutely attuned to the nuances of these commercial strategies, recognizing immediately when we are being "positioned" within them, whether we are buying chewing gum, mutual funds, automobiles or university degrees. Pop demography is the pseudo-sociology of our times because it represents the world as we are now so relentlessly urged to see it.

Whither history? Historical discourses, those premised on the viability and especially the relevance of coherent narratives that link the past and the present, are in retreat against this monologue of power. What is worse, at least from my vantage point, is that the historians, teachers and others who are deeply worried by this trend have shown a troubling inclination to criticize each other—tinkering with curricula, textbooks and classroom teaching methods—and too little inclination to confront its broader cultural context. Increasingly, I am drawn to the daunting conclusion that history will only be resuscitated by means of a discursive counter-revolution, one that takes place, not in the classrooms, where we already preach to the converted, but in the streets, as it were. Short of an economic or political crisis of truly "historic" proportions—which would no doubt expose pop demography as the fanciful propaganda that it is—there must be a renewed emphasis upon history, not as a sterile academic exercise, but as the organizing principle of Canadians' lived experience. J.L. Granatstein is quite correct to call for a return to history as the prism through by which people "learn who they are," but any such restoration will require a great deal of "unlearning," as we attempt to deconstruct and subvert the dominant discourses of our times and to affirm the tangible, life-affirming narratives to which Canadians have a right.

NOTES

1. J.L. Granatstein, *Who Killed Canadian History?* (Toronto: Harper Collins, 1998), p. 3. See also David Jay Bercuson, Robert Bothwell and J.L. Granatstein, *The Great Brain Robbery: Canada's Universities on the Road to Ruin* (Toronto: McClelland and Stewart, 1984); David Jay Bercuson, Robert Bothwell and J.L. Granatstein, *Petrified Campus: The Crisis in Canada's Universities* (Toronto: Random House, 1997); Ken Osborne, "Review of Granatstein, *Who Killed Canadian History?*", *Canadian Historical Review* 80: 1 (1999); A.B. McKillop, "Who Killed Canadian History? A View from the Trenches," *Canadian Historical Review* 80:2 (1999); and Bryan D. Palmer, "Of Silences and Trenches: A Dissident View of Granatstein's Meaning," *Canadian Historical Review* 80:4 (1999).

2. *Hansard* Number 72 (12 March 1998).

3. *Hansard* Number 3 (24 September 1997).

4. McGill University, *Giving the Past a Future: Conference on the Teaching and Learning of Canadian History* (January 1999).

5. At an international conference on federalism held in Quebec in October 1999, Chrétien pegged the date of Confederation at 1864 and Bouchard, at 1868.

6. Michael Bliss, "Privatizing the Mind: The Sundering of Canadian History, The Sundering of Canada," *Journal of Canadian Studies* 26 (1991–2), pp. 5–17. See also Gregory S. Kealey, "Class in English-Canadian Historical Writing: Neither Privatizing, Nor Sundering," *Journal of Canadian Studies* 27: 2 (Summer 1992), pp. 123–9; and Linda Kealey, Ruth Pierson, Joan Sangster and Veronica Strong-Boag, "Teaching Canadian History in the 1990s: Whose 'National' History are We Lamenting," *Journal of Canadian Studies* 27:2 (Summer 1992), pp. 129–31.

7. Ted Byfield, "How Come We're Paying People to Inflict Social Amnesia on Us?" *Alberta Report/Western Report* (12 June 1995), p. 52. See also Virginia Byfield, "History, Beaten to Death by a Gang," *Alberta Report/Western Report* (4 May 1998).

8. Ted Byfield, "We Don't Teach Canadian History Because It's Incompatible with Canadian Culture," *Alberta Report/Western Report* (4 May 1998), p. 52.

9. David Frum, *What's Right: The New Conservatism and What it Means for Canada* (Toronto: Random House, 1996), Introduction.

10. Ian Angus, *A Border Within: National Identity, Cultural Plurality and Wilderness* (Montreal: McGill-Queen's University Press, 1997), p. 5. See

also Gary Teeple, *Globalization and the Decline of Social Reform* (Toronto: Garamond Press, 1995).

11. See, for example, John Gray, *Lost in North America: The Imaginary Canadian in the American Dream* (Vancouver: Talonbooks, 1994); Richard Gwyn, *Nationalism Without Walls: The Unbearable Lightness of Being Canadian* (Toronto: McClelland and Stewart, 1995); Peter C. Newman, *The Canadian Revolution: From Deference to Defiance* (Toronto: Viking, 1995); Franklin Griffiths, *Strong and Free: Canada and the New Sovereignty* (Toronto: Stoddart, 1996); Tom Henighan, *The Presumption of Culture: Structure, Strategy and Survival in the Canadian Cultural Landscape* (Vancouver: Raincoast, 1996); James Laxer, *False God: How the Globalization Myth has Impoverished Canada* (Toronto: Lester, 1993) and also Laxer, *In Search of a New Left: Canadian Politics after the Neoconservative Assault* (Toronto: Viking, 1996). James Laxer's *The Undeclared War: Class Conflict in the Age of Cyber Capitalism* (Toronto: Viking, 1998) is nothing less than a single-minded attempt to reverse this discursive shift. See also Linda McQuaig, *Shooting the Hippo: Death by Deficit and Other Canadian Myths* (Toronto: Penguin, 1996); and Maude Barlow and Bruce Campbell, *Straight through the Heart: How the Liberals Abandoned the Just Society and What Canadians Can Do about It* (Toronto: HarperCollins, 1996).

12. See "The Year for Kids," *Maclean's* (21 December 1992), p. 58.

13. See "The Serene Teens," *Maclean's* (15 April 1991), p. 52.

14. See Alan Bloom, *The Closing of the American Mind* (New York: Simon & Schuster, 1987); Neil Postman, *Amusing Ourselves to Death: Public Discourse in the Age of Show Business* (New York: Viking 1985); Postman, *Technopoly: The Surrender of Culture to Technology* (New York: Random House, 1992); and Herbert I. Schiller, *Culture Inc.: The Corporate Takeover of Public Expression* (New York: Oxford University Press, 1989).

15. Henry Fassbender, cited in Gary Trudeau, "*Amistad* is Important. Discuss," *Time Canada* 150:27 (December 1997–January 1998), p. 116. See also Karen Paul, "*EL* Takes You to the Movies," *Emergency Librarian* 25:2 (November/December 1997).

16. See Robert Fulford, "1960s Prophet Saw the Internet Vision, But Not Its Scale," *Globe and Mail* (29 October 1999). Canada's best known "futurist" text, one that anticipated David K. Foot and *pop demography*, is perhaps John Kettle's *The Big Generation* (Toronto: McClelland and Stewart, 1980).

17. Nathan Keyfitz, "Demography," in Adam Kuper and Jessica Kuper, eds., *The Social Science Encyclopaedia*, second edition (London: Routledge, 1989), pp. 188–191. In the Canadian context, see Roderic Beaujot, *Population Change*

in Canada: The Challenges of Policy Adaptation (Toronto: McClelland and Stewart, 1991).

18. Books in the *genre* include, but are no means limited to, the following: Rob Nelson and John Cowan, *Revolution X: A Survival Guide for Our Generation* (New York: Penguin, 1994); Jason Cohen and Michael Krugman, *Generation Ecch!* (New York: Simon & Schuster, 1994); Karen Ritchie, *Marketing to Generation X* (New York: Lexington, 1995); David K. Foot (with Daniel Stoffman), *Boom, Bust and Echo: How to Profit from the Coming Demographic Shift* (Toronto: Macfarlane Walter and Ross, 1996); Robin Bernstein and Seth Clark Silberman, *Generation Q: Gays, Lesbians and Bisexuals Born around 1969's Stonewall Riots Tell Their Stories of Growing up in the Age of Information* (Los Angeles: Alyson, 1996); Michael Adams, *Sex in the Snow: Canadian Social Values at the End of the Millennium* (Toronto: Viking/Penguin, 1997); Robert Collins, *You Had to Be There: An Intimate Portrait of the Generation that Survived the Depression, Won the War and Re-Invented Canada* (Toronto: McClelland and Stewart, 1997); Danny Seo, *Generation React: Activism for Beginners* (New York: Ballantyne, 1997); and Don Tapscott, *Growing up Digital: The Rise of the Net Generation* (New York, McGraw-Hill, 1998).

19. See, for example, Angus Reid, *Shakedown: How the New Economy Is Changing Our Lives* (Toronto: Doubleday, 1996); Reginald W. Bibby and Donald C. Posterski, *Teen Trends: A Nation in Motion* (Toronto: Stoddart, 1992); Reginald Bibby, *The Bibby Report: Social Trends Canadian Style* (Toronto: Stoddart, 1995); and especially Adams, *Sex in the Snow*.

20. Foot, *Boom, Bust and Echo*, pp. 2–7.

21. Ibid., pp. 16–25.

22. Ibid., Chapter 8 "Rethinking Education."

23. Ontario premier Mike Harris, for one, would seem to agree with Foot's estimation of the province's educational priorities. Speaking in February 2000 to an audience of high-tech workers, Harris quipped: "Some of the traditional academics say 'Well, Harris doesn't understand university. It's for higher learning. Unless you study Greek and Latin and all these things, you'll never be a real true thinker'." See "Harris Hits Back at His Critics in Academia," *National Post* (11 February 2000).

24. Adams, *Sex in the Snow*, pp. 32–9, 126–139.

25. Ibid., pp. 105–8.

26. For evidence of the bona fide socio-economic plight of young Canadians in the 1990s, see Marlene Webber, *Street Kids: The Tragedy of Canada's Runaways* (Toronto: University of Toronto Press, 1991); Paul Anisef and Paul Axelrod, eds., *Transitions: Schooling and Employment in Canada* (Toronto:

Thompson, 1993); John F. Conway, *The Canadian Family in Crisis* (Toronto: Lorimer, 1993); Anthony N. Doob, et al., *Youth Crime and the Youth Justice System in Canada: A Research Perspective* (Toronto: University of Toronto Centre of Criminology, 1995); and Burt Gallaway and Joe Hudson, eds., *Youth in Transition: Perspectives on Research and Policy* (Toronto: Thompson, 1996).

27. Collins, *You Had to Be There*, pp. ix–5, 105.

28. Collins quotes Canadian broadcaster Roy Bonisteel: "Canadians tend to discard the elderly whenever we can." (p. 251).

29. For an alternative to the pop demography paradigm as it applies to the recollections of Depression-era Canadians, see Victor Howard, *We Were the Salt of the Earth! A Narrative of the On-to-Ottawa Trek and the Regina Riot* (Regina: Canadian Plains Research Centre, 1985); and Barry Broadfoot, *Ten Lost Years 1929–1939: Memories of Canadians Who Survived the Depression* (Markham: Paperjacks, 1975). See also James Struthers, *No Fault of Their Own: Employment and the Canadian Welfare State 1914–1941* (Toronto: University of Toronto Press, 1983).

30. Tapscott, *Growing up Digital*, pp. 1–5, 10, 39. Tapscott is the chairperson of the Alliance for Converging Technologies.

31. In place of any serious evidence showing that computer-driven pedagogy improves learning at any level, Tapscott provides a lengthy anecdote about a four-year-old named Ryan who taught himself to read using a computer program called *Reader Rabbit* (p. 128). For a thoroughgoing critique of the collapsing boundary between education and commerce, see Heather-jane Robertson, *No More Teachers, No More Books: The Commercialization of Canada's Schools* (Toronto: McClelland and Stewart, 1998).

32. Vicki Saunders, cited in Tapscott, *Growing up Digital*, p. 156.

33. This new discourse — one that privileges young people's opinions above all else — has become increasingly evident in my undergraduate classes, where students now routinely substitute autobiographical anecdote for evidence from their assigned readings. The influence of "talk show" discourses, including the ostensibly democratic notion that all opinion carries equal weight, is also noteworthy in this respect.

34. Doug Owram, *Born at the Right Time: A History of the Baby Boom Generation* (Toronto: University of Toronto Press, 1996), pp. ix–xii. The same tendency informed earlier work on the counterculture in Canada. See Myrna Kostash, *Long Way from Home: The Story of the Sixties Generation in Canada* (Toronto: Lorimer, 1980) and also Kostash, *No Kidding: Inside the World of Teenage Girls* (Toronto: McClelland and Stewart, 1987).

35. Owram, *Born at the Right Time*, pp. xi–xiv, ch. 9.

36. See, for example, Lawrence Grossberg, *We Gotta Get Out of This Place* (New York and London: Routledge, 1992). In the Canadian context, see Mary Louise Adams, *The Trouble with Normal: Postwar Youth and the Making of Heterosexuality* (Toronto: University of Toronto Press, 1997). Adams notes that, in the 1950s, "business interests responded to economic and demographic changes by nurturing teen consumerism and targeting youth as a specific market. Teen magazines, rock and roll, teen films, teen columns in newspapers, teen sections in department stores were all products of the 'discovery' of the teenager." (p. 42).

37. Jacques Attali, *Noise: The Political Economy of Music* (Minneapolis: University of Minnesota Press, 1985; originally published in 1977), p. 9.

CHAPTER FIVE

THE WAY WE WERE?

HISTORY AS INFOTAINMENT IN THE AGE OF HISTORY TELEVISION

To judge from the scholarly literature, the rise of history television—which now reaches millions of Canadian television viewers every week and tens of millions in the United States—has not been of much formal concern to historians. I find this surprising, partly because such cable services are enjoying enviable success but also because history television executives now routinely take credit for doing what academic historians are no longer thought capable of: making history interesting, entertaining, relevant and popular. History television ought to interest us for any number of reasons, but I shall limit myself to an exploration of the discursive means by which it legitimizes itself as the last best hope for the historically challenged. In the end, I must say that although my research has not tempered my opinion that corporate-controlled, profit-driven history television is a poor—and sometimes dangerous—surrogate for professional historiography, it has certainly added a curious twist to my understanding of the current crisis in Canadian history. If J.L. Granatstein really believes that there are no longer "heroes in our past to stir the soul, and no myths on which a national spirit can be built,"[1] at least one inescapable conclusion may be drawn: J.L. Granatstein does not have cable.

LAUNCHING HISTORY

According to *American History Illustrated*, the idea of a cable channel devoted entirely to history was inspired by the "immense popularity" of Ken Burns' 1991 television series on the US Civil War, which was viewed by roughly 14 million people. In the fall of 1993 two "competing cable companies" announced that they were planning to launch history channels: the Liberty/Cox/Advance-owned Discovery Channel proposed a service called The History Network, while the Hearst/ABC/NBC-owned Arts & Entertainment (A&E) organization proposed The History TV Network. Both groups were said to be planning schedules of "documentaries, mini-series, and movies with historical themes" — a generic programming menu virtually guaranteeing that only one of these proposed services would make it to air.[2] For reasons that are not entirely clear, A&E prevailed: The History TV Network was re-christened The History Channel and launched on 1 January 1995, with an initial audience of 1 million cable subscribers. The service has since exceeded even its own executives' initial projections; by the spring of 1996 The History Channel had 16 million subscribers; currently, it has in excess of 62 million subscribers.[3]

That The History Channel was an idea whose time had come had been suggested both by polling data on Americans' historical knowledge and by A&E's own market research. In April 1994, for example, the Gallup organization published data showing that for 21 per cent of Americans "television was their primary source of historical information." Books (which for the purposes of the poll excluded school textbooks) scored only slightly higher, at 23 per cent. Roughly half of those Gallup had polled said that they were "somewhat or very interested" in history, and fully two-thirds said that "television had not done enough to promote an interest in history." A&E was said to be "buoyed by the [Gallup] findings" as it set about to launch The History Channel.[4] According to Dan Davids, Senior Vice President and General Manager at History, "focus groups and quantitative research" had revealed the same trend: "Americans are more interested in history now than they were five years ago."[5]

From the outset, The History Channel was conceived as a cable service that would be both educational and entertaining, making it a leading exemplar of the Nineties trend in televisual mass media towards "infotainment." As History Channel Vice President Charles Maday put it in 1995, just a month after launch, the new channel provided "viewer-friendly, original historical programming that stimulates the mind and creates a level of historical awareness in an entertaining and informative way."[6] With respect at least to this imperative to "stimulate the mind," The History Channel may be said to bear a greater resemblance to "public" television (PBS, TVO, etc.) than to its myriad commercial competitors. Unlike The Learning Channel, for example, which has abandoned any pretence of pedagogical value in favour of highly sensationalised natural disaster footage and paramedical reportage, The History Channel is predicated on the twin notions that history is a weighty business and that its programming cannot be "dumbed down" *ad infinitum* to appeal to a mass audience.

The History Channel is thus a "niche" service in the strictest sense, with strong appeal to a minority viewership. Practically, this means subsidizing the "hard core" historical content—particularly documentaries—with more popular fare, most notably feature films with "historical themes." This has, in fact, turned out to be a winning strategy. Within a year of its launch, The History Channel ranked as "the network most [cable] operators intended to add," beating ESPN2 (sports), Home and Garden, TLC, the Cartoon network and the Sci-Fi Channel. When asked about their intentions to add the History Channel, cable executives cited the channel's "program quality." As Jack Myers, Chairman and CEO of Myers Communications, put it: "There's a strong perception of the brand from its marketing. And it has a high perceived value in terms of revenue potential for operators."[7] More significantly perhaps, anecdotal evidence suggests that The History Channel was making converts. Writing in 1997, Mark Vittert praised History's appeal to "folks just like us, the ones who 'don't know much about….' It's a reprieve for goof-offs like me who sat through Mr. Alverson's history class drawing mazes. It's also a second chance for those of us who thought the Gettysburg Address was too long and drawn out. All of a sudden, I like history—a lot…."[8]

However much this infotainment strategy has fattened the bottom line at The History Channel, and even helped to attract "goof-offs" like

Vittert, it has not resolved the deep tensions inherent in its efforts to be both a thinking person's pastime, on the one hand, and a competitive commercial broadcaster, on the other. From the outset, for instance, History was intended to feature blockbuster Hollywood movies. But because Hollywood filmmakers have been known to be cavalier about the historical accuracy of their work, the network inaugurated après-film panels of "guest historians and journalists whose commentary will provide historical context, reveal any dramatic license taken by the director, and explore myths that may surround the subject being presented."[9] This is, of course, a case of having one's cash-cow and eating it too. A more serious challenge to the integrity of The History Channel has been the perception that its relationship to its own corporate sponsors is too cosy. In late 1996, for example, History commissioned a documentary series called *The Spirit of Enterprise*, which was to have profiled the growth of American corporations. When it came to light that the series' corporate underwriters—Boeing, Du Pont and AT&T—were to be given "editorial content over their own profiles," a media furore ensued and History quickly cancelled the series.[10] In the press release that followed, the network justified its decision by reminding people that "Our mission at the History Channel is to adhere to the highest programming standards which our viewers have come to expect."[11]

HISTORY TELEVISION

History Television, the Canadian cable service launched in October 1997, was not only conceptually derivative of the US History Channel but also owed much of its early success to the cross-border promotion of its American forebear via A&E.[12] In the fall of 1996, the CRTC approved the addition of 28 new specialty channels to Canadian cable television. Of these, only four were granted "immediate priority," namely CTV News One, History Television, the Comedy Network and Teletoon; the others were reported as having to wait "until new digital-compression technology expands the potential of the cable universe."[13] Originally a partnership between Alliance Broadcasting and CTV, History Television was tagged from the outset as "a Canadian version of A&E's The History Channel," though in true Canadian broadcasting fashion network executives were at pains both to differentiate their service from the American and to imbue this differentiation with ideological import. Asked prior to launch how History Television would differ from The History Channel, Janet Eastwood, Vice President of Marketing and Communications at Alliance, observed: "It's going to be less jingoistic than the US service in that it will be less focused on wars. The focus is going to be on the real people who made a difference in the lives of Canadians."[14] Notwithstanding the fact that History Television had adopted the same sort of "branding" strategy that had made The History Channel such a success in the US, it was a matter of some pride to Alliance executives that their service was "all Canadian" and especially that they had "bought nothing from the American History Channel."[15]

In truth, like both A&E and The History Channel before it, History Television was dominated at the outset by World War II programming. Norm Bolen, Vice President of Programming, said unapologetically in early 1998: "We are doing a lot of World War II. And a lot of people are watching.... When people don't want to watch war, we won't run those programs." Bolen added: "If we only ran war, we might do very well with older men. Whereas we need the 25 to 49 age group which is most attractive to advertisers. And we are getting them as well."[16] World War II documentaries may have been delivering History Television's primary audience in its inaugural phase, but such programming had already gone a long way towards alienating viewers and critics who had harboured high hopes for the new channel. In the spring of 1998, *The Beaver*, a popular Canadian historical magazine, asked its readers "What should lovers of history make of History Television?" and invited them to submit their comments.[17] The History Television schedule "struck them as too predictable, too foreign, and particularly too militaristic—an endless diet of old war footage." Peter McFarlane, a Montreal journalist, was quoted as saying, "The impression I have gotten is that history began in the summer of 1945." He added suggestively: "Even the non-World War II stuff tends to treat the past as a simple known thing that has been adequately recorded and only need to be assembled and related. Coming to grips with our history, it has always seemed to me, is a struggle."[18] Some women respondents noted that History Television was "hugely dominated by men and by male views of history." *Beaver* author Christopher Moore weighed in with critics of the network but inclined to give Bolen the benefit of the doubt on the question of History Television's long-term prospects.[19]

For History Television, as for all private sector interests operating within Canada's heavily regulated broadcasting environment, decisions about "the kind of content we want to offer" are never as straight forward as Bolen's comment might imply. In this country, television and radio broadcasting licences are subject to the myriad conditions imposed by the federal regulator, the CRTC; and they include powerful provisions for the maintenance and promotion of "Canadian content." Television licensees in Canada must make explicit commitments, not only to a specified quantity of Canadian programming, but also to the expenditure of a fixed proportion of revenue on its production. The CRTC is empowered by the *Broadcasting Act* to make licences subject to strict limits on vertical integration, allowing it to mandate that a fixed percentage of the programming *broadcast* by a licensee be *produced* at "arms' length" from it or its parent company.

Whether this seemingly strenuous regulatory apparatus in Canada is as heavy-handed in practise as it appears in law has been the subject of considerable debate over the years. Whatever one's position on this question, it is important to note that the mere existence of the federal regulatory apparatus has fashioned a unique "civic" broadcasting discourse in this country, one which centres on the rather earnest question of whether or not the programs aired by licensees *edify* Canadians. Needless to say, this discourse tends to sit uneasily alongside other, competing discourses, most notably those which are oriented towards the bottom line. In fact, what is aired on History Television is understood differently by different constituencies, and these discursive differences are carefully managed by those whose task it is to fashion a history channel that must appear to be all things to all people.

One of the most important constituencies to which any publicly traded commercial broadcaster must appeal is its corporate shareholders and the "investment community." From an investment perspective, it is important to note that History Television is but one small element—albeit a profitable one—within a highly diversified film and television empire, one which is openly attempting to transcend its national origins and join the ranks of the global entertainment giants. In the spring of 1999, History Television's parent company, Alliance Communications, was granted regulatory approval to merge with its erstwhile domestic rival, Atlantis Communications.[20] With a market capitalization of roughly US$370 million, the merged company, Alliance Atlantis Communications Inc., trades on both the Toronto Stock Exchange (TSE) and the Nasdaq. The corporation's operations now encompass virtually every phase in the production and distribution of "filmed entertainment," hence its organization into three broad operating "groups," Television, Motion Pictures and Broadcasting. Significantly, according to Alliance Atlantis Chairman and CEO, Michael MacMillan, the Broadcasting Group is the "most profitable" division of the company, implying that the profits generated within Canada by the specialty channels are being deployed to subsidize interests elsewhere in the corporation.[21] The Broadcasting Group now includes History Television and Showcase (both formerly Alliance properties), The Life Channel and Home & Garden TV (formerly of Atlantis) and Historia (the "French version" of History Television, launched in January 2000).

What, then, does Alliance Atlantis tell investors about History Television? Here is an introduction that was available at the corporation's online Investors' Overview site in June 2000:

History Television, launched in October 1997, features an entertaining and informative blend of movies, biographies and original historical documentary programming from Canada and around the world.

History Television reaches 60% of English Canadian cable households, with 4.14 million paid subscribers. History

Television reaches almost 4 million Canadian viewers each week. The network's programming spans a wide range of time periods as is evident by its theme nights: "20th Century Mondays," "Ancient History Tuesdays," "Canadian History Wednesdays" and "History of War Thursdays." Three nights a week, viewers turn to History Television for some of the greatest stories ever brought to film. History on Film delivers top-notch entertainment with a fascinating historical perspective.

History Television is ranked among the top 5 Canadian Specialty networks in Average Minute Audience. History Television's audience has grown a dramatic 73% for Adults 25–54 Winter 2000 over Winter 1999.[22]

Clearly, Alliance Atlantis is interested in impressing upon investors the solid performance and especially the growth potential of one of its flagship broadcasting properties. Here, the news is all good. Reduced to its performance statistics History Television is an unmitigated success story, reaching *four million* Canadians weekly and almost doubling its viewership in the lucrative 25 to 54 age group in a single year. Whatever J.L. Granatstein may think, to the international investor the case is clear: Canadians are fanatical about their history!

According to the Specialty Board of the Canadian Association of Broadcasters (CAB)—a lobby which bills itself "the representative of the majority of Canadian programming services, including private television and radio stations, and networks, and specialty television services"—the news is not nearly so good. In a detailed presentation to the CRTC in November 1998, the Specialty Board painted a grim picture of precariously situated Canadian specialty channels besieged by foreign competition, technological change and even regulatory indifference. Indulging heavily in the "civic" Canadian broadcasting discourse noted above, the Board prefaced its remarks by reminding the Commission that "specialty and pay services play an increasingly important role in the Canadian broadcasting system," by providing jobs, by making available "new resources for Canadian program production" and, above all, by "providing Canadians with access to niche programming that speaks to them, tells their stories, and reflects their realities." The Board emphasized that the Commission must be vigilant in safeguarding the specialty channels' access to cable subscribers because nothing less than Canadian culture hangs in the balance:

> Fair and equitable access is of central concern to Canadian specialty channels. Cable is the dominant distributor of television services, and will remain so for at least the next five years and probably beyond. Broad, fair, and equitable carriage on high-penetration tiers is thus essential to the success of Canadian specialty services, and to their ability to contribute to Canadians' demand for more and better programming. *If they are to continue to play a role in supporting Canadian cultural objectives, fair and reasonable access to cable subscribers is essential.* (emphasis added)

Under the ominous heading of "Competition from Non-Contributing US Service," the Board told the CRTC bluntly that "once US services 'occupy the turf', it is almost impossible for a competitive Canadian service to launch." This is because audiences for "highly specialized niche services" can be "fickle" and because they face increasing competition from "non-Canadian satellite services, and even the Internet." The Board concluded:

> The most meaningful contributions specialty services make to the system is through expanding diversity, increasing the number of hours of available Canadian programming, viewing to Canadian programming, and the resources available for producing such programming, particularly in niche areas [*sic*]. The CRTC must continue to ensure that Canadian specialty services are able to offer distinctive programming in well-defined niches, that is complementary to the programming offered by other services, and that Canadian specialty services "occupy the turf" in as many niches as possible.[23]

CANADIAN CONTENT

When History Television executives appear before the CRTC, they tell a similar story and, moreover, they indulge precisely the same sorts of discourses as the CAB. In stark contrast to the rosy picture the company places before investors, the version to which the federal regulator is subjected takes the form of a longsuffering but absolutely vital national institution, one whose selfless mission it is to shepherd Canadians out of the historical darkness and into the grandeur that is their own past. Consider, for example, History Television's presentation to the CRTC's Television Policy Review in October 1998. Appearing before the Commission on behalf of History Television were Phyllis Yaffe, then President and CEO of the service, Norm Bolen, Vice-President of Programming, and Jennifer Fong, in-house regulatory counsel. It fell to Bolen to bring the Commissioners up to date on the important work the channel was doing, and he did so in superlatives, emphasizing the contribution History Television was making in the realm of independent Canadian film production and in the lives of ordinary Canadians:

....We believe that the type of programming shown and origi- nated by History Television is of tremendous value or quality. *Our programs give a voice to the stories that make up our heritage, which we have all too often ignored.* (emphasis added)

We are particularly proud of series, such as *The Canadians. The Canadians* is a History Television original biography series which presents real stories of the men and the women who built this country and established its character. Another series is the award winning *A Scattering of Seeds.* This series documents the lives of ordinary immigrants who came to Canada to make a better life for themselves, from the Schumiatcher family in Calgary who gave us Alberta's famous white cowboy hat to Mary Ann Shadd, the first black woman to edit a newspaper in North America.

A program entitled *Our House* is a unique documentary presentation about the story of the Canadian House of Commons hosted by the Honourable Gilbert Parent, Speaker of the House of Commons. *Our House* was broadcast proudly on July 1st this year as part of History Television's special all-Canadian Canada Day schedule. These are just a few examples of how History Television attracts viewers with quality Canadian programming.[24]

CRTC Commissioner Andrew Cardoso then posed a convoluted but fascinating question for Bolen:

In terms of *A Scattering of Seeds*, we have heard a lot about the absence of cultural diversity being aired on our airwaves and one of the long-standing views has been that the diversity, if portrayed, is portrayed as something relatively recent, problematic and so forth, and that our diverse history is not shown and, indeed, most of our history books don't do that, either. With *Our House*, I think it's particularly interesting because we don't popularize our political history. I think more kids know about the fifth amendment [*sic*] and will plead it if ever arrested, not knowing that we don't have it. I suppose part of it has to go to the particular Speaker in office now who is also interested in popularizing the House of Commons, but I wonder if you could do a couple of things. Share with us how you came to the conclusion that these documentaries were important, were useful, were worth buying and airing, and, second, how you got the financing together.... [25]

This exchange between Bolen and Cardoso raises any number of questions. Firstly, what is one to make of the total absence of reference to non-documentary programming at History Television? Although no formal content analysis of History Television programming has yet been undertaken, it may be surmised that programs aired on the channel are of four general sorts. The most popular (and lucrative) fare consists in imported movies and popular series, which presumably reach large, broadly based audiences with no particular investment in history nor loyalty to History Television. The second could be characterized as filler—*Rat Patrol* and *Combat!*, for example—inexpensive re-runs lacking a significant viewership or appeal to advertisers. The third consists in prime-time light fare, typified by Canadian-made shows like *It Seems Like Yesterday* and *History Bites*. The fourth are the documentaries—serious, fact-based programs which clearly constitute the "hard core" historical content at History Television and undoubtedly attract the service's most dedicated history aficionados. That nothing whatsoever was said in this ostensibly broadly based review of Canadian television policy, of History Television's regularly scheduled airing of American patriotic chestnuts or blockbuster Hollywood movies illustrates something of the power of the civic discourse I described above.

Of the four genres, it is clearly the documentaries that carry the lion's share of the channel's obligatory "Canadian content"—a strategy calculated not only to demonstrate History Television's commitment to Canada's indigenous film industry but to draw symbolically upon Canada's historic pedigree in the *genre* of documentary film-making.[26] The channel's airing of documentaries also gives it a high degree of intellectual credibility in the low-common-denominator world of commercial broadcasting. It may well be that, given the historic domination of the Canadian broadcasting market by American shows, neither regulators nor licensees perceive any great need to dwell upon the obvious, namely that cheap American programming has always been a cash-cow for Canadian broadcasters. It is also true, moreover, that the discursive means by which History Television couches its appeals to the CRTC have been fashioned by network executives in such a way as to maximize their perceived contribution to the nationalist "goals" of the *Broadcasting Act*—a strategy for which they can hardly be faulted. What is striking, however, is the extent to which the regulator itself appears to have accommodated to this discourse. That Commissioner Cardoso should grant History Television the absurd but symbolically invaluable virtue of being the only bulwark against total historical ignorance in Canada, for example, speaks volumes about the ways in which this discourse works to marginalize other sites of historical inquiry. Indeed, the Commissioner's remarks give explicit credence to the notion that "most of our history books" are inadequate, particularly when it comes to the question of Canadian "diversity" — a comment which constitutes a wholesale indictment of the historical profession.

A second, related question is what to make of the extraordinary emphasis in the Bolen/Cardoso exchange upon independent documentary film-making generally and on *A Scattering of Seeds* in particular. Transcripts of the hearings reveal that Bolen's comments were meant largely as a prologue to History Television's main lobbying effort, aimed at persuading the Commission that, as CEO Phyllis Yaffe put it, the existing conditions of Alliance's broadcasting licenses put "conventional broadcasters... at a considerable competitive advantage over Showcase and History." Yaffe's remarks centred on the relationship between state-funded production subsidies, in the form of grants from Telefilm's Equity Investment Program (TEIP), and the Commission's prohibition on vertical integration — or what is known in industry shorthand as "self-dealing between broadcasters and producers." Three questions now faced the Commissioners, she argued:

> First, should conventional broadcasters be able to access Telefilm's Equity Investment Program for their own drama or under-represented category productions; second, should specialty services owned by producers continue to be prohibited from triggering Telefilm's Equity Investment Program for its owners' productions; and, furthermore, should these same services continue to be prohibited from running their owners' productions in first window regardless of whether Telefilm money is involved[?]

The essence of Yaffe's argument seems to have been that, as long as the CRTC continued to be vigilant in thwarting the vertical integration of its specialty channel licensees and Canadian content-providers, conventional broadcasters — who have always been allowed to "produce for themselves" — should have no claim on TEIP financing. On the matter of vertical integration itself, however, Yaffe was prepared to be ambiguous. Having explicitly questioned whether specialty services ought to "continue to be prohibited from running their owners' productions," she then assured the Commissioners that "Regardless of this difference in regulatory treatment, Showcase and History Television are prepared to live with the current self-dealing rules. Under the current situation, we accept the self-dealing rules because they continue to be a necessary protection to ensure that Canada's independent production industry remains strong."[27]

Clearly, while Alliance executives' repeated claims of support for independent documentary film-making in Canada can be read as a function of Canada's civic broadcasting discourse, they also constitute a crucial *strategic* element in the corporation's more broadly gauged approach to regulatory politics. It is no great stretch of the imagination to suppose that executives within vertically integrated conglomerates such as Alliance Atlantis would much prefer to privilege the airing of their own companies' productions to the purchase of others'. After all, this is practically a working definition of the currently fashionable idea of "synergy" in the entertainment sector. Within the Canadian regulatory environment, however, as Yaffe's comments attest, concessions on vertical integration constitute a sort of *quid pro quo*, in which broadcasters are favoured by other, sometimes less obvious material benefits; these include the highly profitable pricing schedules the regulator grants cable providers (through which specialty channels generate most of their revenue) and the protection of the specialty channels' content monopolies in the domestic market. Ingratiating themselves with CRTC commissioners on the question of the regulator's strict "self-dealing" rules was especially important to Alliance executives in October 1998, moreover, since formal application to merge with Atlantis was filed with the CRTC the following month. Indeed, as the Commission's published account of its decision to allow the merger shows, the onus on Alliance Atlantis to avoid *even the appearance* of favouring its own productions was made a condition of the regulator's acquiescence.[28]

None of this is to suggest that History Television is disingenuous in its commitment to independent Canadian documentary film-making.

However, this commitment can only be understood in the discursive context of Canada's regulatory broadcasting environment. The truth is that, however exemplary they might be with respect to the stated goals of the *Broadcasting Act*, Canadian-made documentaries are extremely expensive to produce and notoriously difficult to "sell" on commercial television. *A Scattering of Seeds: The Creation of Canada*, one of the documentary series venerated by Norm Bolen in his remarks before the Commission, is an especially noteworthy case in point. Its production was chronically underfunded and, when finally aired, it failed to recoup its costs. According to a document filed with CRTC by the Canadian Independent Film Caucus (CIFC) in June 1998, the producers were still scrambling to "recoup [their] investment through international sales," most notably by selling single episodes "to the mother countries of several immigrant groups whose stories are told in the series....."[29] Indeed, the "best distribution news" had come, not from television at all, but from "the educational market." Jerry McNabb of McNabb and Connolly, the series' educational distributor, was quoted as saying that the sales of the series were "... great! The best thing since *The Kids of Degrassi Street* series." According to McNabb the series "meets a great need in the education system for Canadian historical material," hence his expectation that "one million children a year for the next three years will see at least one episode of the series in the classroom."[30] *A Scattering of Seeds* was, at the time of the CIFC presentation, said to be "ready to begin production of its much-anticipated second season but it is in crisis. Despite its critical success, its proven popularity, and its importance to the educational system, the series may not be able to raise its budget."[31]

Whatever else may be said about *A Scattering of Seeds*, the salient point is that this account of the series is a far cry from the confident, self-aggrandizing language of History Television's *Investor Relations* précis. It is true that this description of *A Scattering of Seeds* was intended — as were three other similarly styled "case studies" — to persuade the federal regulator to decisively "increase the quantity of documentary programming available in the schedules of both private, conventional broadcasters and specialty services."[32] But even so, there remains a great discursive gulf between the Cardoso/Bolen exchange, in which the series was said by the latter to represent "the very essence of what we are about at History Television," and this rather more troubled rendering by the CIFC. The case of *A Scattering of Seeds* also shows that the Canadian regulatory apparatus itself makes strange bedfellows. At one level, the interests of independent Canadian film-makers are quite at odds with those of commercial entertainment giants like Alliance Atlantis: not only are the broadcasters largely prevented from airing their own productions, but they are required by the federal regulator to capitalize the films of the independents and later to air them—often to relatively small, unprofitable, even "fickle" audiences. Yet the CIFC insisted in its brief to the CRTC that "[d]ocumentary programs are a prominent part of many broadcasters' schedules and *the primary reason for the success of Canadian specialty services* Discovery, History Television, and VisionTV" (emphasis added). The fact remains that, however much Canadian-made documentaries may serve to edify History Television, they do not reach large numbers of viewers and they do not pay the bills. Therein lies the deep, perhaps irreconcilable tension between the civic discourse with which the channel conducts its business with the federal regulator and the bottom line discourse with which it placates its shareholders.

REVIVING HISTORY

The arbiters of these competing pressures at History Television are Sydney Suissa, Vice President of Programming, and Cindy Witten, Director of Independent Programming. Given their control over programming at History Television—which does, after all, reach four million Canadians weekly—Suissa and Witten may be said to exercise an extremely important gatekeeping function with respect to what passes for history in Canadian popular culture.[33] Suissa holds an Honours BA in history from the University of Calgary, as well as a Master's degree in journalism. In my correspondence with him I was impressed, not only by the seriousness with which he takes his responsibility for delivering historical content to Canadian television viewers, but with his keen sense of the relationship of History Television to the academic study of history. Indeed, I was struck by his confident, unapologetic conviction that a profit-driven history-based television service has an extremely important contribution to make in the lives of Canadians, not least because professional historians have abandoned the field. I opened our correspondence by asking him to elaborate on History Television's mandate to enhance Canadians' understanding of their own history. He did not mince his words:

> We have played a central role and will continue to in telling stories from our past. This is a very strong commitment, both personal and regulated. The greatest challenge is not coming up with those stories or making them, but rather in getting Canadians to watch them. By and large I agree with Jack Granatstein: the political and social agendas that have weighed history down (whether in schools or in other public policies and arenas) have made it boring and comatose. The greatest contribution History Television can make is to revive Canadians' interest in our history. That is the true mandate and it can only be done through well researched, well told stories that are rich in narrative, drama, and character.[34]

History Television employs no historians but Suissa affirmed that they are "used extensively on nearly all the documentaries we commission" and also that they are regularly invited "to discuss movies after they've been aired." He added: "In a more informal way, I have a circle of historians that I feel free to consult with on specific historical questions or issues."[35] Like Norm Bolen and Andrew Cardoso, Suissa subscribes to the notion that History Television is the solution to the crisis of relevance in Canadian history. That History Television was one of the sponsors, along with Angus Reid and the Dominion Institute, of the famed November 1998 history quiz—in which "60% of respondents failed a 15-question test about basic historical facts"—speaks directly to this claim.[36]

Ought historians to take this usurpation personally? Frankly, I think not. As Suissa himself put the case to me: "History Television is not a school, it is a television channel."[37] That professional historians play a strictly adjunct role at History Television does, however, bring one back to the decisive issue of programming. Given that the living rooms of Canadians are no place for the "political and social agendas" of professional historians nor for the "boring and comatose" products of their labours, the question arises as to what kind of "history" History Television actually offers. Here, too, Suissa is dauntless. When asked whether "decision-makers at History Television distinguish between entertainment and educational content," he replied, evincing yet again the discursive ease with which documentaries are made the standard-bearers for History Television: "The distinction is in the treatment, in the way the documentary is told. I avoid pedantic styles, where the emphasis is on explanation and analysis rather than on dramatic storytelling. Any well told story is educational, though its primary objective is not necessarily educational." When asked whether the bulk of his audience share derives from the screening of Hollywood films, Suissa conceded that blockbuster movies are popular because of their "marquee value" but insisted that "there is also great appetite for documentaries from Canada and the rest of the world." He did admit, however, that "documentaries will always be a harder sell, and will draw a smaller audience than movies. This is the reality throughout television and is not specific to History Television."[38] Lastly, when invited to comment on the "popular" series *History Bites* and *It Seems Like Yesterday*, he anticipated my scepticism regarding their historical worth, volunteering: "Their mandates are to look at history with a sense of humour and satire, to give viewers a sense that human history at times can be silly, random, and absurd."[39]

In fairness to Suissa and his colleagues at History Television, it is important to recall the vote of confidence the CIFC gave the channel as a dedicated programmer of Canadian-made documentaries. Moreover, there is evidence to suggest that History Television's reputation for airing the best international documentaries is deserved. In February 1998, for example, when the Oscar documentary nominees were announced, the channel was in the enviable position of having scheduled two of the nominated films for the period before the award show, namely Spike Lee's *4 Little Girls* and Mark Jonathan Harris' *The Long Way Home*.[40] That History Television does indeed have its moments of profundity is undeniable. I would cite, for example, its extensive programming in "remembrance" of Hiroshima as a most impressive case in point. As Canadian media mogul Moses Znaimer once remarked, however, what matters on television is not the show but the flow—an aphorism that seems to me to carry special poignancy for History Television. Having taken so much credit for broadcasting the sublime, surely the channel's executives may be taken to task for also airing the ridiculous. What is one to make, for example, of its four-part "soap" on the life of British fascist Oswald Mosley, in which the subject's love life figured more prominently than his politics?[41] What about the weekly spectacle of having Ann Medina—formerly one of the CBC's most respected foreign correspondents—say the words "Hello there. I'm Ann Medina. Welcome to *History on Film*, a discovery of our past through the movies"?[42] What about Rick Mercer's "hope that his reference to Adolf Hitler having one testicle will one day make it to air" on *It Seems Like Yesterday*?[43] What about History Television underwriting the Credo documentary *Pioneer Quest: A Year in the Real West*, in which two couples were paid $100,000 each to "build and share a shelter where they have to live off the land without any modern conveniences, including running water, for one full year"?[44] For that matter, what about *Rat Patrol* and *Combat!*?

In short, in spite of Sidney Suissa's confident claims about the pedagogical and civic virtues of History Television, I am not persuaded. Nor do I believe that my calling into question the channel's mix of documentary versus more popular programming is a case of academic hair-splitting. There is a vast difference between History Television's enormously profitable overall market penetration and the modest audience it generates for indigenous documentary programming. According to data published by the CIFC, the largest first-run English-language audience for *A Scattering of Seeds*, never exceeded 135,000 viewers, and some "episodes" did not even reach this number. This is a mere fraction of the 4.14 million paid subscribers History Television boasts in its *Investor Relations* précis, a ratio which seems to speak for itself. While it is the Canadian-made documentaries that History Television executives privilege when speaking to the federal regulator and academic historians, it is clearly other kinds of programming that constitute the channel's most popular—and profitable—fare. History Television may even be said to be a commercial success in spite of—rather than because of—its commitment to indigenous documentary film-making. In the absence of harder data on audience share and especially advertising revenue, I can only conclude that the channel's extraordinary emphasis on Canadian-made documentaries constitutes a discursive and ultimately a strategic valorization of a cable service whose real bread and butter consists, like most of its competitors', in delivering historically inconsequential programming to an undiscriminating mass audience.

CONCLUSION

I have not taken Sidney Suissa et al. to task because I believe them to be disingenuous. On the contrary, one can hardly blame History Television executives for indulging Canada's longstanding civic broadcasting discourse, nor especially for spinning their programming schedule for maximum regulatory and critical effect. My point is that, ironically perhaps, Suissa and the historians he claims to be usurping today find themselves in precisely the same boat, trying to keep history alive and vital in an age in which—as the Swedish poet Kjell Espmark put it—"we have quietly accepted the disappearance of the past."[45] The most telling line in my correspondence with Suissa, arguably, is that "the greatest challenge is not coming up with stories [from our past] or making them, but rather in getting Canadians to watch them." This seems to confirm my view that history is indeed a hard sell these days, whether in the classroom or on television; it also attests to the cultural dislocation I described in Chapter Four, namely that history has largely ceased to provide the social and cultural architecture within which Canadians contextualize their lived experience.

As for Canadian-made documentaries like *A Scattering of Seeds*, perhaps the heirs to the historiographical throne in our televisual age, it is heartening to discover that they continue to reach *millions* of Canadians in the classroom but only tens of thousands in prime time. The subtext of so much of the politicking that takes place in front of the CRTC appears to be that—to paraphrase the American philosopher Kevin Costner—if you air it, they will watch. Yet, for all of their goodwill and civic rectitude, the combined weight of History Television, the CRTC and even the CIFC cannot draw more than a handful of television viewers to even the most celebrated of Canadian-made productions. I conclude from this pattern that the rumoured usurpation of historians and history teachers by commercial television broadcasters has been greatly exaggerated.

The CBC series *Canada: A People's History* has been heralded as a revolutionary breakthrough in historical television programming since its launch in October 2000, and it has clearly struck a chord with large numbers of Canadians. Only Canada's public broadcaster could have realized such an ambitious and lavish project, which sets *A People's History* well apart from anything that Canada's independent documentarists and private-sector broadcasters could together deliver. Even so, in the absence of consistent data on the series' market penetration, it is not easy to gauge its true impact among Canadian television viewers. In early 2001, CBC publicity claimed, for example, that "[e]pisodes 1–5 of the series, produced in both English and French, attracted audiences of roughly 2.3 million Canadians to CBC and its French-language counterpart Radio-Canada" in its inaugural season.[46] Later the same year the CBC made the even more grand boast that *A People's History* was "the most watched documentary in Canadian history: one of every two Canadians watched some part of the series."[47] Given the enormous publicity that accompanied the launch—and hence the likelihood that some viewers tuned in simply to see what all the fuss was about—it is impossible to gauge the extent of Canadian viewers' episode-over-episode loyalty to the series or, more pointedly, to get any sense of the impact these programs have had on their understanding of (or fondness for) Canadian history. What does seem noteworthy, however, is that the strongest market for *A People's History* is expected to be, as it has been for most of its predecessors, in the schools. By the autumn of 2001, according to the CBC, "approximately 80% of schools across the country are expected to have access to the series, either from purchasing the series themselves or through their School Board's licensing of duplication rights."[48]

Certainly Mark Starowicz, the much-celebrated executive producer of *A People's History* and director of the CBC's Canadian History Project (of which the series is a part), envisages a grand future for historical programming at CBC-TV. Working from the premise that "[j]ournalism is a sub-set of the historical profession," he intends to "establish the Project as a permanent history department [at the CBC], similar to that which is maintained at the BBC."[49] Such a development would without question be good for Canadians and good for Canadian history, but many questions remain. Of these, the most compelling is whether *A People's History* was in fact the harbinger of a revolution in television broadcasting or something far more ephemeral.

NOTES

1. J.L. Granatstein, *Who Killed Canadian History?* (Toronto: Harper Collins, 1998), p. 3.

2. "Cable Companies Plan History Networks," *American History Illustrated* 28:4 (September/October 1993), p. 15.

3. John Flynn, "It's All History Now," *Adweek* 46:18 (29 April 1996), p. 6; "History Channel to Debut," *History Today* 29:6 (February 1995), p. 12.

4. "History Channel to Debut," p. 12.

5. Dan Davids, cited in Flynn, "It's All History Now," p. 6.

6. Charles Maday, cited in "History Channel to Debut," p. 12.

7. Jack Myers, cited in Flynn, "It's All History Now," p. 6.

8. Mark Vittert, "Thankful for History," *Triangle Business Journal* 13:13 (28 November 1997), p. 39.

9. "History Channel to Debut," p. 12.

10. "History Channel Dumps Corporate Profile Series," *Advertising Age* (10 June 1996), p. 2.

11. Cited in "History Plan Rewritten," *Advertising Age* (7 June 1996).

12. Alliance executives acknowledge that they benefited greatly from The History Channel's promotional blitz in 1997, i.e., the US $10 million dollar ad

campaign spearheaded by the New York firm Moss/Dragoti and centring on the slogan "Where the past comes alive."

13. John McKay, "Four New Cable Outlets Getting Ready to Launch," *Canadian Press* (11 May 1997).

14. Janet Eastwood, cited in ibid.

15. Norm Bolen, cited in Christopher Moore, "History Television: Stay Tuned," *Beaver* 78:1 (February/March 1998), p. 50.

16. Ibid., p. 50.

17. Ibid., p. 50.

18. Peter McFarlane, cited in ibid., p. 50.

19. Norm Bolen, cited in ibid., p. 50.

20. See *Decision CRTC 99-106* (19 March 1999).

21. Michael MacMillan, in conversation with Fred Langan on *Newsworld Business News* (27 June 2000).

22. Alliance Atlantis Communication Inc., *Investors' Overview* (posted at allianceatlantis.com).

23. Canadian Association of Broadcasters, *A Submission to the Canadian Radio-television and Telecommunications Commission with Respect to Public Notice CRTC 1998-44* (18 November 1998).

24. Norm Bolen, cited in *Transcript of Proceedings for the Canadian Radio-Television and Telecommunications Commission Canadian Television Policy Review* 14:9 (14 October 1998).

25. Andrew Cardoso, cited in ibid.

26. In its 1998 presentation at the CRTC's Canadian Television Policy Review, The Canadian Independent Film Caucus lauded the work of John Grierson and the National Film Board, which "...led the world in the development of compelling new documentary film making techniques — styles which became renowned as 'cinema direct' and 'candid eye'." See *A Level Playing Field for the Documentary* (29 June 1998).

27. Phyllis Yaffe, cited in *Transcript of Proceedings for the Canadian Radio-Television and Telecommunications Commission Canadian Television Policy Review* 14:9 (14 October 1998).

28. See "The Commission Approves the Applications by Alliance Atlantis Communications Inc...." *CRTC Public Notice 1999-48* (20 May 1999). It is also worth noting that the merger was conditional on increased "Canadian content" provisions. Sydney Suissa told me that this minimum content requirement is likely to be exceeded by Alliance Atlantis over the term of its licences.

29. According to the CIFC's "case study" of *A Scattering of Seeds*, the initial capitalization of this thirteen-part series was so precarious that the producers

"had to defer their entire fee." *A Scattering of Seeds* went on to enjoy both great critical acclaim and "popular success," winning top prize (the Gold Medal for Best Documentary Television Series) at the Worldfest in Houston, Texas. In Canada, the series was said to have been "well publicized," translating into "excellent" ratings on both *History Television* and *Historia*. See *A Level Playing Field*.

30. Jerry McNabb, cited in *A Level Playing Field*.

31. Cited in ibid.

32. Cited in ibid.

33. It is perhaps testimony to the mystique of televisual media that Suissa's name appears nowhere in recent Canadian historiography, even though he is clearly one of the country's most influential historical popularizers. It is worth recalling in this connection that an earlier generation of popularizers—most importantly Pierre Berton and Peter C. Newman—enjoyed no such anonymity.

34. Sydney Suissa, personal correspondence (June 2000).

35. Ibid.

36. Jason Botchford, "Canadians Flunk out in War History: Poll," *Toronto Sun* (11 November 1998).

37. Sydney Suissa, personal correspondence (June 2000). As for the criteria by which documentaries are selected for broadcast on History Television, Suissa listed the following: "i) the quality of the storytelling; ii) the quality and originality of the research; iii) the production values; iv) and the subject."

38. Sydney Suissa, personal correspondence (June 2000).

39. Ibid.

40. Claire Bickley, "Nominated Documentaries Air before Oscars," *Toronto Sun* (17 February 1998).

41. Claire Bickley, "Fascist Immersed in Soapy Froth," *Toronto Sun* (13 November 1998).

42. Christopher Moore correctly observed that most of *History Television*'s on-screen personalities were "refugees from the bloodlettings of recent years in CBC and CTV current affairs departments" and noted "...a painful hint of Ted Baxter about them when they suddenly became historians." See "History Television: Stay Tuned," p. 50.

43. Rick Mercer, cited in Claire Bickley, "Shedding a Little Lite on the Past," *Toronto Sun* (3 December 1997). Recounts Mercer, of History Television's refusal to sanction this bit of historical speculation: "They say, 'You can't say that', and I'm saying, 'Why? Is the Hitler family going to get upset?' [They say to me] 'Is that true? This is the History channel and we want to be accurate.' [I

say] 'For the point of this show, he only had one ball, okay?' Then we picture the Grade Eight student writing the paper, 'Hitler only had one ball. Footnote: History Television'."

44. Pat St. Germain and Bill Brioux, "Sex Charge Kills Pioneer Dream," *Sun Media* (7 June 2000). See also Robert Williams, "Pioneers Press On," *Winnipeg Sun* (27 June 2000).

45. Kjell Espmark, cited in John Ralston Saul, *Reflections of a Siamese Twin: Canada at the End of the Twentieth Century* (Toronto: Penguin, 1998), p. 30.

46. CBC Press Release "CBC Delighted by Response to *Canada: A People's History*" (2 January 2001).

47. CBC Press release "CBC Announces BCE Sponsorship of Season Two of *Canada: A People's History*" (7 August 2001).

48. CBC Press Release, "Season Two Fact Sheet" (1 September 2001).

49. Tod Hoffman, "Making History," *McGill News Alumni Quarterly* (Fall 2001).

CHAPTER SIX

L'ÉTAT, C'EST MOLSON?

YOUTH AND THE DECLINE OF CANADIAN NATIONALISM

Nationalism appears to be a declining force in English Canada and nowhere more so than among Canadian teenagers and young adults. Generally speaking, young people outside of Quebec do not identify with the state, nor with established nationalist traditions (most notably the "left-nationalism" of the Trudeau era); they have little stake in the rights and responsibilities of citizenship; and they are notoriously indifferent to conventional political activity, voting in meagre numbers and evincing a disquieting level of ignorance about Canadian history and politics. As children of globalized mass media, they are wary of cultural protectionism and unapologetic about their preferences for non-Canadian entertainment products; as children of NAFTA, they are neither anxious about continental economic, cultural and military integration nor fretful about post-September 11 talk of "common borders" and "dollarization." Their primary axis of travel is north-south rather than east-west; their preference as travellers, to hopscotch quickly between cities rather than to traverse the broad spaces between them. They have been trained in postmodern fashion to embrace diversity, to imagine their own identities as subjective, fluid and socially constructed, to be suspicious of "in-group versus out-group" distinctions, and to distrust reductionist notions like "national identity." They inhabit, in short, a post-nationalist world of globalized, mass-mediated youth culture—a culture in which the experience of being young, urban and hip has become transnational, cosmopolitan and self-referential, and in which "the national" as a pole of identity formation is in decline. Little wonder, as Professor Terry Goldie has lamented recently, that "twenty-something students look at me as if I were a dinosaur when I assert the necessity of nationalism to the Canadian consciousness."[1]

The purpose of this chapter is to explore the dissolution of nationalism as it applies to English-Canadian youth. I argue that traditional nationalist ideologies carry little currency among young people in Canada not merely, as is commonly thought, because they have become irrelevant in an era of globalization, but because they no longer speak to the lived experience of youth. In contrast with the Trudeau era, when young Canadians were central to nationalist formations, full participants in the organizations they inspired, and immediate beneficiaries of the massively expanded state apparatus they produced, youth today are silent on the great national issues of our time, their citizenship status is precarious, they are demonized rather than celebrated in the popular imagination, and they have been singularly disadvantaged by the retreat of the welfare and regulatory state. In contrast with those who believe that the ground is now fertile for a revival of "left-nationalist" fervor among Canadian youth, I am drawn to the worrying conclusion that young people, having been denied full participation in the life of the nation but hyper-exposed to its symbolic vestiges ("I am Canadian"), are far more likely to find right-wing nationalist formations agreeable.

THE GOLDEN AGE

The high-water mark for English-Canadian nationalism coincided, somewhat paradoxically, with the years in which Canada's famously anti-nationalist prime minister, Pierre Trudeau, held power. As Sylvia Bashevkin has shown, prior to the late 1960s English-Canadian cultural nationalists could bring little institutional pressure to bear on governments and on Canadian society at large because they were represented only in occasional royal commission reports and because "few organizational vehicles existed other than the CBC and NFB."[2] Those whom Bashevkin calls "investment" nationalists, Walter Gordon most prominent among them, had had greater opportunity to affect public policy but their ideas had done little to fire the public imagination and, more to the point, they had been successfully challenged by business. By the 1970s, however, Canada was awash in "a flood of nationalist books and organizations," while polls showed that ordinary Canadians had embraced nationalist ideas in unprecedented numbers. Bashevkin argues that it was the mutually reinforcing coincidence of nationalist fervor, student protest, environmentalism, feminism, peace activism and anti-colonialism that cemented Canadian nationalists' historic left-leaning tendency in these years:

> Although a stream of trade nationalism existed in the business community, at least until the Canadian Manufacturers' Association changed its position in 1984, and although a Tory nationalist streak was present in the ideas of John Diefenbaker, Donald Creighton and George Grant, it is clear that the organized mainstream of modern pan-Canadianism would remain ideologically left-of-centre. Most nationalists, particularly since the end of the Second World War, endorsed assertive federal intervention to defend national culture, to resist continental trade flows and to assert domestic economic control in the face of growing foreign investment.[3]

That young Canadians were central to the growth of left-nationalism in the late 1960s and the 1970s—and that they stood to benefit enormously from it—was evident even to its contemporaries. As Philip Resnick observed in his seminal *The Land of Cain* (1977), it was the "new petty bourgeoisie" which played "*the decisive role* in the eruption of English-Canadian nationalism after 1965," in large measure because of the extraordinary expansion in these years of Canada's state bureaucracy, universities and research institutes. It was members of this new middle class—many of them university-aged—who came to dominate the Committee for an Independent Canada (CIC) and the Waffle movement, and whose publications gave the movement at large its "ideological direction and coherence." Resnick emphasizes not only the strength of the new nationalism within the youth Counterculture—evinced strikingly when "academics and students were signing petitions, marching and occupying university placement offices" — but also the "steady growth of government expenditure for health, education, pension plans and other social services." Left-nationalist policies were thought to be good for Canada, in short, but they were also good for the young members of the new middle class "who benefited from these changes, and came to see statism, by which we mean a strong interventionist state, as in their interests."[4] Young Canadians were also well positioned to benefit from the surge of cultural "protectionism" that accompanied the rise of political nationalism, most notably as the result of new (or strengthened) federal legislation mandating "Canadian content" in the broadcasting, publishing, film and music industries. Indeed, the complaint is now commonly heard that the baby boomers who were initially advantaged by protectionist policies have come to dominate the "cultural industries" so thoroughly that younger artists, writers and filmmakers coming up behind them have been shut out.[5]

As Marc Cousineau has suggested, there is a vast difference between citizenship and "belonging." Insofar as "I do not have to like my country or admire its policies and practices to be a citizen," he observes, belonging must be regarded as "an essential component of any meaningful concept of citizenship."[6] Although Cousineau's work is concerned primarily with the role of the state in mediating minority-majority relationships, his idea of "belonging" is useful in assessing the strength of nationalist discourses within various social groups. If, as I shall argue below, many young Canadians have been denied access to the traditions that might make them feel like valuable contributors to the national project — or to institutions and processes that are available to others around them — then it follows that they are experiencing a hollowed-out form of citizenship in which, as Cousineau remarks of his own Franco-Ontarian community, they know that they do not belong.

In the late 1960s and the 1970s young Canadians' unprecedented "sense of belonging" vis-à-vis the Canadian state was evident not only in their privileged position within the new petty bourgeoisie and the nationalist organizations it spawned, but in the obvious truth that Pierre

Trudeau and many of his senior ministers both understood and admired young people. As Habeeb Salloum has recalled, Trudeau owed much of his meteoric success in federal politics to his "flamboyant reputation... among a majority of Canada's youth," and he governed with a careful eye to nurturing their ongoing support.[7] Asked in 1971 how he felt about young people "hitchhiking around the country... instead of taking a job," Trudeau answered:

> I think it's great. I think that more and more young people are discovering that gainful employment isn't the only thing in life, that they can perhaps be just as useful to society and themselves by traveling across the land or around the world, learning more about humanity and going through the various experiences which will make their adulthood more productive.... I think I was much better advised to bum around the world for a few years than to stay around Canada knocking people's hats off. And I think a lot of the young people today are realizing that.[8]

Jacques Hébert, Trudeau's friend and ally since their days at *Cité Libre* in the 1950s, recalled with pride in 1992 that the Trudeau years "remain a kind of golden age for the youth of Canada."[9] Breaking with the past—when, as Hébert put it, the state had paid young Canadians "little attention"—the Trudeau Liberals deliberately, and in the face of considerable opposition, sought to listen to youth and to respond directly to their needs. The $24.7 million Opportunities for Youth program (OFY), which ran from 1971 to 1974, was the standard-bearer for this new approach, explicitly encouraging young people to "experiment with innovative and creative ideas" while providing "a means of involving youth in the community." Although social service professionals were said to be "wholeheartedly behind the program," it is significant in retrospect that the media response was "almost uniformly critical" and that "businessmen" believed that the OFY had utterly failed to teach young Canadians "the value of perseverance and aggressiveness."[10] That the corporate media and especially business would only a few years later play a leading role in the transformation of the relationship of youth and citizenship in Canada — recasting it in the image of consumerism and the free market — is central to understanding not only the erosion of young people's sense of "belonging" but the policy environment in which this erosion took place. Other Liberal initiatives for youth in the Trudeau era included Canada World Youth (launched in 1971) and Katimavik (begun in 1977), two programs aimed at "character development, involvement in community projects (many related to environmental problems), the learning of another language, discovery of various regions of Canada, and in the case of Canada World Youth, awareness of international development problems."[11] Pierre Trudeau also created the post of Minister of State for Youth in 1984 (a portfolio later paired with sport under Brian Mulroney and literacy under Jean Chrétien). So great was Jacques Hébert's commitment to these Liberal initiatives for youth that he staged a hunger strike in the lobby of the Senate in 1986 to protest the termination of Katimavik by the Tories.

LAMENT FOR A NATION

The decline of nationalism that has accompanied the retreat of the state since the Trudeau era has occasioned in recent years an outpouring of anguish from the many English-Canadian artists, intellectuals and public figures for whom it was a formative ideology. Borrowing from George Grant's *Lament for a Nation* (1965), the bulk of this literature is explicitly backward-looking and more than a little of it verges on the nostalgic. The tone is uniformly grave. Philosopher Ian Angus, for example, prefaced his recent study of national identity in Canada, *A Border Within* (1997), with an elegy: "Globalization has finished the English-Canadian left-nationalist politics to which the more philosophical project with which I aligned myself was bound. To this extent the book is a swan song. This is a sad fact, and it is one that I take no pleasure in stating."[12] Although Angus claims to have undertaken this study in order "to construct a new beginning for the politics of identity in English Canada," it is his emphasis upon the seemingly irrevocable destruction of the postwar social order in Canada that sets the elegiac tone for the book — a tone that also permeates the recent work of James Laxer, Gary Teeple, Jody Berland, Tom Henighan, Robert Lecker, Jeffrey M. Ayres, Terry Goldie and others. The worry is not merely that left-nationalism is dead but, as Angus puts it, that "national identity will be a decreasing pole of identity in the future." Because of the predominance of this interpretation of recent Canadian history on the left — and because it bears so directly on young people's experience of the nation — it is worth excerpting at length:

> The emphasis on national identity in Canada pertains to the postwar period especially. Throughout the capitalist world, a new hegemonic formation came into being that is variously called Keynesianism, the welfare state, Fordism, and so on. This formation has been coming apart in the last decades with the attack on government social spending, globalization of the economy, and the creation of competing free trade zones around the world. One key aspect of this contemporary transformation is the declining influence of the nation-state. Though this change was clearly already in the making in the mid-1970s, we may conveniently and symbolically date the post-war consensus from the end of the Second World War in 1945 to the beginning of the Free Trade Agreement in 1989.... *In this period the national pole of identification held sway over other social identities....* Given this background, we should not be surprised that with the dismantling of the post-war consensus in recent years, new social actors have entered the picture and have come to vie with national identity as significant poles of identification. Growing regionalism, increased power of provincial governments, Quebec separatism, Native land claims, all indicate that the ability of national identity to hold sway over other identifications has significantly weakened. As well, the new forms of identification allied to new social movements, such as feminism, environmentalism, and sexual and minority liberation movements, indicate the possibility that national identity will be a decreasing pole of identification in the future (italics added).[13]

Generally speaking, left-nationalist anxieties about the erosion of Canadian political and cultural sovereignty are today bound up with a more broadly based critique of globalization and neo-liberal economics. As I argued in Chapter Four, Canadians have been weaned off their earlier ideas of "social citizenship" as commercial discourses have usurped older civic ones. State complicity in this process has been singled out by progressive critics, not only to emphasize the apparent abandonment of nationalist goals and strategies but also to expose the sometimes cynical exploitation of what might be called the residual symbols of the nationalist tradition. Culture critic Jody Berland has put this case especially strongly:

> You will need no reminder of the stunning violence of the current economic and political assault on public space. In the present climate of globalizing and privatizing frenzy, the premise that government should represent the rights and interests of its citizens—historically, in Canada, the common foundation of economic, political, and cultural nationalism—is widely represented as anachronistic and simple-minded.... Today, Canadian nationalism is more readily manifested as a symbol of political autonomy, than as a basis for genuinely different political direction. The way nationalism is signified in beer commercials and patriotic government promotions parallels the way many other values—family, art, love, nature, loyalty, redemption—function as transitive signs in commercial discourse rather than in the context of negotiable programmes for their realization. In this situation, culture comes to stand in for the political trajectory which is already lost. We may not have fiscal or political autonomy but we do have our own beer, our own writers, our own mountains, our own flag....[14]

The implication of this critique for Canadians who came of age in the 1980s and 1990s is clear: having inherited this postmodern world of "transitive" nationalist signs, they may be ill-equipped to resist (or even recognize) the "stunning violence" of globalization, or to contribute to cultural and political strategies that might realize genuine nationalist goals.

While many older left-nationalists continue to work for the reversal of the "current economic and political assault on public space," and to formulate strategies of resistance, others have begun to explore the matter of what this new, admittedly unwelcome social order will mean for the young Canadians who are inheriting it. Myrna Kostash's recent book, *The Next Canada: In Search of Our Future Nation*, is a most remarkable text in this respect. Set squarely in the left-nationalist tradition, this work builds on the generational emphasis that characterized *Long Way from Home* (1976), her retrospective on the Sixties student protest movement in Canada, and especially *No Kidding: Inside the World of Teenage Girls* (1987), in which she discovered that she had "fallen victim to the fallacy that *my* generation was still at the cutting edge of youth...."[15] *The Next Canada* finds Kostash interviewing twenty-five to thirty-five year-olds to discover what it means to come of age in a Canada in which "the corporatist language of markets supersedes any particular language of Canadianness, open borders and mobility are privileged over traditional settlement, and globalization and mass communication deliver the benefits of dissolving difference." The subtext of the book, however, never well concealed, is characteristically autobiographical and takes the form of a long and sometimes tortured meditation on the lost world of her youth:

> As a university student in the late 1960s, and as a writer who began publishing in the 1970s, I was a beneficiary of the nationalism that championed made-in-Canada social, political and cultural policy. I wrote for subsidized magazines and public radio, received arts grants from governments, and reached audiences who themselves were increasingly patriotic. But, as I began the research for this book, that kind of Canada seemed in retreat.

Kostash confesses that, despite her best intentions, she was not unbiased in her encounters with her interviewees:

> Although I have declared that this project of mapping the "next Canada" was completely open-ended as to the conclusions I

would draw from it, I admit that I was always especially alert to evidence that the people I was talking with represented some continuity with the political culture that I grew up in — the postwar culture that preceded what I think of as the Great Rupture of 1988, the year of the federal election that decided Canada would sign the Free Trade Agreement.

She understates the case. Her subjects are allowed to speak for themselves but their musings are set squarely within a narrative dominated both by Kostash's own impassioned testimony and by older left-nationalist voices — Dalton Camp, Bob White, Linda McQuaig, Peter Gzowski, Richard Gwyn, Ian Angus and others. Moreover, the narrative itself takes the form of a quest:

Where would they come from, I was wondering, the "next Canadian" radicals for whom everyday politics has been articulated by Brian Mulroney, Jean Chrétien, Ronald Reagan, and Bill Clinton, and framed by the language of free trade and transnational capitalism?

Try as she might to be fair and open-minded about her subjects' views of Canada and the world, in the end they are so alien to her own as to be both perplexing and disappointing. Kostash cannot rise above her initial preconception, namely that the fusion of youth and nationalism that characterized the Trudeau era was a wonderful crucible for her generation and hence that those who have been denied it occupy a pitiable cultural space. She writes respectfully of her interviewees' "postnationalist" and anti-nationalist views, even giving her young subjects the benefit of the doubt on that which is for her the unthinkable:

More than once in the course of conversations with the next generation of Canadians I was told that, unlike my generation, the younger Canadians aren't "scared" of American culture. They've lived with it all their lives and still haven't been vaporized into the American ether. Others, postnationals, seemed sanguine that "Canada" as a site of identity may disappear.

But in the final analysis, Kostash cannot bring herself to accept that sensible, well-educated young Canadians might have come to adopt such "revolutionary" views were it not for the relentless propaganda of corporate media and the "failure" of Canadian political élites to provide a countervailing national vision:

It is not an internal failing in our youth that has put us on this dangerous road to communal eclipse. For they, like the rest of us, have been betrayed by the faint-of-national-heart who cannot or will not see that it is vital for the biodiversity of the human community that Canada survive as a distinct society.[16]

That young Canadians are likely to be "post-nationalist" has, as Kostash's analysis illustrates, contributed to the perception that youth and young adults today are *alien* to the nationalist tradition in Canada, and perhaps even beyond the pale of progressive politics. There is more than a little irony in this observation, at least insofar as depicting youth as alien is commonly thought to be the exclusive prerogative of the Canadian Right. Jeffrey M. Ayres has argued, for example, that the rise of the anti-globalization movement as the dominant strain in contemporary social protest has, like globalization itself, done a good deal to render the nationalist movement obsolete. Social protest, he argues, has evolved from "national to transnational" as a result of "the decline in state power and its concomitant national political opportunity structures." This "evolution" is especially obvious in the changing character of opposition to liberalized trade: "From the highly nationalist anti-FTA campaign, to the transnationalist anti-NAFTA mobilization, to the post-NAFTA context of community-based resistance and anti-corporate campaigns, social groups across Canada have had to rethink traditional methods of protest in an era of shrinking governmental power and resources."[17]

Are we, then, in the presence of a generation gap on the Canadian left, one in which newer ideological formations and political strategies are incompatible with the more traditional? The recent dispute over the New Politics Initiative (NPI) within the NDP—with its global/local axis of political protest and especially its emphasis upon youth—suggests the possibility. Consider James Laxer's critique of the NPI:

> The NPI does not face up to the fundamental fact that Canada lives in an American Empire under the sway of American corporate and state power. The vision statement is so tepid on the issue of the American domination of Canada that half the members of the Liberal caucus in Ottawa could easily sign off on it. The failure of the statement to align itself solidly with the aspiration of Canadians to run and shape their own society, free from domination south of the border, is no small matter.[18]

This excerpt can be read as a classic left-nationalist critique of the new anti-globalization movement. Although the NPI—led by veteran progressives Judy Rebick, Svend Robinson, Jim Stanford and others—was never the sole preserve of the young, it is clear that disaffected youth—"those who hope most fervently for a just and sustainable future"—comprised one of its crucial constituencies. ("Reinventing democracy" in Canada, according to the NPI's media manifesto of June 2001, would have to include "reducing the voting age to 16.")[19] Like Laxer, many older left-nationalists now openly acknowledge this essential paradox: that the young activists in the anti-globalization movement now think and act as globally as the transnational corporations they demonize, and that this may not be good for Canada. As Terry Goldie notes sardonically of his activist students: "When I suggest that their claims to 'transnationalism' will just contribute to American imperialism, their eyes glaze over at the evidence of my creeping senility."[20]

The greatest irony of all, of course, is that the choice between "Globalization or Canadianization," to cite a recent headline from the *Alberta Report*, has emerged as a key rhetorical weapon in the neo-conservative counter-assault against the anti-globalization movement, against the left, and against the young. Columnist Paul Bunner speaks for many self-styled conservatives in Canada who resent the high-minded claims and "boneheaded" antics of the anticorporate movement. "Back before multinational labour unions recruited, funded and armed (with rhetoric) the youthful front-line troops who now serve as cannon fodder in the war against globalization," he asserts, "the cause of preserving national sovereignty had friends on the right too." But now, after the "chaos at the Summit of the Americas in Quebec City... the unions and their juvenile middle-class lemmings are on their own." For Bunner, the anti-globalization movement represents the culmination of all of the worst attributes of the older "left liberal" tradition with which, he claims, conservatives could once make common cause:

> How dare *Globe and Mail* columnist and anti-globalization evangelist Naomi Klein and her husband Avi Lewis, host of CBC Newsworld's increasingly monocratic screechfest *Counterspin*, present themselves as oracles of the popular will? If the summit organizers had not built the fence and buttressed it with a small army of police, it is unthinkable that those two privileged products of Canada's left-liberal intelligentsia would have risked their necks to protect the people and property who would otherwise have been vulnerable to rock-throwing anarchists.[21]

Leading voices on the Canadian right have also found it expedient to take advantage of post-September 11 sympathy for the United States and to claim, like Bunner, that young critics of US foreign policy are little more than the witless dupes of leftist teachers and parents with an anti-American axe to grind:

> Most [Canadian] kids have not mastered the bill of indictment in very much detail. Nonetheless, they know for a fact that America sucks, and that George W. Bush really sucks.... Among these kids, reflexive Anti-Americanism is as much a fashion statement

as the jeans they wear.... Chances are their teachers and their parents think George Bush sucks, too. They've all been raised in a country where recreational bitching at the United States is just as much fun as going to Disney World. And they've never learned how much their lives depend on the liberal democratic values our nations share.[22]

However uncharitable, these are not voices crying in the wilderness. Conservatives now dominate popular discourse in Canada—in the corporate media (where they have always found a home) and increasingly in the public media, where the historically dominant "left-liberals" are under siege. In November 2001 the CBC ombudsman ruled that "anti-war and anti-American sentiments expressed during a National Town Hall broadcast a week after the deadly events of Sept. 11 largely reflected the views of the university students and public sector employees who made up much of the downtown Toronto studio audience, but failed to represent a national cross-section of Canadians."[23] Conservative opposition to left-nationalism is not new, of course; and it is worth recalling in this respect, as Sylvia Bashevkin reminds us, that "the nationalist world view" has always been "a minority perspective."[24] Gone are the days, however, of easy distinctions between left-leaning nationalists and right-leaning continentalists, when it was obvious to progressives that—as George Grant put it in *Lament for a Nation*—"the wealthy lost nothing essential to the principle of their lives in losing their country."[25] In Canada today, it is bank presidents who advocate "smart nationalism" and corporate executives who urge upon us a "mature exercise of sovereignty" that includes a recognition of the "rewards" that come from our close relationship with the United States.[26]

YOUTH AND THE CANADIAN STATE

Any serious discussion of the applicability of nationalist ideology to young Canadians must start not with the many misleading stereotypes that have plagued them of late—"Generation X," "the MTV generation," "the slacker generation"—but with the conditions of their lived experience. The crucial fact of life for contemporary Canadian youths and young adults—anyone born after 1965—is that they have been mired in an economic crisis unprecedented since the Great Depression. Public perceptions that young people are "whiners"—or that "alienation" from "McJobs" is a pose that they have assumed as a kind of lifestyle accessory—has helped to silence the victims of this crisis, while the indifference (and in some cases, the antipathy) of public policy towards young people—cracking down on "squeegee kids," for example, or "toughening up" the *Young Offenders Act*—has helped to divert attention away from its root causes. Throughout the 1990s, young Canadians had the highest unemployment rate of any group in Canada, sometimes twice that of the national average, a crisis that has only recently begun to register on the national agenda.[27] As bad as they are, what the raw unemployment statistics tend to obscure is the long-term, systemic degradation of the value of the labour of young Canadians. For Canadian men aged 18 to 24, real annual earnings dropped 36 per cent between 1979 and the 1990s, while the earnings of women in this age group fell 29 per cent. Among 25- to 34-year-old men men, real earnings fell 14 per cent in the same period—an extremely significant trend since it affirms that young men today have downward mobility and declining socio-economic status in common with Canadian teens.[28] Not only are wages down, but labour force participation has also declined dramatically. In early 1999, a report released by the Canadian Council on Social Development noted that "[m]ore than half of today's 16-year-olds have never found paid work, compared to only about a quarter in 1989."[29] Canadians aged 15 to 24 are today among the most likely to live in poverty.[30]

As I shall show in greater detail in the next chapter, the Canadian state has played a critical role in the socio-economic marginalization of young people since the 1970s, and this fact alone raises serious doubts about the degree to which they enjoy a sense of "belonging." Most obviously, the abandonment of the postwar "Keynesian" commitment to low unemployment—a central element in the neo-liberal economic revolution throughout the West since the 1980s—has meant that youth ("last hired, first fired") have been disproportionately affected both by cyclical changes in the Canadian economy and especially by the deep structural changes that have accompanied globalization. Anti-globalization activist Naomi Klein has argued, in fact, that "the erosion of a commitment to steady employment is the single most significant factor contributing to a climate of anti-corporate militancy" today.[31] Relatedly, in stark contrast to the Trudeau era, when the civil service was expanding and providing good jobs for young Canadians, the public sector has been downsizing for so long that young people, especially university graduates, no longer regard the state as a likely site of employment. The federal Auditor General, Sheila Fraser, stated recently that the failure of the civil service to renew itself now constitutes a serious "human capital challenge" for Canada, and to a greater or lesser degree the same may be said of various provincial bureaucracies.[32] As Anton L. Allahar and James E. Coté, co-authors of *Generation on Hold* (1994) and *Richer & Poorer* (1998) have argued, public policy has played a central role in the economic marginalization of young people:

> [M]any of the policy adjustments undertaken by the Canadian state have made government a key mediator between the interests of capital and young workers. One such policy is the setting of minimum wage levels. In the mid-1970s, the minimum wage would put a person about 40% above the official poverty line; now it puts a person 30% below that line. Notably, two-thirds of minimum wage earners are under 24 years of age. Here, government policies have clearly contributed to age-based discrimination. Few people seem to be aware of the role the state has played in mediating the interests of capital in this regard, and many of those who are aware seem to see nothing wrong with it.[33]

One of the most thoroughgoing recent analyses of young Canadians' relationship to the state takes the form of a *Literature Review on Youth and Citizenship* written by Caroline Beauvais, Lindsey McKay and Adam

Seddon. Like Marc Cousineau, these researchers distinguish between the nominal citizenship rights of Canadians and "full citizenship," by which they mean "*actively seeking to engage* so as to realize one's rights, exercise one's responsibilities, have access to political institutions, be empowered, and share a sense of belonging to the community—national as well as local." Building on the extremely important observation that "youth" as a social construct has been extended in recent years so as to include people in their twenties and even their thirties, these researchers show how young people's acquisition of full citizenship status has been retarded by the prolonging of the period in which their relationship to the state is "mediated by their parents." Establishing an autonomous household, for example, is obviously "fundamental to full citizenship," yet the number of Canadians aged 20 to 34 who live with their parents has been increasing steadily since the 1970s. This process constitutes a systematic download-ing of financial responsibility for dependent adult children from the state to the family, and is the direct result of public policies that range from "denying social assistance benefits to young people" and forcing them into "workfare" programs on the basis of age alone, to the "artificial distinction between student debt and commercial debt" in the *Bankruptcy and Insolvency Act*. Beauvais, McKay and Seddon conclude bluntly that

> an increasing number of young people are experiencing a citizen-ship status that is precarious due to various "holes" in the policy environment. The abandonment of the nominal commitment to full employment, increased difficulties in accessing higher education because of tuition hikes, a lack of affordable housing, limited access to health and social services, and cutbacks to social assistance are all increasing the number of gaps through which young people may fall. Many youths are therefore en route to exclusion.[34]

In contrast with the Trudeau era, moreover, when young people were accorded a great deal of latitude when challenging adult authority—re-call the extent to which the Counterculture was indulged by teachers, public officials, even the police—young people today inhabit a world of "zero tolerance," in which strict conformity to "adult" social norms constitutes the only acceptable behaviour. As *Ottawa Citizen* columnist Dan Gardner puts it: "'Zero tolerance' is the buzzword that captures the belief that we can punish our way to a world of perfect safety. Drugs threaten our kids? There will be 'zero tolerance' for drugs. Violence? Zero tolerance. Weapons? Zero tolerance."[35] Originally the sole preserve of extremists in the Reform party, "zero tolerance" and its corollary, "getting tough" on youth crime, have in the last decade moved to centre stage in Canadian political theatre. The Klein and Harris governments in Alberta and Ontario, respectively, have taken great electoral advantage of increasing public worry about youth crime; and in concert with sensational media stories and the relentless attacks of the Canadian Alliance party, they have prodded the Chrétien Liberals into replacing Pierre Trudeau's *Young Offenders Act* with the more punitive *Youth Criminal Justice Act*. Although there is debate among Canadian criminologists as to whether or not youth crime is actually on the rise, all agree that youth crime as a proportion of crime in general remains "relatively low."[36] University of Toronto criminologist Anthony Doob reminds us that between 80 and 90 per cent of Canadian adolescents "commit crimes"—few of them more serious than minor acts of vandalism—and presumably always have.[37] That young people's occasional engagement in "rule-breaking and illegal behaviour" is simply part of growing up would not have surprised earlier generations of Canadian adults; today, however, as Bernard Schissel has argued in *Blaming Children* (1997), "Canada's war on crime… is quickly becoming a war against youth."[38]

The state is also implicated in any number of lesser demonization strategies when it comes to the young. Heavy metal, hip-hop and more recently industrial and goth music have been blamed for inciting violent, suicidal and even murderous behaviour in young Canadians.[39] Rave culture has been impugned for its connection to what public officials are now calling "ecstasy-related" deaths (Toronto police chief Julian Fantino believes raves are "threatening the very fabric of Canadian society").[40] That teens appear to be smoking in increasing numbers has produced a melodramatic feud between the federal health minister and the tobacco industry, enhancing a public perception of Canadian youth as naive or reckless. Various education ministries have radically reformed public school curricula, complete with standardized testing, mandatory literacy testing as a prerequisite to graduation and — in Ontario — "plans to get tough on failing kids."[41] Marginalized, demonized, downsized, toughened up — little wonder that young Canadians' citizenship is precarious, and their identification with the Canadian state weak.

DEPOLITICIZATION

The defection of youth from conventional electoral politics has caused a good deal of hand-wringing of late, and not only in Canada. Throughout the industrialized West young people have been opting out of the political process since the 1970s. Recent studies in the United Kingdom show that six out of ten young people there do not vote. In the United States, the situation is even worse: in the 1994 midterm elections, fewer than one in five Americans aged 18 to 24 voted, and in 1996 — a presidential election year — fewer than one in three did so.[42] According to *Guardian* columnist Jonathan Freedland, what is most disturbing about this trend is its longitudinal pattern. Citing data from BBC polls, Freedland notes that "what used to be an under-twenty-five problem a decade ago is now an under-thirty-five problem and fast becoming an under-forty-five problem." The worry is that young people's defection from electoral politics signifies not merely an erosion of democratic values but evidence of their profound, perhaps permanent detachment from national life:

> [A] large slice of the country, especially the young... is tuning out of the national conversation altogether. The things which preoccupied dinner tables in London and broadcasts on the BBC passed them by; whether shut out or having dropped out, they are on the outside. Not voting is just one more proof of their exclusion.[43]

In 1999 the *Atlantic Monthly* published a lengthy cover story by 30-year-old Ted Halstead entitled "A Politics for Generation X." This article has since become one of the most frequently cited texts on contemporary youth culture (in large measure because Western youth are commonly thought to occupy many of the same impoverished cultural, political and especially socio-economic spaces vis-à-vis the dominant mass-mediated, commercial culture). Halstead acknowledges that "postboomers" in the US are "less politically or civically engaged, exhibit less social trust or confidence in government, have a weaker allegiance to their country or to either political party, and are more materialistic than their predecessors." Their "general knowledge about public affairs is uniquely low," they "see partisan boundaries blurring into irrelevance," and they are "the group least likely to favor maintaining the current two-party system." Even more fundamentally,

> Xers have internalized core beliefs and characteristics that bode ill for the future of American democracy. This generation is more likely to describe itself as having a negative attitude toward America, and as placing little importance on citizenship and national identity, than its predecessors.... Moreover, there is a general decline in social trust among the young, whether that is trust in their fellow citizens, in established institutions, or in elected officials. These tendencies are, of course, related: heightened individualism and materialism, as Alexis de Tocqueville pointed out, tend to isolate people from one another, weakening the communal bonds that give meaning and force to notions of national identity and the common good.

Halstead's explanation for Gen X apathy hinges on young people's grim socio-economic inheritance: falling wages, shrinking benefits, the inflation of educational credentials, growing economic inequality, child poverty, and a "daunting array of fiscal, social, and environmental debts." He believes that for American youth neither the historic left-right ideological model nor the two-party electoral system is relevant.

Rather, young people advocate a pragmatic approach to politics he calls Balanced-Budget Populism: "Fiscal prudence, economic populism, social investment, campaign reform, shared sacrifice, and environmental conservation—this constellation of beliefs transcends the existing left-right spectrum."[44]

"Twenty-something" *Globe and Mail* columnist Leah McLaren concurs with Halstead's sense of contemporary youth politics:

> When we were in high school a friend asked me, what was the difference between the left wing and the right wing? This particular friend was a bisexual vegan anarchist who went ballistic when the green peppers at her local organic fruit market were needlessly wrapped in plastic. Floored, I wondered how could this pierced-and-dreadlocked virago be so militant and so moronic at the same time? I drew a little diagram and explained, in my teenspeak, the difference between, like, tax-and-spend social democracy and, like, a more fiscally restrained conservatism. So okay, I said, you can either be a crunchy liberal, a middle-of-the-road liberal, a red tory or blue tory. She said it didn't matter: She planned to spoil her ballot anyway.
>
> I have since learned that my friend, although particularly ill-informed, was typical of my generation. It wasn't that she was stupid, or without politics of her own. Rather, the old right-left political spectrum simply held no meaning for her.[45]

McLaren's claim that youth in Canada have a "politics of their own" may be overly sanguine. In a recent study for the Institute for Research on Public Policy (IRPP), Brenda O'Neill analyzed "generational differences among Canadians in their political attitudes and behaviours" only to find that "[t]he young appear at best to be politically passive and at worst politically apathetic." Canadian youth are today "participating in the political system at lower levels than previous generations did at the same age, suggesting that recent declines in voting turnout and other measures of political participation will not be reversed in future years." Of her sample group of 1278 Canadians, whom she polled in 2000 (an election year), O'Neill found that 59 per cent of Canadians 18 to 27 "do not follow politics at any level." In dramatic contrast with the young Americans described by Halstead, however, she discovered that "younger Canadians reveal higher levels of satisfaction with a number of institutions, including Canadian democracy and elections generally and they hold healthier opinions of the federal government." Significantly, O'Neill also found that political parties are more attractive to older Canadians while interest groups appear to be much more attractive to the young: "The ratio of interest group participation to political party participation is 4.5 to 1 for the youngest age group but only 0.3 to 1 among the oldest age group." O'Neill concludes that in general "although younger Canadians appear to be less politically engaged, this disengagement appears less as a conscious decision to turn away from politics than a failure to see the importance of political participation, combined perhaps with a belief that traditional politics may not be providing effective mechanisms for translating desire into action." Her prescriptive advice for the Canadian government is to suggest that it would "do well to address these findings, both by increasing dialogue with Canadians generally and by implementing measures designed to increase political participation among Canadian youth."[46] Meanwhile, Elections Canada officials report that getting young people out to vote remains their "greatest challenge," while even MuchMusic admits that its voting-aged viewers are "having trouble achieving an election."[47]

CONSERVATIVE YOUTH

In contrast with the public perception that Canadian youth are "wild" and "out of control," the dire economic circumstances of their lives has fashioned Canadians under 35 into a more *conservative* group, taken as a whole, than their elders. Education, especially higher education, is also a conservatizing force in the lives of young people, emphasizing discipline, delayed gratification and, to a greater or lesser degree, identification with the promise of upward mobility. With more young Canadians than ever in school, youth are more likely to identify with the socio-economic *status quo* in Canada than to challenge it. Debt alone — which many young university and college graduates must now bear as a kind of mortgage, sometimes running into the tens of thousands of dollars — is a sobering, conservatizing force, notwithstanding the sensational claims frequently made in the news media that defaulting is a common strategy for young Canadians.

The declining strength of nationalism among Canadian youth and young adults is inextricably connected with this trend towards conservatism and with the socio-economic marginalization that informs it. If affluence and a keen sense of "belonging" were the preconditions of the nationalist inheritance of the youth Counterculture in the 1960s and the 1970s, then the contrary holds for the youth of today. The evidence is unambiguous. Sociologist Reginald Bibby has been sampling the attitudes of young Canadians for two decades, and his books on Canadian youth — *The Emerging Generation* (1984), *Canada's Youth* (1987), *Teen Trends* (1992) and *Canada's Teens* (2001) — constitute an invaluable "longitudinal" record of their evolution. Although he remains a tireless defender of Canadian youth, Bibby's work demonstrates a clear correlation between young people's increasingly conservative attitudes, their worsening economic prospects, their increasing materialism, and the declining importance of nationalism in their thinking. The central thesis of *Teen Trends*, for example, a book Bibby co-authored with Donald Posterski, was that Nineties youth exhibited virtually none of the idealism that characterized the Sixties Counterculture, nor did they have much reason to do so: "Canadian young people in the 1990s do not see themselves as agents of change. They are like mirrors on the wall of society. Their attitudes and behaviour mainly reflect the *status quo*. They have not been able to carve out much of a world that is uniquely their own." The subtext of this study was that young Canadians were being "Americanized" at an alarming rate, primarily via the influence of mass media, and that their failure to identify with Canada constituted an historic rupture:

Canadian young people, exposed as they are to American thought, complete with American self-confidence, power, and energy, are buying the idea that Canadians tend to rate behind Americans when it comes to a number of valued traits.... The sense that "American is best" is pervasive.

Significantly, Bibby and Posterski speculated in *Teen Trends* that the legacy of Trudeau-era left-nationalism for the young Canadians following in its wake was one of disappointment and even disillusionment:

Perhaps the fatal flaw in our post-60s social reconstruction efforts was our failure to lay out a national dream that would enable Canadians of all ages to pursue together what they have been saying they value the most: good relationships and economic prosperity. In opting to emphasize the "just society" over the "best society," we left millions of young people and others with the message that our national objective is equitable co-existence.[48]

By 2001, when *Canada's Teens* was published, the decline of nationalism among young Canadians was so far gone as to obviate any serious discussion about resuscitating it. In contrast with *Teen Trends*, in which young Canadians' declining identification with Canada in the early 1990s was a major preoccupation, Bibby now appeared resigned to the fact that the issue was a dead letter: "As Canadians we have not made a lot of nationalism, especially in post-Trudeau years." He did not pull his punches:

[O]ur national effort to establish a rich Canadian culture through championing a multicultural country has contributed to a cultural blank in most of English-speaking Canada. Outside Quebec, people have a questionable sense of where they have come from, few heroes and a passive acceptance of being inferior to the US. In lieu of having our own Canadian culture, the tendency has been to fill the void with American culture, contributing to the Americanization of Canadian life.

Asked who they regard as "the greatest Canadian of all time," Bibby reports, roughly 60 per cent of Canadian youth surveyed in 2000 either indicated that "no one comes to mind" or left the item blank.[49]

While there has been a tendency on the Canadian left to attribute young people's conservatism, depoliticization and Americanization to the baneful influence of corporate media and the decline of civic discourses noted above, there is also evidence of a bona fide ideological reaction among young Canadians against what they view as the excesses of left-nationalism and the "entitlemania" with which it is commonly identified. This trend has been fuelled in the 1990s by the increasing popularity of political parties, think tanks and pundits espousing neo-liberal economics (smaller government, debt reduction, balanced budgets, tax cuts) and more recently by the perception that Canada is a country in decline. As pollster Allan Gregg observed in *Maclean's* in 1998, Canadians' postwar belief in progress and particularly in unlimited upward mobility appears to have come crashing to a halt:

> We started to question that belief for the first time with the erosion of real income brought on by rampant inflation and interest rates in the early '80s. The failure of time-tested solutions (mainly governmental) to provide relief further eroded the belief that progress was normal. Today, Canadians accept that we live in a world of diminished opportunities. The public has also concluded that not everyone in society will share equally in the diminished opportunities that are available.[50]

Speaking to the Fraser Institute in November 2001 as a former "Canadian nationalist," Conrad Black opined that Canada has become "a plain vanilla place" compared to other G-7 countries.[51] Historian Michael Bliss (backed by the editorial writers at the *National Post*) has asserted recently that the country is mired in mediocrity: "When it comes to being committed to excellence, to real achievement, to making real contributions to the life of the world, it is increasingly hard to be proudly Canadian."[52] In February 2002 federal Minster of Industry Allan Rock admitted in *Achieving Excellence*, part of his newly unveiled "innovation strategy," that "real incomes in Canada have been steadily falling relative to the U.S. over much of the last two decades"—a confession interpreted on the Canadian right as a vindication of its longstanding critique of Liberal economic policies.[53]

Such claims have not been lost on young people. Weaned on the notion that government deficits and debt meant "mortgaging our children's future," for example, many young Canadians today agree with the likes of Gregg and Bliss that Canada is a land of diminishing opportunity, and that the overweening Canadian state is to blame. *Youthquake*, written by 24-year-old Ezra Levant and published in 1996 by the Fraser Institute, suggests the extent to which at least some young Canadians have embraced this neo-liberal critique. With an introduction by Jason Kenney (then president of the Canadian Taxpayers Federation and now a Canadian Alliance MP), this polemic sets out the now-familiar nononsense case against the Canadian welfare state and in so doing takes on some of the left-nationalists' historic sacred cows. Alluding to the well-known claim that the pension and healthcare needs of retiring baby boomers will have to be financed on the backs of younger Canadians, Levant asserts:

> There is no way there'll be any free plums left on the health care tree by the time I am sixty. And today's luxurious social services won't continue either. It's a mathematical impossibility. The whole deal is raw. It was stacked against all of us but against young people in particular.

He is categorical in his rejection of the notion that the state might serve as the locus of reform, couching his critique explicitly with reference to the expansion of the welfare state in the 1960s:

Government, supposedly the problem-solver of the sixties, has turned into the problem-maker of the nineties.... That's the twentysomething zeitgeist—government's a con, so you either get in the game or become the mark. We recognize Entitlemania for what it is. You can translate these sentiments into economic jargon if you like: welfare programs are a disincentive to work.

That Levant knows he is stomping over hallowed nationalist ground is evident in his qualified debt of gratitude to earlier nation-builders:

Were the patriotism and nation-building of the past exerted in exchange for the expectation of a retirement payoff? Of course they weren't. Young Canadians are grateful to those who came before. They built this country: that's true. But our genuine thanks do not translate into a wholesale intergenerational transfer of resources from tomorrow's workers to today's retirees."[54]

Young Canadians' conservatism is not only translating into votes for the right but, according to some observers, contributing to the realignment of political coalitions in Canada. In the 1995 provincial election in Ontario, for example, Mike Harris' Tories took 46 per cent of young and first-time voters, leaving only 28 per cent for the Liberals and 15 per cent for the NDP. According to Brooke Jeffrey, author of *Hard Right Turn* (1999), this electoral success was attributable in part to the Tories' promise to reduce taxes and eliminate the deficit, but more particularly to the way in which Mike Harris offered "a politically acceptable outlet for the growing frustrations of the economically endangered middle class and their adult children."[55] Yet of the four "hot button issues" that animated the Common Sense Revolution in its first term—welfare, employment equity, young offenders and photo radar—two (welfare and young offenders) targeted youth explicitly. How to explain this apparent paradox?

On the one hand, it is likely that many of the young Canadians who vote for neo-conservative parties are, in fact, voting their parents' interests. The downloading of state responsibility for dependent adult children onto families has been so thoroughly naturalized since the 1970s that many young voters are today unable to distinguish between their own political stake in Canadian society and that of their parents. How else to explain the appeal of tax cuts to a generation of youth impoverished by sinking wages and indebted by consumer over-spending and soaring tuition fees? On the other hand, "zero tolerance" has been so relentlessly trumpeted by the media, the schools, parents and the state that many young people appear to have themselves internalized the prevailing distinction between "good kids" and "bad kids," and they now vote accordingly. Reginald Bibby discovered, for example, that almost "three in four" Canadian teens believed in 2000 that the *Young Offenders Act* should be "toughened."[56] Since, as noted above, it is known that most Canadians break the law at some point during adolescence, this statistic implies that young Canadians neither empathize with those of their peers who run afoul of the law nor believe, more to the point, that they will ever end up in trouble themselves. The point is not that young Canadians today privately believe that their misdeeds will go unpunished—this has always been true—but that this belief informs their public selves and their politics. When it comes to social attitudes, many Canadian youth have found the vindictiveness of the neo-conservative right agreeable, but only by exempting themselves from its opportunistic attacks on the weak and the marginal.

NATIONALIST OPTIONS FOR YOUTH?

There is yet another explanation for the attractiveness of neo-conservative policies for the minority of young Canadians who participate in conventional politics, and it derives from what Jeffrey M. Ayres calls "the deteriorating symbolic position and identity of English Canada." Borrowing from Philip Resnick, whose work continues to explore the ways in which the English-Canadian nation might be "imagined," Ayres observes that the demands of "separatist, aboriginal, and other, often multicultural, voices" have forced the state to recognize "the new cultural realities in Canada." These new realities, in turn, have undermined the historic dominance of English Canadians, causing uncertainty, worry and even bitterness: "English Canadians no longer see themselves and their way of life consistently reflected in societal institutions, celebrated in public events, and upheld by public authorities—they have become to some degree 'social strangers.'" Ayres argues convincingly that this "spirit of this uncertainty" in English Canada has directly informed the rise of the Reform/Alliance Party—a "populist" movement which has "tapped into English Canadian national concerns by opposing Quebec nationalism, the distinct society clauses of the Meech Lake and Charlottetown Accords, and the broader government policies of the previous decades which have granted greater cultural recognition to minority groups."[57] In short, the ideological element in neo-conservatism that makes it attractive to English Canadians who believe that they are losing status in their own homeland may well be nationalism—not the historic nationalism which has sought to "channel state action in directions that are meant to strengthen national sovereignty and to reinforce the autonomy of state institutions," but nationalism of the paranoid, defensive and ultimately nativistic variety.[58]

It is impossible at this juncture to know whether Ayre's linkage of nationalism and neo-conservatism applies to large numbers of Canadian youth. Some observations may be ventured, however. The first of these is the perhaps obvious point that the Reform/Alliance movement has long recognized that its ability to rise to "national party" status has been hobbled not only by its regional roots and its reputed "bigotry" but by the public perception that it represents mainly older white English-speaking men. One of Stockwell Day's presumed advantages over Preston Manning was his ostensible "youthfulness," and polls did indeed reveal that Day had drawn unprecedented numbers of young Canadians into the Reform Party after winning the leadership. What the polls showed by mid-2001, however, is not only that he had lost the support of youth but that the Alliance "has reverted to its early Reform days when it drew support from older males, who generally earn less money and were less likely to have graduated from university than the general population."[59] However enthralled they might have been with Day as the "fresh face" in national politics, young people in this instance at least proved themselves fickle fellow-travellers.

In one important sense, the abandonment of the Canadian Alliance by youth and young adults should come as no surprise. Notwithstanding their well-documented political ignorance and apathy, the fact remains that they are not only the best-educated Canadians but the most tolerant.[60] In addition, as countless marketing analyses, surveys and polls have shown, young Canadians are notoriously disloyal and difficult to "brand"—in politics as in music, jeans and soft drinks. On both counts, then, one might well expect that their allegiance to the Reform/Alliance movement would be tentative and ultimately impossible to cement.

There is also the matter of young people's apparent indifference to nationalist politics, whether it takes the form of neo-conservatism, left-nationalism or some Halsteadian hybrid of the two. The Canadian Alliance is not the only "grey" party failing in its efforts to tap the ostensibly rich vein of English-Canadian national identity. Mel Hurtig's National Party of Canada, for example, campaigned on a nationalist platform in the federal election of 1993 and utterly failed to capture the public imagination; Paul Hellyer's nationalist Canadian Action Party is, if anything, even less well known. The Liberals under Jean Chrétien have been criticized heartily in some quarters—especially since the eruption of the post-September 11 "sovereignty crisis" in Canada—for refusing to engage in a national debate about Canada's relationship with the United States. Toronto *Star* columnist Richard Gwyn, for one, has suggested that this reluctance is clear evidence of political cowardice, asserting that Ottawa has become "an intellectual and emotional black hole."[61] It seems far more likely, however, that Chrétien has opted for a Mackenzie King-like approach to the matter, meaning that he would rather say nothing than provoke a deep fissure in the country at a time of crisis. That the Chrétien Liberals understand—as Hurtig and Hellyer apparently do not—the political dynamite of nationalist ideology in the present international climate is perfectly obvious, not least because the only minister with the temerity to criticize the United States since September 11, Heritage Minister Sheila Copps, has been pilloried in the press and abandoned by her Cabinet colleagues. Recalling Sylvia Bashevkin's notion that the success or failure of nationalist organizations rests on their capacity to serve as collective "carriers of meaning," the question thus remains: even if young Canadians wanted to attach themselves to an explicitly nationalist movement, where might they turn to see themselves and their interests represented? As Terry Goldie has observed, even in relatively successful lobby groups like Maude Barlow's Council of Canadians, nationalism has devolved—by design or by accident—into a pragmatic, confused and lacklustre affair:

> The Council of Canadians seems to be a self-evidently nationalist organization, but the last time I checked its main target was genetically modified foods. Pardon? Back in the days of the Waffle and the Canadian Liberation Movement, there was no such diffusion. I was a student of Robin Mathews, and my problem with him was that he seemed to have no focus other than nationalism. At present, not even the nationalists are nationalist.[62]

The finest analysis to date of young Canadians' inchoate, ambivalent nationalist yearnings is Nicole Nolan's "Isn't it Ironic?," published in *This Magazine* in 1996. Nolan, who appears to be a member of the contemporary "urban youth" cohort she describes, is interested in exploring the apparent paradox that Canadian youth are today both deeply suspicious of "official" nationalist discourses—particularly those which originate in Ottawa—but enamored of the nationalist allusions that today permeate Canadian popular culture. Correctly noting that a "half-dozen different national visions have gone down the tubes since the Second World War," Nolan asserts bluntly that "national identity has been left in the hands of Canada's gruesome TV Heritage Moments and Sheila Copps' $23-million dollar flag giveaway campaign." Of Copps' public posturing, in particular, she writes:

> Like [American presidential candidate] Bob Dole, with his white shoes and his old World War II record, Copps and her flags seem

trapped in an agonizingly archaic dance, recycling dusty notions in a desperate attempt to fuel national spirit. It's a scheme guaranteed to leave younger generations utterly disaffected with nationalism. They could hardly need more reason to find the emotion distasteful; after you have seen some of the atrocities committed in the name of nationalism in Bosnia, the US or Burundi, the very idea of waving a flag seems offensive. No doubt Copps' flags hold strong appeal for my grandmother, but at the age of eighty-one, she hardly represents the future of the nation.

Nolan argues that the advertising of Molson and Labatt—populated by "unshaven explorers who crack withering jokes as they traverse early Canada, and young urbanites who travel the world in a whirl of Gen-X hipness"—is not only more sophisticated in its use of ambiguous nationalist signifiers but far better attuned to the postmodern ways in which their young viewers consume popular culture:

> Underneath the various chunks of cultural grot one might expect from productions aimed at twenty something white boys, these ads are some of the most compelling things I have seen in the area of national identity. Witty, cosmopolitan, simultaneously proud and self-deprecating, the Molson and Labatt ads are the only blips on the radar that are even attempting to rethink what "Canadian" means in the late Twentieth Century. They're witness to an appetite for a redefined Canadian identity (particularly in the youth market) that lavishly rewards anyone who feeds it. And like any original idea, they're drawing deeply on tradition—in this case, the strain of withering, self-parodying irony and ambiguity that has long run through the country's culture. Unlike our flat-footed government, Labatt and Molson seem actually to be listening to Canadians' often ambivalent feelings about their country.

Nolan is by no means unambiguous in her praise, however, asserting not only that the ads' "mutilations of history are truly among the most brutal ever produced" but that they constitute compelling proof that "Canadian education is in deep shit." But the lamentable fact remains—for Nolan and for others—that "Molson and Labatt have done a shockingly good job of tapping into the national zeitgeist." It is a pity, she concludes, that this "proven Canadian appetite for multiplicity and irony has been left in the hands of beer companies."[63]

Ads show what people are listening to in culture at the time — you can see various demographics

CONCLUSION

Generally speaking, young Canadians' precarious citizenship, their declining socio-economic status and especially their *de facto* exclusion from the "national conversation" have put them beyond the pale of traditional nationalist formations in Canada. There are, of course, exceptions but, as Beauvais, McKay and Seddon have argued, they tend to prove the rule. The retreat of the Canadian state and the usurpation of "civic" discourses by those of the "free market" have polarized youth, enhancing the citizenship status of the minority who enjoy access to private resources and social capital, while marginalizing those who do not.

In contrast with Myrna Kostash and others on the Canadian left who today hold out the hope that young people's idealism, tolerance and good sense might translate into a renaissance of the left-nationalist tradition in Canada, I take the view that the era in which "the national" represents a significant pole of identity formation for progressive Canadian youth is all but over. Ezra Levant's accusation that the baby boomers used the state to enrich themselves at the expense of younger Canadians is but an extreme version of a view more widely held among many young people today—not all of them neo-conservative ideologues—that the era of "bloated" governments constituted a mortgaging of their future. Young Canadians also seem receptive to the idea that the sovereignty of the nation-state is eroding so dramatically as to call into question its continuing viability as a continuing site of social reform—a claim that puts them in the intellectual company of older Canadian Marxists like Gary Teeple who believe that the Keynesian welfare state represented only a temporary "compromise" in postwar societies, one which was possible only because capital was still national (rather than global) in its reach.[64] Many progressive, idealistic, activist youth and young adults in Canada have found a home in the transnational anti-globalization movement and some, most obviously Naomi Klein, are in its intellectual vanguard; and while it is true that this movement has enjoyed some success in allying with older left-nationalists—as in the New Politics Initiative—it is also apparent that the two movements are in some critical respects incompatible. Left-nationalism is greying, in short, and there is little evidence to suggest that progressive youth can be mobilized around an ideology that today seems so anachronistic.

The relevance of nationalist formations for the majority of young Canadians who are neither progressive nor even politically self-aware in any conventional sense is much more difficult to gauge. Although mostly silent on the great issues of our time, young Canadians are today afflicted with a crisis of "belonging" that has no historic equal save perhaps for the disaffection of the cohort that came of age during the 1930s. The current crisis—even now largely hidden from public view—points to the possibility that, like the Depression generation, alienated young people might well find the politics of the right agreeable, especially now that the left seems so thoroughly discredited. As Eric Hobsbawm reminds us in *The Age of Extremes*, however accustomed we have become to viewing all youthful protest through the lens of the 1960s Counterculture, there is nothing inevitable about young radicals' preference for the left. Until World War II, he writes, "the great majority of students in central and western Europe and North America had been non-political or Right-wing."[65] In this context, Ian Kershaw's description of young Germans' disaffection under the Weimar Republic also has an eerily contemporary resonance:

For young people, the Depression years had both in material and in psychological terms been appallingly damaging. Hopes and ideals had been blighted almost before they could take shape. By the end of 1932, four consecutive cohorts of pupils had left school to miserable prospects. Those lucky enough to find work had done so in deteriorating conditions, and were usually dismissed at the end of their apprenticeships. The youth welfare system was close to collapse. Growing suicide and youth criminality rates told their own tale. Those from more well-to-do backgrounds faced greatly diminished chances of launching a career in the professions to match their ambitions. Above average support for the Nazis among university students was one indication of middle-class youth's alienation from the Weimar Republic. In fact, the attractiveness of extremist parties of Right and Left—the NSDAP and the KPD—to young people is an indication of their different forms of alienation from Weimar democracy and their readiness to resort to political radicalism. In many respects, it was a generational revolt against a system and a society that had failed them.[66]

As Canada's political culture shifts to the right and as neo-conservative politicians position themselves to take advantage of English Canadians' unease—their sense, to borrow Jeffrey M. Ayres' phrase, that they are "social strangers" in their own land—the uses to which Canadian nationalism are being put in everyday life should be of more than academic interest. How nationalist discourses resonate for Canadian youth and young adults is especially significant, since these cohorts seem to not only occupy but revel in the world of postmodern ambiguity, dissonance and irony, a world in which meaning is not only socially constructed but fluid and provisional. In such circumstances, the struggle for the hearts and minds of Canadians will take place increasingly in the realm of identity and fought over symbolic "carriers of meaning." Canadian youth may know little Canadian history and even less of Canadian politics, but they remain strikingly receptive to the invocation of certain national myths and icons. The Tragically Hip inspires fanatical loyalty in their fans because they are "a great Canadian band"; a movement is launched to draft Don Cherry as Governor General; Team Canada defeats the US in the gold-medal Olympic hockey game and young Canadians with maple leaves painted on their faces pour into the streets in ecstasy; "Joe Canada" recites "The Rant" — Molson's latest advertising hook — at theatres and hockey games and young audiences holler their approval. However ironic, however superficial, however frustrating to the likes of Jody Berland and others who worry that while we are busy celebrating hockey victories and Canadian rock stars we are losing our country, the question remains: are these symbolic investments merely the vestiges of an ideology in eclipse (the proverbial corpse kicking) or evidence of something far more profound?

NOTES

1. Terry Goldie, "Blame Canada," *Essays on Canadian Writing* 71 (Fall 2000), pp. 224–31.

2. Sylvia B. Bashevkin, *True Patriot Love: The Politics of Canadian Nationalism* (Toronto: Oxford University Press, 1991), p. 9. The commissions to which she refers were Massey-Lévesque in 1951, Fowler in 1957 and O'Leary in 1961.

3. Ibid., p. 28.

4. Philip Resnick, *The Land of Cain: Class and Nationalism in English Canada 1945–1975* (Vancouver: New Star Books, 1977), pp. 167–170.

5. See Robert Wright, *Hip and Trivial: Youth Culture, Book Publishing and the Greying of Canadian Nationalism* (Toronto: Canadian Scholars' Press, 2001), esp. ch. 4.

6. Marc Cousineau, "Belonging: An Essential Element of Citizenship — a Franco-Ontarian Perspective," William Kaplan, ed., *Belonging: The Meaning and Future of Canadian Citizenship* (McGill-Queen's University Press, 1993), pp. 139–40.

7. Habeeb Salloum, "Pierre Trudeau's Visionary Prime Minister," *Contemporary Review* 277 (December 2000), p. 329.

8. Pierre Elliott Trudeau, *Conversation With Canadians* (Toronto: University of Toronto Press, 1972), p. 30.

9. Jacques Hébert, "Legislating for Freedom," in Thomas S. Axworthy and Pierre Elliott Trudeau, eds., *Towards a Just Society* (Toronto: Penguin, 1990), pp. 184–5.

10. *Youth '71: An Inquiry into the Transient Youth and Opportunities for Youth Programs in the Summer of 1971* (Ottawa: Canadian Council on Social Development, 1971), pp. 69–91.

11. Hébert, p. 185.

12. Ian Angus, *A Border Within: National Identity, Cultural Plurality and Wilderness* (Montreal: McGill-Queen's University Press, 1997), p. ix.

13. Ibid., pp. 8–34.

14. Jody Berland, "Politics after Nationalism, Culture after 'Culture'," *Canadian Review of American Studies* 27:3 (1997), pp. 36–7.

15. Myrna Kostash, *No Kidding: Inside the World of Teenage Girls* (Toronto: McClelland and Stewart, 1987), p. 7.

16. Myrna Kostash, *The Next Canada: In Search of Our Future Nation* (Toronto: McClelland & Stewart, 2000), pp. ix–x, 309–27.

17. Jeffrey M. Ayres, "From National to Popular Sovereignty? The Evolving Globalization of Protest Activity in Canada," *International Journal of Canadian Studies* 16 (Fall 1997), pp. 107–23.

18. James Laxer, "The Left Reinvents the Zeal," *Globe and Mail* (26 July 2001), p. A17.

19. Morna Ballantyne, Dave Meslin, Judy Rebick, Svend Robinson and Jim Stanford, "The Left Needs New Voices," *Globe and Mail* (7 June 2001).

20. Goldie, "Blame Canada," pp. 224–31.

21. Paul Bunner, "Globalization or Canadianization: Take Your Pick," *Alberta Report* (14 May 2001).

22. Margaret Wente, "They Had It Coming?" *Globe and Mail* (15 September 2001), p. A21.

23. Heather Sokoloff, "CBC National Town Hall Too Local: Ombudsman," *National Post* (26 November 2001).

24. Bashevkin, p. 25.

25. George Grant, *Lament for a Nation: The Defeat of Canadian Nationalism* (Toronto: McClelland & Stewart, 1970; originally published in 1965), p. 47.

26. Charles Baillie, cited in David Crane, "Banks Have Role to Play in Nation's Success," *Toronto Star* (18 December 2001); and Yves Fortier, "Time to Grow Up," *National Post* (25 January 2002).

27. Dana Flavelle, "Firms Ignore Jobless Youth," *Toronto Star* (25 June 1999).

28. Garnett Picot, *What Is Happening to Earnings Inequalities and Youth Wages in the 1990s?* (Ottawa: Statistics Canada, July 1998).

29. Cited in Elaine Carey, "Jobs Elude Most Teens, Report Says," *Toronto Star* (19 January 1999).

30. Caroline Beauvais, et al., *A Literature Review on Youth and Citizenship*, (Ottawa: Canadian Policy Research Networks, 2001), p. 10.

31. Naomi Klein, *No Logo: Taking Aim at the Brand Bullies* (Toronto: Vintage, 2000), p. 266.

32. Sheila Fraser, cited in "Hire More Full-Time Federal Workers: Auditor General," *CBC.ca* (5 December 2001).

33. Anton L. Allahar and James E. Coté, *Richer & Poorer* (Toronto: Lorimer, 1998), p. 128.

34. Beauvais, et al., *A Literature Review*.

35. Cited in Jane Taber, "The Threat of Zero Tolerance," *National Post* (27 November 2001). See also Stephen Cole, "Saying No to Zero Tolerance" *Globe and Mail* (30 August 2003), p. F6.

36. Anthony N. Doob, et al., *Youth Crime and the Youth Justice System in Canada: A Research Perspective* (Toronto: University of Toronto Centre of Criminology, 1995), pp. 37–8.

37. Ibid.

38. Bernard Schissel, *Blaming Children: Youth Crime, Moral Panics and the Politics of Hate* (Halifax: Fernwood, 1997), p. 9.

39. See Robert Wright, "I'd Sell You Suicide: Pop Music and Moral Panic in the Age of Marilyn Manson," *Popular Music* 19:3 (Autumn, 2000).

40. Julian Fantino, cited in Donna Laframboise, "The Sky Isn't Falling," *National Post* (16 May 2000).

41. Louise Elliott, "Ontario Rekindles Debate over Repeating Grades," *Canadian Press* (29 April 2001).

42. Jonathan Freedland, "The Rise of the Non-Voter," *The Guardian* (12 December 2001); and Ted Halstead, "A Politics for Generation X," *Atlantic Monthly* (August 1999).

43. Freedland, "The Rise of the Non-Voter."

44. Halstead, "A Politics for Generation X."

45. Leah McLaren, "Leah McLaren Looks Both Left and Right," *Globe and Mail* (13 September 1999).

46. Brenda O'Neill, "Generational Patterns in the Political Opinions and Behaviour of Canadians," *Policy Matters* 2:5 (October 2001).

47. See Mark MacKinnon, "Young Voters Feel Disaffected," *Globe and Mail* (6 November 2000); and Lynda Hurst, "Are Young Voters Down for the Count?" *Toronto Star* (15 September 2003).

48. Reginald W. Bibby and Donald C. Posterski, *Teen Trends: A Nation in Motion* (Toronto: Stoddart, 1992), pp. 68–9, 185.

49. Reginald W. Bibby, *Canada's Teens: Today, Yesterday and Tomorrow* (Toronto: Stoddart, 2001), pp. 104, 111–12.

50. Allan R, Gregg, "Brave New Époque," *Maclean's* 11:114 (6 April 1998), p. 56.

51. Conrad Black, "I Dreamt of Canada," *National Post* (16 November 2001).

52. Michael Bliss, "Is Canada a Country in Decline?" *National Post* (30 November 2001); and "True Patriot Love," *National Post* (17 December 2001).

53. *Achieving Excellence: Investing in People, Knowledge and Opportunity* (Ottawa: Industry Canada, 2002), p. 14.

54. Ezra Levant, *Youthquake* (Vancouver: The Fraser Institute, 1996).

55. Brooke Jeffrey, *Hard Right Turn* (Toronto: HarperCollins, 1999), pp. 205–7.

56. Bibby, *Canada's Teens*, p. 44.

57. Jeffrey M. Ayres, "National No More: Defining English Canada" *American Review of Canadian Studies* 25:2–3 (Summer-Fall 1995), pp. 181–201.

58. See, for example, Christine Dallaire and Claude Denis, "'If You Don't Speak French, You're Out': Don Cherry, the Alberta Francophone Games, and the Discursive Construction of Canada's Francophones," *Canadian Journal of Sociology* 25:4 (Fall 2000).

59. Tim Harper, "Alliance under Day Losing New Young Backers: Poll," *Toronto Star* (4 June 2001).

60. Wright, *Hip and Trivial*, ch. 2.

61. Richard Gwyn, "Ottawa Fails to Lead Border Debate," *Toronto Star* (28 November 2001).

62. Goldie, "Blame Canada."

63. Nicole Nolan, "Isn't It Ironic?… The Slickest New Nationalism Is in the Latest Wave of Beer Ads," *This Magazine* 30:3 (November-December 1996), pp. 22–5.

64. Gary Teeple, *Globalization and the Decline of Social Reform* (Toronto: Polestar, 1995), p. 21.

65. Eric Hobsbawm, *Age of Extremes* (London: Abacus, 1994), pp. 299–300.

66. Ian Kershaw, *Hitler*, volume I (London: Penguin, 1998), pp. 407–8.

CHAPTER SEVEN

ZERO TOLERANCE

CANADIAN YOUTH IN THE CHRÉTIEN ERA

"[W]e put more young people in jail than
any other industrialized country."
ANNE MCLELLAN, MINISTER OF JUSTICE (2000)

"Raves [are] a threat to the very fabric of Canadian life."
JULIAN FANTINO, TORONTO POLICE CHIEF (2000)

"[J]ob opportunities for young people are more plentiful than
they have been in a very long time. Indeed, it is a time of
boundless opportunity in Canada."
PRIME MINISTER JEAN CHRÉTIEN (2000)

For young Canadians "zero tolerance" has been the defining slogan of the Chrétien era. Once the most privileged social groups in postwar Canada, children and youth have in the last decade been abandoned to the margins of a public culture that cynically flatters the middle-aged and patronizes the elderly. Stigmatized and silenced by poverty, debt and dependency, young people emerged in the 1990s as the scapegoats for Canada's painful transition to the discipline of neo-liberal economics and law-and-order politics. Liberal apologists in Ottawa have understood this, but claim that the government has had to make some "tough choices." The recession they inherited from Brian Mulroney had to be fought, then the deficit had to be exorcised. Just when it appeared that the federal surplus would allow "comprehensive

new spending programs for children, youth and families,"[1] the terrorist attacks of September 11th forced massive security spending to the
top of the Canadian agenda, diverting resources once again from the
young. Now, at the eleventh hour and with an eye firmly fixed on his
own legacy, Prime Minster Jean Chrétien has pledged to rescue young
Canadians from the myriad crises his government did so much to foster
and so little to alleviate. In so doing, he has sought to salvage his own
record at the expense of his successor, leaving young people and their
advocates wondering whether the next Liberal regime will make good
on his promises.

In two important respects, it has been easy for the Chrétien Liberals
to neglect young Canadians. On the one hand, the demonization of
young people emerged in the 1990s as one of the central elements in
North American political culture, where it remains. Self-styled neo-con-
servatives have put "getting tough on youth" at the heart of their assault
on North American liberalism since the 1980s, relentlessly pitching their
"common sense" palliatives to an increasingly fearful public and forcing liberals onto the same ideological terrain. In the United States, for
example, as sociologist Mike Males has noted, the Clinton Democrats
actually escalated "the anti-youth bias of the Reagan and Bush years":

> Increasingly, Clinton's health and welfare policy has consisted of
> blaming teenagers for nearly all major social ills: poverty, welfare
> dependence, crime, gun violence, suicide, sexual promiscuity,
> unwed motherhood, AIDS, school failure, broken families, child
> abuse, drug abuse, drunken driving, smoking, and the breakdown
> of "family values".... [2]

Canadian politicians like Preston Manning, Stockwell Day, Ralph Klein
and Mike Harris—along with their allies in law enforcement and the
media—have adopted the same anti-youth agenda to spectacular effect.
Boot camps, workfare, the crackdown on squeegee kids, toughening up
the Young Offenders Act, banning raves, policing schoolyards, reform-
ing education to "get tough on failing kids"—these have been hallmarks

of zero-tolerance politics in Canada. In a healthy political culture, scape-goating powerless children and youth might be expected to generate a credible opposition (as it has, for example, in Europe). But in Canada, where the left has been all but vanquished from federal politics, the once "centre-left" Liberals have, like the Clinton Democrats, found it expedient to adopt the law-and-order agenda of their right-wing critics. When Anne McLellan acknowledged in May 2000 that "Canada imprisons young people more often than the United States"—a statement that in an earlier era might have embarrassed a Liberal Justice Minister—she was in fact attempting to refute the claim that her government was "soft on crime."[3]

On the other hand, the Chrétien era has been one in which policy reforms stressing the social context of Canadians' lives have been displaced by those which centre almost exclusively on the individual. This is as much a cultural shift as a political one and here, too, the impact on youth has been dramatic, if more subtle. Social solidarity, never very strong in Canada, has evaporated in the rush to embrace the free market and a consumerist model of public policy. What were once understood as public goods are now private commodities. Post-secondary education, for example, which was once thought to benefit Canadian society at large and was therefore almost entirely subsidized by the state, has been reconceptualized as something from which students gain a competitive advantage in the labour market and for which therefore they ought to pay the lion's share. Canadian taxpayers have learned to expect less from governments, governments have learned to do with less from taxpayers, and both have made their peace with the ever-widening gulf between the rich and the poor. Thus, it is not merely the case that the most tenacious social problems faced by young Canadians—poverty and unemployment—have ceased to inspire the sort of hand-wringing they did a generation ago but, far more tellingly, that the language of equality and social justice that once framed our public conversations about such problems has itself been supplanted by the headline-grabbing language of private morality and individual culpability. The youth-related issues that have preoccupied Canadians in recent years are those which can be framed almost entirely within the rubric of "individual responsibility": violent crime, street gangs, drinking and driving, childhood obesity, illiteracy, cigarette smoking, Ecstasy use, bullying and "extortion," teen suicide, dropping out of school, etc. The Chrétien Liberals are not solely responsible for this cultural shift, of course, but they have benefited enormously from it, offering predictable platitudes about the small minority of "at risk" kids while quietly allowing poverty and unemployment to ravage the lives of millions.

THE DEMOGRAPHIC CRUNCH

Understanding the tenuous place of children and youth in contemporary Canada begins with something that Jean Chrétien and his government have long known but have been reluctant to express publicly: the country has an unprecedented demographic crisis on its hands.

The problem is not merely that the Canadian population is ageing or that the national fertility rate is in a nosedive but that, as a Statistics Canada study put it in 1999, children are now widely regarded as a "luxury many average income-earners feel they cannot afford."[4] For the most part the Liberals have emphasized immigration as the crucial element in the maintenance of population stability and economic growth in Canada. This has not been an unambiguously successful approach. The 1993 Red Book promised to increase immigration to 1 per cent of the population annually (roughly 300,000 immigrants and refugees) but the government has never come close to delivering that number, clear evidence of the continuing strength of anti-immigration sentiment in Canada. Liberal ministers have been more aggressive in pitching higher immigration quotas of late, partly because of renewed strength in the Canadian economy but also because fertility data from the 2001 census have prompted an outpouring of anxiety nationwide. Immigration remains the "key to Canada's demographic, economic and social future," Immigration Minister Denis Coderre reassured Canadians in 2002.[5] He is probably correct. There appears to be very little governments can do to directly influence Canadians' family-planning decisions, something

Quebec's ill-fated and expensive "baby bonus" policies demonstrated in the late 1980s and the 1990s.[6]

The numbers tell the story. The national birth rate began its steep descent in the mid-1960s, which has meant significantly fewer children and youth as a proportion of the overall population since roughly 1980. In 2000 the number of babies born to Canadian women fell to its lowest level since 1946, marking the tenth straight annual decline in the birth rate. The Canadian fertility rate (which measures the average number of babies born to women of childbearing age) today stands at 1.49, well below the 2.1 necessary to sustain a population. The fertility rate in the United States, by contrast, stands at precisely 2.1, prompting some Canadian observers to worry about a "fertility gap."[7] Only 40 per cent of the discrepancy between the Canadian and American rates can be explained with reference to larger black and Hispanic families in the US; the remainder is a function of Canadian women's postponement of childbearing. Significantly, statisticians point to unemployment as one of the key factors behind the lagging Canadian rate. In 1980, the jobless rates for Canadians and Americans in their early twenties were roughly equal; but by the late 1990s the Canadian rate was roughly one-half to two-thirds higher. If fertility rates and unemployment rates are indeed closely correlated, the best demographic policy for Canada might well be a full-employment policy for youth, something the Chrétien Liberals have abandoned along with the other tenets of the postwar liberal consensus.

Statistics Canada researchers Alain Bélanger and Geneviève Ouellet have studied the earning power of young and old Canadians dating from the census of 1921. They report, predictably, that "the number of children per woman has varied with the incomes of young Canadian couples for the last eighty years." What their research also shows, however, is a more direct correlation since the 1970s between the national fertility rate and Canadians' earnings in the first five years of paid employment. In 1971, young men earned on average one-third of the household income of a middle-aged couple (aged 45 to 54) with one or more children. By the mid-1990s, young men were earning only 16 per cent of their older counterparts' income. Young women with full-time jobs suffered a relative drop in earnings as well. Bélanger and Ouellet have calculated that if the Canadian fertility rate continues its present trajectory, it will reach 1.3 children per woman by 2010. They have made another provocative calculation as well. If for the next fifteen years the annual earnings of young Canadian adults were to increase by only 3 per cent of their parents' incomes, Canada would again have a self-sustaining population.[8]

It is a sure sign of the times that young people are themselves being blamed for Canada's plummeting fertility rate. Jim Frideres, sociologist and Associate Vice-president Academic at the University of Calgary, told the *National Post* in 1999 that "selfish values" lay behind young Canadians' cautious family-planning strategies. "This is the Me Generation," he claimed. "It's, 'I want it now, don't give me this delayed gratification stuff.' They have a 'what's in it for me?' mindset." Here we get a glimpse at the cruel sleight of hand that turns Canadian youth into the agents of national decline. Older Canadians have enjoyed "incredible economic prosperity," Frideres mused, while youth today have modeled their own "self-centered behaviour" on the "casual prosperity that children enjoyed in the 1960s and 70s."[9] The problem is not that young people are singularly poor in a society of great wealth, but simply that they have unrealistic expectations. Charles Dickens would have recognized this logic.

not fair — we cannot do what are parents could.

GENERATION GAPS

That children and youth represent a declining proportion of the Canadian population (and will continue to do so for the foreseeable future) helps to explain how it has been so easy for all levels of government to ignore their interests in favour of those of older voters. There is much truth in the familiar cliché that baby boomers, by virtue of their numbers alone, dominate the Canadian political and economic landscape at the expense of younger cohorts, as I shall show below. Less well known perhaps is the steady economic progress the elderly have made in Canada in the last thirty years, thanks largely to federal programs like

Q — when all baby boomer cohort is gone — what will happen?

the Canada Pension Plan, Old Age Security, Spouses' Allowance and especially the Guaranteed Income Supplement. As economist Krishna Pendakur has shown, the "consumption poverty" rate for elderly Canadians dropped from 31 per cent in 1969 to 2.8 per cent in 1997, a direct result of "the retrenchment of income support programs for the non-elderly over the 1990s and the increasing share of public pensions among social expenditures."[10] Canada's success in significantly increasing the standards of living of the elderly puts the lie on the claim that the state is no longer capable of (or interested in) seriously combating systemic poverty. It attests as well to the thesis, now widely accepted among Canadian sociologists, that in the Chrétien era older Canadians have shamelessly enriched themselves at the expense of the young.[11]

This syndrome appears to be growing even more blatant. In 2003 the Tory government in Ontario announced that it was eliminating the education portion of residential property taxes for homeowners over 65, cynically affirming the general rule that in Canadian politics old people matter and young ones do not. "Ontario owes much to its seniors," said Tory Finance Minster Janet Ecker during her made-for-TV budget speech. "They are our grandparents and parents, our aunts and uncles." They are also among the wealthiest Canadians. The property-tax credit, worth an average of $475 to each of Ontario's 945,000 seniors' households, is not geared to income; thus it will leave an estimated $22,500 in the pocket of media mogul Ken Thompson and another $17,000 in that of folksinger Gordon Lightfoot. Again, the Chrétien Liberals are not responsible for this policy; but they have clearly benefited from a political culture in which the redistribution of wealth from poor young Canadians to comparatively affluent adults is thought—in the words of the *National Post*—"prudent."[12] Regardless of whether or not the Ontario Tories actually end up reducing the provincial education budget as a result of this tax break, it is clear that some extremely important principles—some would say "defining" principles for Canadians—have been compromised. Is it really the case that Canada's seniors have ceased to enjoy the myriad advantages of living in a well-educated society, or that as parents and grandparents their financial obligations to that society are no longer relevant? And if in Canada's biggest province it is acceptable for the childless not to pay for public education, is it reasonable to continue to ask the healthy to underwrite public healthcare?

As I suggested in Chapter Four, there are significant differences of wealth and status within cohorts, something worth bearing in mind when generalizing about this or that "generation." To perhaps state the obvious, the famed riches of the baby boomers are by no means evenly distributed, and there remain pockets of serious social and economic dislocation among middle-aged Canadians.[13] At an aggregate level, however, it is clear that Canadian boomers—especially the "early boomers," born between 1943 and 1957—have enjoyed levels of wealth attainment that both their children and their parents can only dream of.[14] Their social and economic success has had a great deal to do with good luck and even better timing; but, as a comparison with the youth of today shows rather bluntly, baby boomers have also been singularly well-served by the largesse of the Canadian state. Vastly expanded and improved public education, inexpensive post-secondary education, expanding government bureaucracies requiring huge numbers of new workers, a heavily subsidized cultural and public broadcasting sector, generous minimum wages and benefits for the unemployed—these unprecedented advantages were the "public" birthright of the baby boom in Canada. Not so for those who have followed. More than any other factor, it has been the retreat of the state from the lives of young Canadians since the 1970s that has driven children, youth and young adults to the margins of society. In some respects, the Chrétien Liberals have merely accepted the neo-liberal economic logic of their Tory predecessors and NAFTA trading partners, adopting *laissez-faire* principles that have been ruinous for young people almost everywhere in the industrialized West. In others, however, it is clear that they have taken political advantage of the "intergenerational warfare"[15] that is one of the defining myths of our times, dismantling the postwar welfare state at the very moment when affluent middle-aged voters believe they need it the least. The baby boomers are safely ensconced in the lifeboat, in short, and Jean Chrétien is helping them to pull up the ladder.

As noted in the last chapter, Canadian teenagers and young adults have since the 1980s faced a largely unacknowledged employment crisis. The official statistics are grim. In 1992, the worst year of the recession, 184,000 Canadians between 15 and 19 (19.7 percent of all labour force participants in this age range) were unemployed, compared with 16.6 per cent of those aged 20 to 24 and 9.9 per cent among those aged 25 and over. For most of the 1990s, youth unemployment hovered in the 16 per cent range, roughly 20 per cent worse than the average for all OECD countries. Between 1998 and 2001, with the Canadian economy boom-ing, the youth unemployment rate fell from 15.8 per cent to 12.8 per cent (the lowest it had been since August 1990). By late 2001, however, it was again on the rise, reaching 13.6 per cent in December 2002. As bad as the statistics are, some studies suggest that the official data significantly understate the depth of the crisis. Allahar and Côté, for example, esti-mate that the real unemployment rate among youth is 50 per cent higher than the official rate, if "discouraged workers" are taken into account.[16] Career Edge, a job-placement agency for Canadian university graduates, estimated in December 2002 that as many as 600,000 young Canadians were unemployed or underemployed.[17]

The long-term, systemic degradation of the value of the labour of young Canadians has been even more grave; indeed Statistics Canada data reveal a dramatic "polarizing trend" in the Canadian economy over what amounts to an entire generation. For Canadian men aged 18 to 24 real earnings dropped 36 per cent between 1979 and the 1990s; among 25 to 34-year-olds, real earnings fell 14 per cent in the same period. The real annual earnings of young women in Canada fell 29 per cent in this period.[18] To put this in perspective, the earnings of Canadian men aged 18 to 24 who were working full-time in the 1990s were the same as they had been for young men in the late 1960s; middle-aged workers were by the Nineties earning one-third more than their Sixties counterparts. What is worse, the decline of young workers' earnings relative to those of older workers has occurred in all strata of the workforce, regardless of industry, occupation, educational level, or union status.[19] Even the *Globe and Mail*, a leading voice in the neo-liberal crusade to allow markets to set wages, recently acknowledged "a striking generational split in the country's paycheques," with "increasingly wealthy, highly skilled baby boomers" seeing great gains and "[t]he youngest workers… either making less or at best the same as their peers of 20 years ago."[20]

THE RETREAT OF THE STATE

The Canadian state is directly implicated in young Canadians' chronic downward mobility. Consider, for example, the resolve with which it has allowed inflation to degrade youth wages over several decades. Workers earning minimum wage in the 1970s were 40 per cent over the official poverty line in Canada; in the 1990s minimum wage put workers 30 per cent below that line.[21] Most of the paid work done by the young is in the low-paying retail and service sectors; two-thirds of minimum wage earners in Canada are under the age of 24. Although the setting of minimum wages is a provincial responsibility, the federal government is directly culpable in the matter. In a concerted effort to allow markets to set wages, the OECD has explicitly urged member countries to replace "statutory minimum wages" with "more direct instruments" for achieving income redistribution. In Canada, such "direct instruments"—a guaranteed annual income or a negative income tax—would fall under federal jurisdiction and would allow, it follows, for a national policy aimed at equalizing or even subsidizing provincial minimum-wage levels for youth. (Not only do provincial minimum-wage levels vary, but in Ontario and Alberta there are discriminatory sub-minimum wages for Canadians under 18.) Under the Chrétien Liberals there has been no such initiative. In the last decade, in fact, Ottawa has allied itself with its provincial counterparts in dramatically "restructuring" welfare and unemployment benefits so as to provide "incentives" for workers to take minimum-wage jobs and to move from high-unemployment regions of the country to those with more job vacancies. The only "direct instrument" the federal Liberals have introduced to assist young Canadians is the National Child Tax Benefit (NCTB), a combination of tax breaks and income supplements for poor families with children; but, as the

National Council on Welfare has noted, the provinces have been free to "claw back" benefits via their "punitive and cruel" social-assistance policies, leaving the poorest Canadian families in "abject poverty."[22]

With respect specifically to employment insurance, the Liberal government has been openly discriminatory towards working youth. In 1996, sweeping reforms to UI/EI specifically targeted young people thought to be at risk of becoming "dependent" on the state. Hours of weekly work necessary to qualify workers for EI benefits jumped from 15 to 35, while the total number of hours required for "new entrants" jumped from 300 to 910.[23] The result: an immediate and precipitous drop in the proportion of young Canadians covered by employment insurance, from 55 to 15 per cent. Obsessed with fighting the deficit and balancing the federal budget, Ottawa also exacerbated the youth employment crisis in the mid-1990s by cutting overall job-creation funding in half, from $1.2 billion in 1993–94 to $532 million in 1996–97.[24] Similarly, by significantly reducing transfers to the provinces in the same period—combined CAP and EPF transfers dropped from roughly $19 billion in 1993–94 to $12.5 billion 1998–99—it indirectly undermined social programs in which youth had a disproportionately high stake. Downsizing the federal bureaucracy has hurt young Canadians as well, especially those with university degrees, since the state has itself served as a crucial site of employment, job security and upward mobility for the middle class.

Although in the mid-1990s there was remarkably little media interest in the desperate economic situation of young Canadians, the Liberals unexpectedly found themselves facing attacks in the House of Commons on the issue (mainly from the Bloc Québécois), the assiduous lobbying of social-welfare advocates, and reports from its own pollsters showing that "91% of Canadian *adults* said they worry about the difficulties faced by youth entering the labour market" (emphasis added).[25] Even Canadian business weighed in, launching the Corporate Council on Youth in the Economy to warn Canadians that the youth unemployment "crisis will have enormous long-term impact on our country's future prosperity and productivity."[26] In 1996, the third year of Paul Martin's "hell or high water" campaign of fiscal austerity (and the very year in which he made EI inaccessible to most young people), the Liberals availed themselves of a time-honoured Canadian method of containing political heat and appointed a Task Force to develop a "youth strategy." Out of this process, which if nothing else gave the appearance of broad and earnest public consultation, came the 1997 Youth Employment Strategy (YES).

A complicated and sprawling initiative with many bureaucratic tentacles, the mandate of the YES was essentially twofold: to increase young people's access to job-related information (via such Net-based initiatives as Youth Resource Network of Canada and the National Graduate Register), and to increase their prospects for entry-level work experience via "partnerships" with the public, private and not-for-profit sectors. Student Summer Job Action, for example, which was itself composed of fourteen initiatives within four distinct programs, was designed to stimulate the hiring of summer students; Youth Internship Canada (YIC) sought to enhance the entry-level job prospects of youth still in high school; and Youth Service Canada (YSC) endeavoured to connect young people with various community service projects. "Internship" programs, of which there were three, were designed to direct unemployed (or underemployed) young workers into the careers for which they had received post-secondary training. The annual budget for the first three years of the Youth Employment Strategy was a relatively paltry $105 million. Taking credit for the improvement in the youth employment rate in 1998, HRDC Minister Pierre Pettigrew announced in December of that year that the YES would become a permanent program with an annual budget of $155 million. In April 2003 a "new" Youth Employment Strategy was announced, presumably to streamline the original into three critical areas: Skills Link, Career Focus and Summer Work Experience.

Sounding more like a McDonald's ad than an official communiqué, a government web site boasted in 2003 that its Youth Employment Strategy, along with "other targeted programs," had "helped over 3 million young Canadians."[27] For her part HRDC Minister Jane Stewart has issued a steady stream of press releases celebrating local YES-based initiatives—some of them involving as few as a dozen young people—in a campaign clearly designed to maximize the public profile of the Strategy. Whether Liberal initiatives like the YES have borne fruit on anything even remotely approximating the scale implied by these public pronouncements is not easy to determine. The explicit target of the original program was "110,000 work experience opportunities," which translates into an average of roughly 37,000 youth placements annually. Amid the literally hundreds of published HRDC documents on the Youth Employment Strategy, however, I could find none that included hard data on whether these targets were met, or what proportion of these "experience opportunities" turned into real jobs.

What can be said of the YES with certainty is that it has cemented a "supply-side" policy approach centring on job-training, school-to-work transitions and especially "partnerships." In so doing, it has foreclosed on all other approaches, including those which might actually create jobs or increase wages, or rescue youth for more than a few months from the mercy of private employers and volatile labour markets. An HRDC review of the Youth Service Canada program in 2000 acknowledged this truth explicitly: "[P]articipation in YSC had no statistically significant effect on annualized earnings, weekly wage, hours worked per week, or annual social assistance benefits. In other words, the estimates of program effect on these measures could easily have resulted from random variation or chance, and cannot be reliably attributed to participation in YSC." The main economic impact of the YSC was, in fact, something that would warm the heart of any Liberal Minister of Finance: it had "reduced reliance on EI benefits."[28]

The truth is that entry-level "internships" and unpaid "voluntarism" serve to keep all youth wages low, since young people willing to accept these sorts of positions constitute a large, cheap labour pool. It is highly likely, therefore, that the Youth Employment Strategy is actually worsening the situation of young workers who are not participants in one of its programs. There is anecdotal evidence, moreover, that internship programs reflect rather than significantly alter the labour market conditions facing young workers. In 2002, for example, IBM Canada reported that it had received 20,000 applications for 500 internships and co-op positions, while at Wilfrid Laurier University the number of employers scouting for young talent dropped from 300 in 2001 to 200 in 2002. Career Edge, the career-counselling service noted above, now boasts a registry of 13,000 Canadian university graduates willing to work for the meagre salary of $18,000 annually "just to get some solid work experience."[29] Meanwhile, six years into the YES, youth unemployment in Canada continues to climb from its 2001 low, and as the economy slows in 2003 it is almost certain to worsen.

The alternative to the Liberals' supply-side Youth Employment Strategy would, of course, be a full-employment policy for youth—a laughable prospect in the current climate of privatization and partnerships. Richard Marquardt has calculated that if Canada adopted an aggressive full-employment strategy like that of Sweden in the 1980s—one which guaranteed every unemployed young person career-counselling, training opportunities and a job—it would cost roughly $20 billion per year, which is 30 times more than all levels of government in Canada currently spend on all youth job creation programs (excluding education).[30] Some Liberals, including Jean Chrétien, have been around long enough to remember that at one time the party actually did take youth job creation seriously—as in the Opportunities for Youth program in the 1970s, for example. No longer. Today the government takes a less-is-more approach: minimize your financial commitment to the young while maximizing your political advantage among anxious adult voters.

THE TUITION SQUEEZE

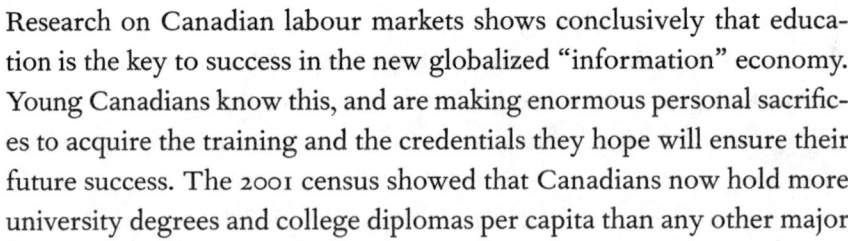

Research on Canadian labour markets shows conclusively that education is the key to success in the new globalized "information" economy. Young Canadians know this, and are making enormous personal sacrifices to acquire the training and the credentials they hope will ensure their future success. The 2001 census showed that Canadians now hold more university degrees and college diplomas per capita than any other major industrialized country, including the United States.[31] The national Youth in Transition survey has revealed, perhaps even more astoundingly, that the Canadian high school dropout rate fell to an all-time low of 12 per cent in 1999 and that 70 per cent of high school graduates today attend post-secondary institutions. In July 2003, an OECD-UNESCO study showed that Canadian teenagers were "among the best in the world on international tests of reading, math and science...."[32] Canadian students should congratulate themselves for these extraordinary achievements, for they have occurred largely at their own initiative and expense. In an era in which young Canadians are commonly thought to be lazy, irresponsible and incapable of grasping the concept of deferred gratification, their world-leading dedication to education is nothing short of breathtaking.

The achievements of post-secondary students in the Chrétien years are especially remarkable in the light of the obstructionist role played by the Canadian state. There is a rather delicious irony here. Jean Chrétien is said to believe that his Millennium Scholarship initiative will be his greatest political legacy, presumably because it casts the federal government in the role of sugar-daddy for college and university students; yet he is almost certain to be remembered as the Canadian prime minister who irrevocably transformed higher education from an inexpensive public good into an increasingly expensive private commodity, in the manner of a Margaret Thatcher. In truth, the federal Liberals' greatest contribution to Canada's impressive educational record in recent years has been to provide young people with such bleak economic prospects that they opt to stay in school.

Although higher education is a matter of provincial jurisdiction in Canada, Ottawa shares control of the purse-strings. Throughout the 1990s, deep cuts to provincial transfers for higher education were among the most public of the Liberals' fiscal austerity measures, prompting a wide-ranging national debate in Canada about whether or not markets should be "allowed" to set tuition fees.[33] Since the ensuing funding crisis in Canadian higher education has been the stuff of headlines for years, the numbers need only be briefly summarized. When the Liberals took office, post-secondary education claimed just under 20 per cent of combined CAP and EPF transfers from Ottawa to the provinces, for a total of almost $4 billion. Between 1993 and 1999, cuts to federal transfers reduced provincial education budgets by roughly $1.2 billion annually. These cuts were in turn passed on to colleges and universities. Between 1993 and 2002 tuition fees increased in Canada by an average of 135 per cent. Tuition fees now represent 50 per cent or more of the average income of one in ten Canadian families, while the average post-secondary student faces a $56 monthly gap between income and expenditures. Paul Martin's own figures show that whereas fewer than 8 per cent of graduates in 1990 had debt over $15,000, by 1998 the number exceeded 40 per cent. In 1990, the average individual student debt-load in Canada was $8,700. By 1996, it had reached $17,000. Paul Martin has estimated that it now stands at about $25,000.

Of the many crises the under-funding of colleges and universities triggered in the 1990s, one of the least studied has been its impact upon those Canadian students (and their families) for whom it came out of the blue. In the 1970s and even the 1980s, cheap tuition was a fact of life in Canada. Thus, with the long term in view, saving money for a "child's" post-secondary education was a relatively modest undertaking. (Though it seems inconceivable today, in the early 1980s university students — and faculty — campaigned for full government funding of post-secondary education in the belief that it was the logical endpoint for a system which boasted "unhindered access" as its *raison d'être*.) The best evidence of the relative manageability of the cost of higher education in Canada — apart from the negligible debts students carried after graduation — is that there was no government-subsidized Registered Educational Savings Plan (RESP) nor any great demand for one.

Remarkably, it appears not to have occurred to Paul Martin and his provincial counterparts that the massive tuition increases they were downloading onto Canadian students and their families after 1993 were the worse for having been unanticipated, and that they thus constituted a serious political liability. Even after his devastating 1995 budget, Martin was oblivious to the gathering storm. By 1998, however, perhaps because he had slayed so many of his fiscal dragons and could now take stock of the general devastation, he had become visibly worried that the student debt crisis his policies had done so much to exacerbate might have serious economic and political consequences. It became clear to the Liberals that something had to be done, and that it was going to require new spending. It also became clear that they now faced an historic fork in the road: they could return to the postwar liberal tradition and restore stable, behind-the-scenes federal funding for colleges and universities, or they could drive their new *laissez-faire* model of higher education to its logical conclusion and, with a great deal more fanfare, put federal money directly into the pockets of the new breed of student-consumers. There was never really much doubt about which way Jean Chrétien and Paul Martin were headed; they opted enthusiastically for the latter.

A flurry of new federal legislation, some of it dating from the 1997 budget, was tabled under the rubric of the Canadian Opportunities Strategy (COS). The overriding purpose of this Strategy, to quote Paul Martin, was to "provide Canadians—especially young Canadians—with greater opportunity to prosper in the new, knowledge-based economy of the 21st century." Five measures specifically addressed the tuition/ student debt crisis. The first was the RESP, which provided a federal grant of up to $400 per child per year to Canadian families who were able to set aside an annual minimum of $2000 per child. Apart from helping affluent Canadian families disproportionately—by 2000 only 15 per cent of Canadian children were registered for RESPs[34]—this measure appears to have been premised on the dubious notion that Canadians are better investors than either the state or professional money-managers. The second initiative took the form of a modest (17 per cent) tax credit on the interest portion of graduates' annual loan repayments. The third was a $100 million addition to the existing Canada Study Grants program, which for the first time made students with children or other dependents eligible for federal grants of between $40 and $60 per week. The fourth took the form of "reforms" to the Canada Student Loans Program, including "interest relief" for graduates with low incomes, an extended repayment period for "those who have exhausted 30 months of interest relief," and reduction of the loan principal if annual payments exceed 15 per cent of a graduate's income. Lest the government appear too soft on its new loan provisions, they were paired with a highly discriminatory change to the *Bankruptcy and Insolvency Act* which made anybody with loans under the Canada Student Loans program ineligible for a bankruptcy hearing for a period of 10 years. The "centre piece" of the Canadian Opportunities Strategy was the $2.5 billion Canada Millennium Scholarship program, first announced by Jean Chrétien in September 1997. Averaging $3,000 per year up to a maximum of $15,000 over four years, these federal scholarships would be available to prospective students who "need help in financing their studies and demonstrate merit."

That the Chrétien Liberals opted for what they believe are "supply-side" solutions to the problem of skyrocketing tuition fees indicates conclusively their new faith in an "entrepreneurial" model of higher education: colleges and universities which could once rely upon direct and stable state funding must now compete for students.[35] It is too early to gauge the long-term impact of the Canadian Opportunities Strategy on young people but several trends are already coming into view. The first is that, despite the government's considerable efforts to pitch the Strategy as a salve for the tuition/debt crisis, the great majority of indebted students still do not qualify for assistance. Claude Proulx, manager of policy for Canada Student Loans, reported in 2002, for example, that federal efforts to bring debt relief to university graduates had been a failure: the government had estimated that 12,000 Canadians would have debts up to $10,000 forgiven but, as it turned out, only 467 persons qualified.[36] Secondly, the Canadian Opportunities Strategy will do nothing to curb rising tuition fees; indeed, the Millennium Scholarship program may well end up providing provincial governments and post-secondary institutions with a pretext for deregulating tuition fees altogether. Thirdly, notwithstanding Jean Chrétien's and Paul Martin's considerable efforts to frame Millennium Scholarships as a panacea, the truth is that they will help only a small minority of students: approximately 100,000 full- and part-time students will receive federal scholarships each year, a fraction of the roughly 1.7 million students enrolled annually in colleges and universities throughout Canada. As the Millennium Foundation's own research shows, Canadian students will face a worsening tuition/debt squeeze for the foreseeable future.[37]

It is fair to say as well that the Canadian Opportunities Strategy has thus far failed in its primary political aim, which was to assuage the fears of worried voters who have children heading into their college and university years. In this important sense, Jean Chrétien and Paul Martin are reaping what they have sewed, paying a potentially high political price for their stoic silence through so many years of cuts to provincial transfers. Polls show that Canadian parents believe the costs of higher education are significantly higher than they actually are: parents with only a high school education believe that tuition is roughly $10,000 per year; those with a university education believe it is closer to $7000 per year.[38] In fact, undergraduate tuition in Canada in 2003 averaged just under $4000 per year. Even if the Liberals attempted to turn this misperception to their own advantage by persuading parents that higher education in Canada is a bargain, the evidence suggests that it would have little impact on the young Canadians who represent the bulk of college and university students. Data published in 2003 showed that, while 80 per cent of students receive some money from their parents for higher education, 60 per cent of parental contributions do not exceed $2000 per year.[39]

In the long run, however, it is possible that none of these political missteps will stick to Jean Chrétien. By the time he leaves office, the crisis atmosphere that characterized college and university life for most of his tenure will have passed. Higher education will have been irrevocably transformed. Colleges and universities now accept the *laissez-faire* logic of the new entrepreneurial model (some of them grudgingly) and are governing themselves accordingly; and now that government deficits have been replaced by surpluses, these institutions are even enjoying expansion and new state funding. No doubt the Canadian Federation of Students will continue to attempt to rally students and faculty to the slogan "Freeze Tuition!" But it is already clear that they are on the wrong side of history. The issue has none of the urgency it once did because Jean Chrétien and Paul Martin have weaned Canadians off the old-fashioned idea that inexpensive, accessible higher education benefits all citizens. In about a decade, the first of the RESP babies will enter post-secondary institutions. They will be the true beneficiaries of current Liberal policies. Indeed, for the affluent minority, whose families can pay for higher education out of private resources, the future looks as promising as ever. As for the vast majority of Canadian young people, who have access neither to private capital nor to decent wages, they will inherit the *status quo*. The lucky ones may pick up a Millennium Scholarship along the way, but this will not change the broader outlook. Impoverished, debt-ridden young scholars will be Jean Chrétien's legacy.

YOUNG AND POOR

If there is a single social-policy crisis that has stuck to Jean Chrétien, it might be "child poverty." In November 1989, with a great deal of fanfare, the House of Commons unanimously passed a resolution affirming that "members of parliament would seek to eliminate child poverty by the year 2000." Since then, the proportion of Canadian children who live in poverty has grown from roughly one in six to one in five. Yet the political fall-out of even this tragic story, retold practically daily in the nation's headlines, has been greatly attenuated to the Liberals' advantage. There are at least three reasons for this. The first is that child poverty is relatively invisible. The second is that it is derivative of adult (parental) poverty, which inspires little public sympathy. The third is that throughout the Chrétien era neo-liberal economists and editorialists have been tireless in promoting the idea that Canada's official poverty line is too high and, hence, that the incidence of "real" poverty has been exaggerated. Anti-poverty activists have worked assiduously to keep the child poverty crisis in public view, and there is evidence to suggest that their efforts have not been entirely in vain. A 1997 Angus Reid poll revealed that roughly 70 per cent of Canadians thought the federal government was doing too little to eradicate child poverty.[40] But critical though the situation of the poor has become, it has not inspired a broad public outcry in Canada nor any concerted program of reform by the state. Child poverty certainly has not hurt the Liberals at the polls. Asked in 1999 whether child poverty would be a priority for his government, Jean Chrétien replied casually: "We debated that…. There were statistics that were given to us that the level of poverty is much less in Canada as in the United States even though they are richer than us."[41]

Not so long ago, child poverty was a high priority for Canadians and for the Liberal party. Although Pierre Trudeau was never prepared to adopt a European-styled model of wealth redistribution, his "Just Society" policies did help to drive the Canadian child poverty rate from 11.7 per cent in 1969 to 3.5 per cent in 1978. In the 1980s, child poverty declined even further, bottoming out at 1.8 per cent in 1992.[42] In the 1990s, under the Chrétien Liberals, all of this progress was undone. Data from the 2001 census showed that roughly 20 per cent of children in Canada were poor, for a total of about 1.5 million kids. According to the Laidlaw Foundation, a youth-oriented public interest organization, the fastest-growing group of users of homeless shelters today is children.[43] In 2002, the Canadian Association of Food Banks' *Hunger Count* reported that almost 750,000 Canadians use food banks monthly, of whom more than 40 per cent are children.[44]

Child poverty is, of course, a function of family poverty. Given that the youngest Canadian adults, those of child-bearing age, have faced severe unemployment, underemployment and plummeting real wages in recent decades, it should come as no surprise that they and their children are growing poorer. In the spring of 2003, Statistics Canada published a detailed "family inequality" analysis based upon 2001 census data. It illustrated clearly what Canadians could see in the streets of their major cities, namely that the situation of the wealthy had improved greatly and the plight of the poor had worsened. As of 2001, the richest 10 per cent of Canadian families took home 28 per cent of total family income; the poorest 10 per cent took home 1.6 per cent. Over the 1990s the incomes of the wealthiest families grew by an average of 14.6 per cent; the poorest experienced no increase in income. Though it is unlikely to happen given the current mania for free markets and low taxes, even a modest income-redistribution policy would today produce dramatic results: if the top 10 per cent of Canadian families—whose incomes in 2001 averaged $261,000—gave up just 1 per cent of their earned wealth annually, the incomes of the poorest 10 per cent would rise by 25 per cent.[45]

Although punitive provincial social-assistance policies have been devastating for the poor, particularly in Ontario and Alberta, the federal government is also directly implicated in their plight. The Tories' abolition of universal family allowances ("baby bonuses") in 1992, for example, marked a symbolic turning-point for the once-cherished principle of "universality" in Canada, even though family allowance benefits had in fact been taxable since 1973. The Chrétien Liberals did nothing to restore universal family allowance benefits after their election victory in 1993, yet they suffered none of the public scorn that had been heaped on Mulroney—a political lesson that boded ill for poor Canadian families. The Tories replaced baby bonuses with a new Child Tax Benefit, which took the form of tax credits for low-income families. They also introduced the "Brighter Futures" initiative in 1992, which promised to provide $500 million over five years for at-risk children, or an average of $100 per child per year. The Chrétien Liberals inherited both.

Deep cuts to the federal CAP and EPF in the mid-1990s were accompanied by expanded provincial discretion in deciding how social transfers would be spent, virtually eliminating national standards for social assistance. This left the poorest Canadians—young parents and their children—at the mercy of the likes of Ralph Klein and Mike Harris, premiers who opportunistically offered up welfare recipients as the scapegoats *par excellence* in their campaign against bloated, wrong-headed government spending. Like the crises of youth unemployment and student debt, child poverty became a Liberal priority only when it started to look like a serious political liability. In the spring of 1997, HRDC Minister Pierre Pettigrew met with his provincial and territorial counterparts to hammer out a National Children's Agenda which would, in the minister's words, give "children in low income families a fighting chance for a better future." Out of this tortuous process came the National Child Benefit (NCB) Supplement to the National Child Tax

Benefit (NCTB), a measure designed to top up monthly payments for the poorest Canadian families. In 2001-02, the government provided $5.2 billion through the NCTB to 3.2 million families (5.8 million children), or approximately 82 percent of Canadian families with children; another $2.5 billion was provided through the NCB Supplement, delivering benefits to 1.5 million families (2.7 million children), or 40 per cent of all Canadian families with children.

Generous though they may seem, such federal benefits are not protected from "claw back" at the provincial level; thus, as noted above, what many poor families gain in federal benefits they lose in social-assistance benefits. Critics point out as well that if the Liberals believed their own rhetoric about giving children a fighting chance, they would ensure that the NCTB cover at least the minimum annual cost of raising a child in Canada, estimated at roughly $4,000.[46] (In 2004, the maximum benefit under the program will be $2,400 annually for the first child.) A 2003 study by Montreal economists Pierre Lefebvre and Philip Merrigan has gone even further, concluding the NCTB policy "is a dead end and should be replaced by a generous universal allowance for each child in the family." Such an allowance, they argue, should be accompanied by policies that "substantially reward the employment efforts of low-skilled parents while decreasing the costs of working...."[47] What Canadian children need from Jean Chrétien and his successor, in short, is what they got from Pierre Trudeau: a full-employment policy for young parents, including adequate wages and job training, and a family allowance policy that allows children not merely to survive but to thrive.

They are unlikely to get it. Canadians continue to live in an extraordinarily wealthy society in which children go hungry, food banks are a growth industry, and a seemingly endless parade of homeless young people sleep in shelters and beg in the streets. The children of impoverished young parents are also poor, presenting Canadians with a scenario they have not known since the Dirty Thirties: two generations of young people locked in a seemingly hopeless cycle of inadequate jobs and wages, daunting educational costs and debts, punitive welfare policies, pitiful public housing and childcare policies, and a Liberal regime willing to let the conditions of their lives deteriorate until they can no longer be contained politically.

CONCLUSION

As noted in Chapter Six, the Liberals' indifference to young Canadians has been reciprocal. Generally speaking, youth outside of Quebec do not identify with the state; they have little stake in the rights and responsibilities of citizenship; and they are notoriously indifferent to conventional political activity. Youth today are silent on the great national issues of our time, and they are demonized rather than celebrated in the popular imagination. If, as Jacques Hébert has suggested, the Trudeau years "remain a kind of golden age for the youth of Canada,"[48] the Chrétien years have marked a return to the dark ages.

Liberal policies have played a critical role in the socio-economic marginalization of young people in the last decade. Most obviously, the government's abandonment of the postwar commitment to low unemployment has meant that youth have been ravaged by the deep structural changes to the Canadian economy that have accompanied globalization. For working-class youth, chronic downward mobility has meant poverty; for the middle class it has meant dependence. Indeed, the very idea of "youth" has devolved in the last decade so as to include people in their twenties and even their thirties. A growing body of research confirms that young people's acquisition of full citizenship status has been retarded by the extension of the period in which their relationship to the state is mediated by their parents.[49] Establishing an autonomous household, for example, is obviously a critical element in full citizenship, yet in 1999 Statistics Canada reported that roughly half of Canadians between the ages of 20 and 34 still lived with their parents. This process constitutes a systematic downloading of financial responsibility for dependent adult children from the state to the family, and is the direct result of discriminatory policies ranging from unequal access to social-assistance and employment-insurance benefits to the artificial distinction between student debt and commercial debt.

Yet what of young Canadians themselves? In contrast with the public perception that youth are "wild" and "out of control," the dire economic circumstances of their lives has in fact fashioned Canadians under 35 into a more conservative group, taken as a whole, than their elders. Education, especially higher education, is a profoundly conservatizing force in the lives of young people, emphasizing discipline, delayed gratification and identification with the promise of upward mobility. With more young Canadians than ever in school, youth are more likely to identify with the socio-economic *status quo* in Canada than to challenge it. Debt alone—which many young university and college graduates must now bear as a kind of mortgage—is a sobering, conservatizing force, notwithstanding the sensational claims frequently made in the news media that defaulting is a common strategy for young Canadians. As sociologist Reginald Bibby concluded in 2001, young Canadians'

> personal resilience in not abandoning [the] relational and success components of the Canadian Dream is, in many instances, quite remarkable.... Despite in many instances having disadvantaged backgrounds, most believe they can transcend those backgrounds—along with national instability, if need be—en route to education, occupational, and financial success. That kind of resilience and determination is something else.[50]

Of course, the worst stereotypes persist. In July 2003, *Globe and Mail* writer Jan Wong devoted an entire column to the "vandalism and violence" of teen parties, casting young Canadians as rich, pampered, lazy and psychopathic: "Rising affluence has created the most indulged generation in history. If a rug is destroyed, well, insurance will cover it. If police press charges, a lawyer will bail you out. Old-fashioned morality has been eclipsed by a sense of entitlement."[51] Here, in a nutshell, is the sort of public misinformation against which young people and their advocates continue to struggle daily—and a clear indication of why public officials in the Chrétien era have felt no great urgency in addressing the critical problems of children and youth. As the kids themselves would say, "Yeah, whatever...."

NOTES

1. *Speech from the Throne* (1999).

2. Mike A. Males, *The Scapegoat Generation: America's War on Adolescents* (Maine: Common Courage Press, 1996), pp. 6–7.

3. Anne McLellan, cited in Luiza Chwialkowska, "Canada Tougher on Youth Crime Than U.S.," *National Post* (8 May 2000).

4. Cited in Elena Cherney, "Families Can't Afford 'Luxury' of Kids," *National Post* (23 December 1999).

5. Denis Coderre, cited in Campbell Clark, "Immigration Targets Virtually Unchanged for 2003," *Globe and Mail* (31 October 2002), p. A4.

6. See Graeme Hamilton, "Quebec's Baby Incentives Cost a Bundle," *National Post* (25 January 2002).

7. Bruce Little, "Ethnicity, Marriage Trends Causing Fertility Disparity with U.S.," *Globe and Mail* (30 September 2002), p. B3.

8. Alain Bélanger and Geneviève Ouellet, cited in ibid.

9. Jim Frideres, cited in Cherney, "Families Can't Afford 'Luxury' of Kids."

10. Krishna Pendakur, "Consumption Poverty in Canada 1969 to 1998," *Canadian Public Policy* (June 2001).

11. See Anton L. Allahar and James E. Côté, *Richer & Poorer: The Structure of Inequality in Canada* (Toronto: Lorimer, 1998); Maureen Baker, *Canadian Family Policies: Cross-National Comparisons* (Toronto: University of Toronto Press, 1995); and Richard Marquardt, *Enter at Your Own Risk: Canadian Youth and the Labour Market* (Toronto: Between the Lines, 1998).

12. Robert Benzie, "A Scripted Appeal to Older Voters," *National Post* (28 March 2003). See also Caroline Mallan, "Mcguinty, Eves Chase 'Gray' Vote," *Toronto Star* (16 September 2003).

13. See Jordan Heath-Rawlings, "Third of Boomers Worry about Retirement Assets," *Globe and Mail* (3 September 2003), p. A8.

14. See Steve Kerstetter, *Rags and Riches: Wealth Inequality in Canada* (Toronto: Canadian Centre for Policy Alternatives, December 2002); and Jeff Sanford, "Blame the Boomers," *Financial Post* (6 September 2003).

15. See Doug Owram, *Born at the Right Time: A History of the Baby Boom Generation* (Toronto: University of Toronto Press, 1996).

16. Allahar and Côté, *Richer & Poorer*, p. 126.

17. See Katherine Harding and Virginia Galt, "Job Market Prospects Chill Young Adults," *Globe and Mail* (14 December 2002), p. B1.

18. Garnett Picot, *What Is Happening to Earnings Inequalities and Youth Wages in the 1990s?* (Ottawa: Statistics Canada, July 1998).

19. Myles Corack, cited in Elaine Carey, "Poor Economy Hit Young Hard, Analysis Says," *Toronto Star* (22 January 1999).

20. Erin Anderssen, "Paycheques Show Generational Split," *Globe and Mail* (12 March 2003), p. A6.

21. Marquardt, *Enter at Your Own Risk*.

22. National Council on Welfare, "Serious Concerns about the Levels of Poverty in Canada," (29 June 2003).

23. Stephen McBride, *Paradigm Shift: Globalization and the Canadian State* (Halifax: Fernwood, 2001).

24. Martha Justus and Mike McCracken, "Securing the Future of Canadian Youth: A Review of the Landscape," *Monthly Economic Review* 16:6 (27 November 1997).

25. Maurizio Bevilacqua (Chair, Task Force on Youth), "Youth and Employment—the Issues," (1996).

26. Anne Cira, cited in Dana Flavelle, "Firms Ignore Jobless Youth," *Toronto Star* (25 June 1999).

27. "About Canada's Youth Employment Strategy" (2003).

28. Human Resources Development Canada, "Summative Evaluation of Youth Service Canada" (18 October 2000).

29. Cited in Harding and Galt, "Job Market Prospects Chill Young Adults."

30. Marquardt, *Enter at Your Own Risk*.

31. Caroline Alphonso, "Canadians Are Now World's Best Educated," *Globe and Mail* (12 March 2003), p. A6.

32. Heather Sokoloff, "Canadian Students among Top in UN Test," *National Post* (2 July 2003).

33. See, for example, "99.5% Should Be So Lucky," *National Post* (7 February 2002).

34. *National Report—Canada: Ten-Year Review of the World Summit for Children* (Ottawa: Government of Canada, 2002).

35. See Marquardt, *Enter at Your Own Risk*.

36. Sue Bailey, "Program To Ease Student Debt Falls Short: Official," *Canadian Press* (27 February 2002).

37. See EKOS Research Associates, *Making Ends Meet: The 2001–2002 Student Financial Survey* (March 2003).

38. Heather Sokoloff and Siri Agrell, "Student Loans Fall Short of Needs: Study," *National Post* (11 March 2003). See also Rob Carrick, "Four Years of University Education Will Cost You $92,292," *Globe and Mail* (30 August 2003).

39. Sokoloff and Agrell, "Student Loans Fall Short of Needs: Study."

40. Cited in Mel Hurtig, *Pay the Rent or Feed the Kids: The Tragedy and Disgrace of Poverty in Canada* (Toronto: McClelland and Stewart, 1999), p. 58.

41. Cited in ibid., p. 68.

42. Pendakur, "Consumption Poverty in Canada 1969 to 1998."

43. Christa Freiler and Paul Zarnke, "Putting the Poor Back on the Political Agenda," *Toronto Star* (26 August 2002).

44. Cited in Allan Thompson, "Food Bank Users Double in Decade," *Toronto Star* (17 October 2002).

45. "Policies Encourage Growing Inequity," *Toronto Star* (17 May 2003).

46. Greg deGroot-Maggetti, "Putting the National Children's Agenda on Hold? Citizens for Public Justice Responds to the Federal Budget." Retrieved 2 March 2000 from the Citizens for Public Justice website: http://www.cpj.ca/budget/00/NCAhold.html.

47. Pierre Lefebvre and Philip Merrigan, "Assessing Family Policy in Canada: A New Deal for Families and Children," *Choices* 9:5 (June 2003), p. 8.

48. Jacques Hébert, "Legislating for Freedom," Thomas S. Axworthy and Pierre Elliott Trudeau, eds., *Towards a Just Society* (Toronto: Penguin, 1990), pp. 184–5.

49. See Caroline Beauvais, et al., *A Literature Review on Youth and Citizenship* (Ottawa: Canadian Policy Research Networks, 2001).

50. Reginald W. Bibby, *Canada's Teens: Today, Yesterday and Tomorrow* (Toronto: Stoddart, 2001), p. 156.

51. Jan Wong, "Party Animals," *Globe and Mail* (12 July 2003), p. F1. See also Roy MacGregor, "The Extended Teen Generation: Why It's Sticking So Close to the Many Comforts of Home," *Globe and Mail* (8 September 2003), p. A2.

CHAPTER EIGHT

TIME TO GROW UP

"ANTI-AMERICANISM" IN CANADA
AFTER SEPTEMBER 11TH

With only two years' hindsight, the myriad implications of the September 11th 2001 terrorist attacks on the United States have only just begun to come into view. From the moment the hijacked planes hit the World Trade Centre, Canadians have been scrambling to come to grips with the crisis—for themselves, for their American friends, allies and trading partners, and for the world. Whether Canadian-American relations were irrevocably changed that day remains an open (and increasingly contested) question. On the one hand, there is compelling evidence that the post-9/11 convergence of North American security, immigration and border policies has cemented NAFTA-era continentalism. On the other hand, there is evidence of a new independence in Canadian foreign policy, evinced most strikingly in Canada's unprecedented refusal to fight alongside its historic Anglo-American allies in Iraq. Certainly, Prime Minister Jean Chrétien appears to have found his "nationalist voice" again at the twilight of his political career, suggesting that Canadians may be entering a new era of nationalist formation.[1]

To an extent that is striking in retrospect, the days, weeks and months that followed the attacks of September 11th were anything but propitious for Canadian nationalism. The suggestion was made in more than one quarter that historic "anti-Americanism" in Canada bore a worrisome resemblance to the anti-Western grievances that appeared to have inspired the attacks, and that Canadians would do well to purge such sentiments from their ideological lexicon. Some prominent

Canadian nationalists recanted, saying that they had awakened from the naive dream of an independent Canada to find themselves inhabiting a new world of "virtual sovereignty." Others acknowledged that in the post-9/11 world, where one was either with the United States or with the terrorists, minor points of difference between Canadians and their American allies appeared to count for little. The purpose of this chapter is to examine the "national conversation" in Canada as it took place in the white-hot emotional aftermath of September 11th. Specifically, I want to address the extremely serious allegation that, instead of inspiring sympathy and comradeship, the tragedy prompted the worst sort of "anti-Americanism" from Canadians, including the view that "they had it coming." I examine this charge not only in the light of nationalist and anti-nationalist cross-currents in Canada, but against the backdrop of the new patriotic orthodoxy that quickly took shape in the United States and, via global media led by CNN, spread inexorably to its allies.

PATRIOTIC ORTHODOXY IN THE US

Owing in part to the unprecedented media saturation occasioned by the events of September 11th, the initial public response of shock, horror and disbelief persisted indefinitely in the United States. Revolted and yet riveted by the filmed images of the planes hitting the World Trade Centre, corporate media outlets led by CNN proved incapable of rising above a purely visceral response to the attacks at the outset, and thereafter, of framing their analysis within any sort of historical or political context. This failure was in part the predictable consequence of the patriotism that the attacks had inspired; but it appears to have derived as well from deliberate obfuscation. The question "Why do they hate us?"[2] was raised, but mainly rhetorically. Osama bin Laden and Al Qaeda were demonized but rarely explained. Indeed, the very notion that the events of September 11th were explicable—that they could be understood as having some kind of historical context—was widely regarded as disloyal, tasteless or naive. Coming as it did from within a media culture that has done so much to obliterate the past, this sentiment had the effect of placing September 11th outside history, where it remains. President George W. Bush's appeal to a Manichean framework of "good versus evil"[3] thus went largely unchallenged in the dominant media, and appears in fact to have cemented his massive popularity in the aftermath of the attacks. The foreign policy doctrine Bush announced before Congress on 20 September 2001 — "Every nation in every region now has a decision to make: either you are with us, or you are with the terrorists" — also went unchallenged in the US, with serious repercussions for America's allies and trading partners, including Canada. For a year after the attacks, American pollsters studiously avoided asking the public whether the United States bore any responsibility for the tragedy.[4]

To be sure, idealism ran high in the United States in the immediate aftermath of September 11th. The hope was commonly expressed, at least within the intelligentsia, that the catastrophe might not only bring Americans together in common cause but serve to attenuate some of the more selfish and frivolous tendencies within American culture. The *New York Times* spoke for many when it opined: "Americans desperately want to commit to something greater than themselves. That was the secret of what we admired in the World War II era, and it is what this new war against terrorism will require as well. The awful week of death and destruction that has just ended might be the invitation to create a great new generation and a finer United States."[5] Some commentators expressed the view that Americans would be jolted into a new awareness of the outside world and of their nation's place within it. *New York Times* columnist Frank Rich wrote: "This week's nightmare, it's now clear, has awakened us from a frivolous if not decadent decade-long dream... that we could have it all without having to pay any price, and that national suffering of almost any kind could be domesticated into an experience of virtual terror akin to a theme park ride."[6]

Within a month, however, such optimism about the attacks' ability to catalyze "a great new generation and a finer United States" had begun to wane. The event that was said to have changed the course of history was naturalized, in fact, in surprisingly short order. In a detailed analysis of Americans' cultural consumption patterns in the weeks after September

11th, for example, the *New York Times* conceded that the crisis had had no measurable effect. (The only noteworthy exception was that books on September 11th were selling well but "it was unclear whether this amounted to a lasting trend or a burst of curiosity....")[7] Similarly, after dropping precipitously in the days after September 11th, the Dow Jones industrial average—ostensibly a crucial barometer of American investors' sensitivity to international instability—had fully recouped its losses by Christmas. Christopher Hitchens, one of the most thoughtful and provocative journalists to regularly probe the deeper meanings of the attacks and their aftermath, wrote bluntly in March 2002 that the "new seriousness" that had been widely celebrated in American life after September 11th had been greatly exaggerated.[8]

Not surprisingly, perhaps, the attacks provided the pretext for a dramatic escalation in the already-heated "culture wars" in the United States—a trend that would spill over into Canada and greatly affect the terms of the debate September 11th would occasion here. On the American Right, liberalism was bluntly accused of having eviscerated patriotism. Liberal education, politically correct history curricula and the pernicious influence of "cult leaders" like Noam Chomsky were singled out. Writing in *Salon*, for example, David Horowitz called Chomsky "without question, the most devious, the most dishonest and—in this hour of his nation's grave crisis—the most treacherous intellect in America." Casting Chomsky as the "ayatollah of anti-American hate" among youth, Horowitz railed: "Schooled in [Chomsky's] big lies, taught to see America as greed incarnate and a political twin of the Third Reich, why wouldn't young people—with no historical memory—come to believe that the danger ahead lies in Washington rather than Baghdad or Kabul?"[9] Elsewhere conservatives attacked the progressive bias that had come to dominate American public education. Writing in *Commentary*, Chester E. Finn Jr. chastised the liberal American intelligentsia *en masse*: "We are no longer surprised at intellectuals and college professors who look askance at any manifestation of love of country. To many of them, after all, patriotism has long connoted McCarthyism, jingoism, American imperialism, excessive spending on defense (and not enough on education), Ronald Reagan, and mindless flag-waving by tattooed workers lacking university degrees."[10]

The *Nation* magazine correctly identified such outbursts as evidence of "the return of good old-fashioned anti-intellectualism."[11] The problem, progressives argued, was not merely that patriotic fever had gripped Americans in the wake of September 11th, but that dissent from this patriotic orthodoxy was viewed with suspicion. Progressive critics of media concentration in the United States argued, for example, that superficial media coverage of September 11th was the inevitable result of corporate owners' dumbing-down of those media over the years—a trend clearly visible in the dramatic decline of international news coverage. In a *Salon* article provocatively entitled "America the Ignorant," Laura Miller explored the myriad reasons why Americans' knowledge of foreign affairs was decreasing, even as the US government has assumed an increasingly activist role in the world.[12] Mark Crispin Miller at *The Nation* went even further, suggesting that concentration of media ownership had allowed for the privatization of censorship, with "heavy hitters of the media Cartel—the owners and major advertisers—themselves acting quickly to shut down critical discussion."[13] It was widely rumoured that CNN had adopted an explicit policy of patriotic bias in its news coverage after September 11th.[14] To all of this progressives added what was arguably the most worrisome indictment of all, namely that the First Amendment right of free speech was routinely being trampled on university campuses.[15]

Veterans of the "culture wars" of the 1980s and 1990s, progressive critics in the US feared that the events of September 11th would be—in Noam Chomsky's words—"a gift to the hard jingoist right, those who hope to use force to control their domains."[16] Thus they were quick to gird their loins not only in defense of free speech and other civil liberties but, more generally, against the imposition from the Right of an agenda of paranoid xenophobia at home and dangerous unilateralism abroad. American progressives wasted no time in opening up the very question the corporate media would not touch: "Why do they hate us so much?" On September 13th, to cite the most dramatic example, Noam Chomsky posted a short piece called "On the Bombings" on the Internet. In it, he explicitly cast the attacks on the World Trade Centre and the Pentagon as a by-product of recent US foreign policy: "In scale they may not reach the level of many others, for example, Clinton's bombing of the Sudan with no credible pretext, destroying half its pharmaceutical supplies and killing unknown numbers of people...." Quoting veteran foreign correspondent Robert Fisk, Chomsky observed that "this is not the war of democracy versus terror that the world will be asked to believe in the coming days. It is also about American missiles smashing into Palestinian homes and US helicopters firing missiles into a Lebanese ambulance in 1996 and American shells crashing into a village called Qana and about a Lebanese militia—paid and uniformed by America's Israeli ally—hacking and raping and murdering their way through refugee camps." Predictably, although Chomsky had qualified his remarks with the observation that the attacks had been "major atrocities," this could not save him from the venom of the American Right.[17]

Whether Chomsky believed that his remarks were apt to provoke a serious national (or international) debate on US foreign policy, or, indeed, whether he believed that the American people were even ready to consider the matter only two days after the attacks remain open questions. That his timing could have been better, or his tone less smug, seems obvious in retrospect, if only because the most salient intellectual theme articulated in "On the Bombings" was subsequently dismissed along with its more inflammatory accusations. "As to how to react," Chomsky wrote, "we have a choice. We can express justified horror; we can seek to understand what may have led to the crimes, which means making an effort to enter the minds of the likely perpetrators."

WE MUST ACCEPT THE INEVITABLE

From the moment the hijacked planes hit the World Trade Centre on September 11th, Canadians' responses to the crisis were animated by three related impulses: their shock and horror at the severity of the attacks, their suspicion (later confirmed) that Canadians had likely been among the victims and, above all, their realization that the "fire-proof house" in which continental North Americans had lived since the eighteenth century was no longer beyond the reach of the ideological, religious and ethnic violence that has always bedeviled much of the outside world.[18]

The outpouring of Canadian sympathy — both for the victims of the attacks and, indeed, for all Americans — was immediate and genuine. All of the major Canadian media, including the CBC, were effusive in their expressions of pity, horror and revulsion; Canadian political leaders expressed their sympathy for the United States in no uncertain terms; and wherever called upon to do so, ordinary Canadians responded to the emergency needs of ordinary Americans — most notably those travellers whose flights had been diverted from closed US airspace — with generosity and forbearance. Polls taken in the immediate aftermath of the attacks showed that "a strong majority of Canadians were personally upset about the tragedy that played out on our television screens and in the news media generally."[19] On 14 September, designated in Canada and elsewhere as a day of mourning for the victims of the attacks, 100,000 Canadians led by Governor-General Adrienne Clarkson and Prime Minister Chrétien assembled to pay their respects to the slain. Chrétien addressed US Ambassador Paul Cellucci on behalf of all Canadians:

> Mr. Ambassador, you have assembled before you, here on Parliament Hill and right across Canada, a people united in outrage, in grief, in compassion, and in resolve. A people of every faith and nationality to be found on earth. A people who, as a result of the atrocity committed against the United States on September 11, 2001, feel not only like neighbours, but like family. At a time like this, words fail us. We reel before the blunt and terrible reality of the evil we have just witnessed. We cannot stop the tears of grief. We cannot bring back lost wives and husbands. Sons and daughters. American citizens, Canadian citizens, citizens from all over the world. We cannot restore futures that have been cut terribly short.[20]

As the emotional intensity of the immediate aftermath of the attacks re-ceded and the nation prepared for war in Afghanistan in late September, polls showed that roughly two-thirds of Canadians continued to feel that the tragedy had "made me personally feel a closer sense of shared values and interests with the Americans." [21]

The most striking aspect of Canadians' outpouring of sympathy and support for the Americans, seen in retrospect, was its apparent invisibil-ity within their own nation. To judge from the op-ed pages of Canada's leading newspapers, for example, Canadians had neither appreciated the extent to which their own values had been assaulted on September 11th, nor had they even extended their beleaguered American neighbours the common courtesy of toning down their "barren, soul-destroying" anti-American rhetoric. Within days of the attack on America, in fact, the national conversation in Canada became unexpectedly hysterical, as some of the country's leading public commentators rallied around the twin propositions that "we are all Americans now" and that any attempt to understand the attacks in an historical or political context represented a public-relations victory for Osama bin Laden and his ilk. Anti-intel-lectualism reared its head. The bogey-man of anti-Americanism was deployed relentlessly, baselessly and out of all proportion to the extent to which it actually manifested itself; the few Canadians who had the temerity to pronounce on the events of September 11th in the light of US foreign policy were pilloried with unprecedented fury; and dissent, most notably at the CBC and on Canadian university campuses, was chilled. Historians were mobilized to denounce Canadians' long-standing paranoia about the United States, their smug sanctimony on the world stage and the pitiful state of their defence commitments. Some Canadian pundits imported the Americans' own patriotic orthodoxy, thereby un-dermining serious debate about the significance for Canada of the new continentalism demanded by the terrorist threat. Others pronounced Canadian nationalism dead—a poetic and immature fantasy from the 1960s that had no place in the post-September 11th world.

Veteran Canadian author and commentator Robert Fulford helped to establish this atmosphere of doubt and recrimination in Canada with several uncharacteristically illiberal columns in the *National Post*. The first, "US Bashing No Longer a Game," appeared on 14 September, casting Canadians in the role of unwitting accomplices in the spread of the same anti-American ideas that lay behind the terrorist attacks. For Fulford the most important Canadian question in the wake of September 11th was this: "Do our views, and those of the world's most dangerous fanatics, have anything in common?" The answer was clear: "we should acknowledge that reflexive anti-Americanism (as opposed to honest disagreement with the United States) is a poison afflicting large parts of the world, a poison we should purge from our own system." Anticipating the Bush Administration's characterization of a world divided between the friends and enemies of terror, Fulford insisted that Canadians make some hard choices:

> As alliances are formed and sides taken in the aftermath of September 11, much of the argument will come down to a relatively simple question: is U.S. influence, in sum, more harmful or more beneficial? It seems obvious to me that it is infinitely more beneficial. Accepting this reality means understanding the United States rather than reinforcing prejudices against it. That being so, the anti-Americanism that we have so casually practised for so long now begins to seem insincere and irrelevant.[22]

Fulford's call for "understanding"—eminently laudable on the surface—was coupled in "US Bashing No Longer a Game" with a scathing indictment of the very intellectuals and artists whose business it is, arguably, to seek understanding. Anti-Americanism, claimed Fulford, is "accepted almost universally in Canada [and] tolerated in university classrooms," while in "the arts" this "ingrained prejudice… flourishes unhindered." This anti-intellectual strain in Fulford's thinking was exposed even more starkly in his column of 24 November 2001, in which he attacked some University of Toronto students for holding a debate on the "fatuous" resolution: "Be it resolved that the terrorists have a point." Comparing this event to the famous 1933 Oxford Union debate on pacifism—which Winston Churchill called "notorious" and Adolph Hitler was rumoured to have interpreted as evidence of British cowardice—Fulford responded with unrestrained contempt:

> Do the heartless mass murderers who attacked the United States on Sept. 11 have a point? Everyone already knows the answer: Yes, of course they have a point. Who doesn't have a point? Hitler certainly had a point, likewise Stalin, also Mao and Pol Pot, too. Nobody on Earth with a grievance lacks a point; it's a non-question. What matters is how the point finds expression. Is there anything legitimate about what happened on Sept. 11, or should the whole world rise up in fury and smite the perpetrators and all those who supported them? That might be worth discussing.

Fulford saved the real venom for Canadians generally and for the federal government in particular, apparently for fostering a national attitude of smug sanctimony and do-nothing effeteness:

> No doubt [the debaters] will approach the issue in the cool and civilized manner for which our nation would like to be famous. It sounds like a perfect Canadian evening. No one will feel called upon to act and everyone will enjoy a brisk discussion. In the struggle between civilization and chaos, Canada will take its place on the sidelines. Meanwhile, our government will be available (as always) to serve as honest broker.[23]

For Robert Fulford, the one-time editor of *Saturday Night* and arguably one of Canada's most respected public intellectuals, September 11th appears to have come as an epiphany, distilling centuries of complex Canadian history (to say nothing of Canadian-American relations) into a singular moral imperative: *Choose.*[24]

Fulford was not alone. Canadians' ostensibly rampant anti-Americanism was also the central theme of Margaret Wente's first *Globe and Mail* column after the attacks of September 11th, and here the tone of anti-intellectualism was even more explicit and malevolent. The piece opened with a quotation: "The Americans are reaping the fruits of their crimes against humanity." Who had made such a statement?

> That's Saddam Hussein speaking. But you don't have to go to Baghdad to hear such views. Just hang around any college campus. Or chat with your well-heeled neighbours in downtown Toronto. Anti-American sentiment is nearly as popular among Canadians — especially well-heeled ones — as Starbucks lattes.

These "anti-Americans," according to Wente, "believe the United States was asking for it":

> The bill of indictment against the United States is both very vague and very specific. Some people blame the gap between rich and poor, which the U.S. is either inadvertently or advertently responsible for creating. The feeling is that the poor are so desperate, so hopeless and so oppressed that it's not surprising they would lash out like this. Other people blame the long record of alleged U.S. atrocities abroad, including its efforts to overthrow Fidel Castro, the war in Vietnam, the secret war in Cambodia, its support for various strongmen and dictators, the Persian Gulf war, the oppression of Palestinians, the deliberate starvation of Iraqi children etc. etc.

At least as troubling for Wente as the ostensible content of this critique was its origins within a Canadian social and cultural élite which "should know better." Bitter "rants against America" in the wake of the terrorist attacks were not "confined to the usual anti-globalization crowd," she claimed, but could be heard from "lawyers, managers, teachers and various other [Torontonians]." "[I]gnorant prejudice against America" was especially common among young Canadians, Wente argued — little wonder, since they had been so thoroughly brainwashed by their older compatriots:

Among these kids, reflexive anti-Americanism is as much a fashion statement as the jeans they wear. Their teachers haven't challenged their beliefs. Their parents haven't, either. Chances are their teachers and their parents think George Bush sucks, too. They've all been raised in a country where recreational bitching at the United States is just as much fun as going to Disney World.

Having disparaged activists, lawyers, teachers, "managers," the university community, youth and "the well-heeled" in general, Wente went on to reassure her presumably working-class *Globe and Mail* readers that "the majority of Canadians" did not subscribe to the sanctimonious "prejudice" of the Toronto "intelligentsia":

Certainly, the cafeteria lady, the liquor-store clerk and the guy who fixes my plumbing don't blame the victim. They're outraged. Their attitude is: "Terrorism must be stopped, so that this never happens again." They think that the United States must strike back and that Canada ought to help them.[25]

Elsewhere in the national press, editorial and op-ed pages for the week of September 11th were similarly acerbic. The *National Post,* for example, claimed bluntly on 15 September that "[m]any Canadians wish America ill":

In recent decades, hostility toward the United States has been most virulent amongst Canada's intellectual and cultural élites. Our painters have made anti-American politics central to their work; university professors have advised generations of students that U.S. imperialism is the root of all injustice; and writers have clothed resentment in eloquence.... The hostility now on display in Toronto cafés and university student centres amounts—in the words of [historian J.L.] Granatstein—to "glib, mindless prejudice" and "a barren, soul destroying conceit."[26]

KNEE-JERK NATIONALISTS

It is worth noting, in the light of this chorus of condemnation for Canadians with an ostensibly anti-American cast of mind, that for the week of September 11th I could find almost no references in the public record to anti-American statements made by members of the Canadian "intellectual and cultural élites." Naomi Klein, a leading light in the anti-globalization movement, wrote what might be called a Chomsky-styled critique of US foreign policy that week. Given that Klein writes for an international audience and does not identify herself as a Canadian nationalist, however—her column "Game Over" appeared in the *Globe and Mail* on 14 September and was reprinted later in the week in both *The Nation* and the *Los Angeles Times*—her critique did not take the form of homespun "recreational bitching at the United States." Much of what Klein had to say about US economic and political power, in fact, echoed arguments that were being put forward by American activists, including her central thesis that "[p]erhaps September 11, 2001 will mark the end of the shameful era of the video game war." Although her comments were strongly worded—she characterized Americans as being "blithely unaffected by, even uninterested in, international conflicts in which they are key protagonists"—they were also qualified by her insistence that the US did not "deserve to be attacked" and, indeed, that the very suggestion that it did was "ugly and dangerous."[27]

Similarly, despite bearing the inflammatory title, "It's the U.S. Foreign Policy, Stupid," Haroon Siddiqui's *Toronto Star* column of 19 September 2001 took aim at international power politics writ large and included explicit indictments of Israel (for trying to "crush the intifadah"), Russia (for "cloak[ing] its brutality in Chechnya as a war against terrorism"), India ("on Kashmir") and China (for "battling Uighur separatists in Xingiang region"), as well as the United States.[28] As even his critics acknowledged, however, Siddiqui was no run-of-the-mill "anti-American." His reputation as a veteran journalist of the utmost integrity and perspicacity (as well as the fact that he was born in India) exempted him from the common accusation that criticism of US foreign policy was coming only from "knee-jerk nationalists" in Canada. More importantly, as the "editor emeritus" of the *Toronto Star*, he had written the paper's impassioned and sympathetic "Letter to Our American Friends" on 13 September, which included the unambiguous advice: "Hit the terrorists hard. Be merciless in going after them. But spare the innocents, both abroad and at home."[29] Even so, Robert Fulford indicted Siddiqui explicitly in his column on the University of Toronto debate, noted above, claiming that he had shored up a conceit widely held by Canadians: "If only Americans would straighten themselves out, and heed our sound advice, these problems would disappear."

Klein's "Game Over" and Siddiqui's "It's the U.S. Foreign Policy, Stupid" were, in any case, the exceptions that proved the rule. As noted above, Canadian print and broadcasting media in the days that followed the attacks were keenly attuned to Americans' confusion and grief, and they took great pains to report the tragedy with sensitivity and tact. Even if some Canadian intellectuals and artists did believe that the Americans "had it coming," which remains a highly dubious contention, they were not saying so publicly during the week of September 11th.

I spent that week on three university campuses in Ontario and I confess, moreover, that I saw none of the smug sanctimony described by the *Post* as having permeated "university student centres." On the contrary, my deep and abiding impression of Canadian undergraduates' response to the terrorist attacks was that they were even more incredulous than either the mass media or Canadian society at large. My own students were literally dumbfounded and heartsick, incapable of processing the enormity of the crime initially and, even weeks later, of framing it as anything other than a tragedy of epic dimensions. Like the great majority of Canadians whose sympathies were being tracked by pollsters that week, they were deeply moved by Americans' suffering and incensed at reports of anti-Americanism that were carried in the media, most notably the images of seemingly jubilant Palestinians dancing in the streets. Campus newspapers confirm that this profound emotional dislocation was the most common response among Canadian university students. To cite but one example, at the University of Toronto's Erindale College in Mississauga, undergraduates had been so traumatized by "the tragic events" of September 11th that college administrators "initiated a series of student support seminars to attempt to alleviate the emotional pressures experienced by students."[30] The Canadian Federation of Students, for its part, collaborated with other like-minded organizations to create the September Eleventh Peace Coalition, which stated publicly: "We … mourn the tragic loss of life resulting from the terrorist attacks on September 11, 2001. We condemn the attacks and want the perpetrators brought to justice."[31]

The question arises, then: who, exactly, were the "anti-Americans" who had provoked the wrath of Robert Fulford, Margaret Wente, the *National Post* and others in the days immediately following September 11th? The only persons cited explicitly by Fulford were John Turner, for fear-mongering during the Free Trade election of 1988, and the late Greg Curnoe, a Canadian artist whose greatest popularity had come in the era of the Vietnam War. Aside from her generalized attack on the bourgeois professions, noted above, Wente's only evidence for rampant anti-Americanism in Canada was her own "crammed" email inbox, the contents of which were quoted but never attributed. The *Post*, which claimed explicitly that the terrorist attacks had "unleashed a stream of anti-American venom" in Canada, cited as evidence excerpts from Farley Mowat and Margaret Atwood circa 1987, when the two authors were campaigning against the Free Trade Agreement, and various letters to the editor from Canadian dailies. In none of these editorials did there appear a single attributed anti-American statement made by a prominent Canadian during the week of September 11th. In light of the vicious recriminations faced by Canadians who later *did* express anti-American sentiments in connection with the terrorist attacks—most notably Professor Sunera Thobani, whose case I shall discuss below—I can only assume that if such statements had been at hand in mid-September, they would have been cited (and damned) explicitly.

THE NEW REALITY

That there was so little evidence of anti-Americanism in Canada the week of September 11th 2001 suggests not merely that Fulford and Wente, et al., had overreacted, but that they were, in truth, using the terrorist attacks on the United States as a pretext for airing longstanding grievances against Canadian nationalists. (An uncharitable interpretation, but a not-unreasonable one given their repeated references to the likes of Margaret Atwood, Farley Mowat and John Turner, is that they were still fighting the Free Trade debate of 1988, which, of course, they had already won.) Clearly, they were also *anticipating* a nationalist response to the tragedy of September 11th. Viewed from this perspective, their hyperbole was intended to serve a prophylactic function, nipping anti-Americanism in the bud and, in so doing, framing the terms of serious debate about Canada's place in the post-September 11th world in such a way as to place nationalists beyond the pale. In this latter respect, they—and their academic and political allies—were successful even beyond their own expectations. In the national conversation sparked in Canada by the events of September 11th, nationalists were thrown immediately onto the defensive, their ideas mocked rather than challenged, their commitment to the right "values" doubted, their motives questioned. Some veterans of the Canadian left-nationalist tradition, like author Richard Gwyn, recanted, confessing that they had been naive in the past and could now see that a new world of realpolitik was upon them. Others, like broadcaster Peter Gzowski and veteran political commentator Dalton Camp, stuck to their nationalist guns but felt obliged to trot out their pro-American pedigrees at every opportunity. Those who continued to use the old-fashioned language of Canadian nationalism, and to speak of the continuing need for Canada to assert its independence vis-à-vis the United States—members of the federal NDP, PC leadership hopeful David Orchard and Heritage Minister Sheila Copps, for example—simply became *non grata*, their ideas backward-looking and embarrassing, if not cowardly and dangerous.[32] Those like veteran social-democrat James Laxer, who warned that Canadians "need to guard against taking hasty decisions in the heat of the moment whose consequences could be felt long after Osama bin Laden is forgotten," were largely ignored.[33]

The case of veteran *Toronto Star* columnist Richard Gwyn is note-worthy. A high-profile foreign-affairs commentator and the author of *Nationalism without Walls: The Unbearable Lightness of Being Canadian* (1995), among other works, Gwyn has always identified himself as a left-nationalist, while questions of Canadian sovereignty and "identity" have always been at the centre of his thinking.[34] For Gwyn, the events of September 11th were nothing short of catastrophic—for the Americans on whom the attacks were inflicted but also for Canadians like himself, who had been deluded for decades in their belief that their nation was actually sovereign. In his column of 29 September 2001, bearing the ominous title "We Must Accept the Inevitable," Gwyn told Canadians: "We have entered the virtual sovereignty phase of our national story." Canada would now have to make its peace with the realities of a post-September 11th world in which, among other things, the security priorities of the United States must dictate Canadian policy:

> [T]he Chrétien government's decision this week to adopt a common North American perimeter—U.S. standards applying everywhere, that's to say—for security and intelligence, for immigration and for our refugee systems represents one of the most significant abandonments of our sovereignty in our history. Abandonment is the wrong term. Accepting the inevitable would be the right way to put it.

Gwyn was critical of Chrétien's handling of the issue, not because he thought Liberal policies were wrong-headed but because the Prime Minister had been cowardly about leading Canadians into the new era of global terrorism. Included in this critique—clear evidence of the profound change of heart that September 11th appeared to occasion for Gwyn—was an uncharacteristic slur on the nationalist tradition in Canada, of which he had himself been a part:

Rather than educate Canadians about these fundamental changes in our national condition, Chrétien has tried to distract the public's attention from what was happening. He declared that no one was going to change our "values and traditions." Rather than talk about the national security crisis, he went on and on about Canadian multiculturalism, worthy enough in itself but irrelevant to the task at hand. All of this was just arm waving on the sidelines, plus a certain calculated playing to the anti-American constituency in Canada (or, more exactly, those Canadians who enjoy being morally superior to Americans). Belatedly, Chrétien has accepted reality.[35]

Three weeks later, on 17 October, by which time the war in Afghanistan was underway, Gwyn elaborated his thinking on the nature of this "change in our national condition." He started with the provocative observation that "The Sixties ended on Sept. 11." What followed was a terse but powerful analysis not only of the distance Canadians appeared to have travelled since the heady nationalism of the Trudeau era, but of the manner in which they understood their own history:

The Sixties were a wonderfully innocent time. Peace and love could conquer all. A perfect world was possible. Tolerance, understanding, dialogue could solve all problems. With occasional variations, those presumptions have dominated our public consciousness ever since. Canadians were convinced of our own moral superiority. Canada, it can be argued, became the most Sixty-ish society in the world. Certainly, we were the most politically correct. We were just about the most moralizing, convinced of our own moral superiority, most especially toward Americans, but also toward the rest of the world since our "human security" foreign policy agenda, in its premise that our values could and should be exported around the world, amounted to a kind of secular missionary undertaking or to cultural colonization. It was all highly idealistic and exceedingly well-intentioned. But it was also more than a little bit self-deceiving. It depended upon the fact that the U.S. guaranteed our national security. It also depended upon the presumption that the rest of the world—the nasty world we occasionally saw on our TV screens, for example, in the Balkans or in Rwanda—would remain safely on the far side of the Atlantic and Pacific while we went about our worthy work. We've now been mugged by reality. And we're changing our assumptions and attitudes more rapidly than has ever happened in our history.[36]

Gwyn's change of heart did not go unnoticed in Canada. Calling him "the grand old man of Canadian nationalism," for example, the right-wing *Alberta Report* cited his about-face as clear evidence that Jean Chrétien, among others, should also face up to "the new reality."[37]

Not all Canadian commentators were "changing their assumptions and attitudes" wholesale in the manner of Richard Gwyn, but those who took a more measured view were extraordinarily few in number in the days and weeks after September 11th. One of the only pundits in Canada to even question the assumption that the world had changed irrevocably on that day—and for this reason alone his writing on the subject remains an extremely important counterweight to the prevailing anxiety of the times—was Dalton Camp, then 81 years old and as committed as ever to the "red Tory" tradition in Canada. In his *Toronto Star* column of 29 September 2001, for example, entitled "Canada Need Not Be Lockstep with U.S.," Camp challenged the assumption that in the wake of September 11th, "[f]ear stalks our country… from the stock market to the classroom, from church pews to shopping malls." Canadians had other things on their minds as well, he observed, notwithstanding the patriotic hyperbole with which the dominant North American media had been stoking public opinion since the terrorist attacks. "It is… not surprising," Camp wrote, "that the American media—from CNN to *The New York Times*—would join so fervently in the task of preparing the American people for a war of undetermined length against a catalogue of hypothetical enemies. In such endeavor, critical judgment becomes consumed in patriotism while being terminally suspended." What did come as a surprise, however, was that the Canadian media were "feverishly joining in condemning anyone who does not have the same degree of zeal for America's 'new war'."

Camp correctly noted that the tendency of the Canadian media to import both the content and the bias of their US counterparts derived from the fundamental problem that they no longer understood the two nations as having distinct interests. He recognized as well that it was the pervasive stigma of anti-Americanism that had foreclosed on virtually all other interpretations:

> It is surely possible to be pro-Canadian without risk of being deemed anti-American. While one can easily comprehend American purposes and interests, these are not necessarily congruent with our own, and we have the right to consider our own interests before determining our course. It is a revelation, to say the least, to find so many Canadian journalists who seem to feel Canadians are subsumed in America's interests and that our role and choices in such matters as those now before us are simply nugatory.

Camp noted provocatively that the United States had been "unimpressed by the threat" Adolph Hitler had posed to democracy in 1939, and thus had watched from the sidelines as the Canadians alone fought for North America for the first two years of World War II. Americans of all people should recognize, therefore, that Canada's interests and their own are not identical, something Canada's leaders would also do well to bear in mind: "Whatever we do to help [with the War on Terror], as help we must, Canada's leaders must put Canada's interests foremost without apology. Our best interest is our self-interest. As settled policy, no people would better understand that than our American friends."[38]

A week after "Canada Need Not Be Lockstep with U.S." appeared in print, Camp was compelled to defend himself explicitly against the charge of anti-Americanism — evidence not only that unnamed "critics" of his position had besieged him in the meanwhile but, ironically, that the very intellectual chill he had been describing now extended to himself:

> I am often accused of being anti-American. In confirming this charge, I am also accused of being a socialist, peacenik, trade-unionist and a supporter of the United Nations. In my defence, I remind my critics that I married an American citizen, have two America-born children, attended both grade school and university in the U.S. and can name all 50 states, something few Americans can do. Besides all that, some of my best friends are American.

What followed was an elegant and powerful articulation — encapsulated in the title "We Like Americans But Not Their Politics" — of Camp's understanding of the historical relationship between the two countries, beginning with a harshly worded critique of those Canadians who failed to understand this distinction: "Our anti-Americanism is misrepresented by the American jingoes and journalists in our midst who, for patronage or other considerations, earn valuable coupons, frequent flier miles, or brownie points, by defending them against us. This overlooks a fundamental hard truth about Canadian anti-Americanism — most of us like most of them; it's their politics we can do without." Most Canadians "revered" Franklin D. Roosevelt, "adored" John F. Kennedy and even "liked" Bill Clinton, wrote Camp. What Americans "should know about us," he argued, "is that while we hold them in the highest regard, as neighbours and friends, we don't feel the same about Trent Lott, Dick Armey, Richard Perle, Henry Kissinger, and the like." This distinction is profound, said Camp, and it is rooted not in Canadian prejudice but in American history: "Canadians can remember when the first president George Bush lit up our Christmas holiday season by bombing the hell out of Panama City, killing and terrorizing uncounted Panamanians, all because the American government was looking for a dope peddler.... Canadians are puzzled by the U.S. government's prolonged official sulk over Cuba while its leaders are now regularly visiting Vietnam...."

Such references to US foreign policy, Camp recognized, were now being "swept aside by our local U.S. government boosters," who claimed that the terrorist attacks had changed everything. He directly challenged the idea being promulgated by the likes of Robert Fulford and Margaret Wente that September 11th demanded of Canada that it abandon the narcissism of small differences in favour of an unambiguous assertion of its essential comradeship with the United States. Such claims, Camp wrote,

> suggest there is some entirely unique and significantly different nature in our present Canadian-American relationship that did not exist in 1812, 1914, 1939, or last month. Obviously, times change and are never precisely the same. The past, however, has been a learning experience in our Canadian struggle to build our own society, one that reflects our values, as we create the imperatives and priorities in our ongoing development of a distinctive Canadian democracy.

Moreover, Camp observed, differences of opinion on US foreign policy were by no means ancient history. Citing the American refusal to sign the Kyoto Protocol on the environment and to join an international embargo on the spread of anti-personnel mines, he reminded Canadians that "as of September 10" it was widely thought that "the Bush administration had pretty well withdrawn from world affairs...." In what would turn out to be an extraordinarily astute insight, he argued that, although it may be "impolitic to raise such matters now, and especially discomfiting to the anti-Canadians in their own country," ordinary Canadians could still "recognize the differences between an apologist and a patriot":

> Not even the most ingenious of pollsters can find a gram of anti-Americanism among Canadians today. It's only that they do not share the awe for the present American government with a number of Canadians whose fealty may be as true as their self-interest. But our Prime Minister had it right, speaking in Kitchener

the other night. Don't worry, he said to his audience, Canada would be there to do its part. That has been its history, something that some Canadians have forgotten or never learned.[39]

Like Dalton Camp, Peter Gzowski, the veteran author and broad-caster whose "Morningside" persona was considered by some the glue that held Canada together, was compelled after September 11th to speak to the matter of anti-Americanism. His ruminations are also worth quoting at length, not only because they were so tortuous but also because this was one of the last occasions before his death in January 2002 on which Gzowski defended his history as a Canadian nationalist. He began by listing in detail the people he had known personally who had perished in the attacks: "Everyone I know knew someone, or knew someone who knew someone, and every story was a terrible reminder that we are all connected to everyone else. . . ." From there Gzowski set out, circuitously and somewhat ambivalently, his own view of what it meant to be both Canadian and American:

These thoughts come from someone who has been described from time to time as anti-American, and who sometimes, even tongue-in-cheek, applies the label to himself. Am I? Oh, maybe, if you look over most of a working life that has been committed to trying to stem the benevolent tide of cultural imperialism that rolls steadily over our southern border—or if not to stem it, then to build shelters from its omnipotence. I wish to limit no one's right to read or watch what they want. I've simply wanted to be—and to give my descendants a chance to be—"as Canadian as possible, under the circumstances," as someone wrote long ago to win a contest I had proposed on CBC Radio. And in recent months, that feeling about the United States has been as strong as ever—maybe even stronger. I think we've been bullied on everything from PEI potatoes to softwood lumber. I'm concerned about selling water like a farm crop. I think our interests are being ignored in our own north. And I wish we'd stand up for ourselves on everything from global warming to racism — a view that is, admittedly, more a criticism of our own government's lack of backbone than of our neighbour's colonialism. But anti-American? Come off it. I am an American. I don't mean just *Ich bin ein New Yorker*, as a short but eloquent letter to the editor on Thursday put it or even in the sense of standing shoulder to shoulder with our best friends, but of literal fact.... I know the lyrics of Ira Gershwin and Bob Dylan (better than Bob does, I sometimes think). I get most of the cartoons in *The New Yorker* and all the jokes on Jay Leno. I'm grateful for jazz, blues, rock 'n' roll, oranges, Broadway, movies, gin rummy, Annie Dillard, George Carlin, hamburgers, Waldorf salads, Muhammad Ali, key-lime pie, A. J. Liebling and Marilyn Monroe. I know more baseball history, state capitals and presidential trivia than most five-time *Jeopardy* champions, at least one of whom, by the way, has been, like its host, a Canadian, and certainly more than any of the numskulls on *The Weakest Link*. I'm an American with a difference, to be sure, but an American still. Being anti-U.S., I have finally figured out, is like being anti-winter. You can whine and bitch all you like, but in the end you have to admit you love it.[40]

HATE SPEECH

Notwithstanding the pervasive consensus in Canada that the terrorist attacks had been an unmitigated tragedy, there were, predictably, some instances in which Canadians expressed contrary views. Like Dalton Camp, they insisted that the events of September 11th must be understood in the context of the imperialistic tendencies of US foreign policy — a critique which, as noted above, borrowed heavily from liberal American critics like Noam Chomsky. Although the dissenters were remarkably few in number and in most cases minor players on the Canadian scene, the backlash they triggered within Canada escalated quickly to an hysterical level, setting in motion a year-long campaign of vilification in which the national press and even respected academics played leading roles. Two events in particular—a CBC "Town Hall" broadcast on 18 September and Professor Sunera Thobani's speech to the Ottawa Women's Resistance Conference on 1 October—became nothing less than *causes célèbres* in Canada, demonstrating the extent to which Canadians appeared to have embraced the patriotic orthodoxy that had done so much to chill debate in the United States.

On 19 September 2001, one week after the terrorist attacks, CBC News broadcast a "National Town Hall" hosted by Peter Mansbridge. The topic under consideration was "Attack on the U.S.A.: The Consequences for Canada." Highly attuned to the sensitivity of this issue, the producers of this broadcast sought explicitly to "elicit informed opinion and analysis" and to convene a broad cross-section of "politicians, military experts, invited guests and the Canadian public."[41] Guests included Janice Stein (Director of the Munk Centre for International Studies), Haroon Siddiqui, Barbara McDougall (former Tory Minister of External Affairs), David Rudd (Chair of the Canadian Institute for Strategic Studies), journalists Brian Stewart and Terence Corcoran, Cheryl Regehr (Professor of Social Work), Art Eggleton (the serving Minister of National Defense), NDP leader Alexa McDonough and Leader of the Opposition Stockwell Day. According to later press reports, the broadcast "was heavily criticized by viewers, *some of them American*, who accused the Corporation of presenting a one-sided, left-wing perspective on the causes and consequences of the terrorist attacks on the United States" (emphasis added).[42] Mr. Pav Penna, identified as a management consultant from Ontario, was sufficiently "offended by the broadcast" that he demanded the Corporation Ombudsman review the program to see whether it had "violated any CBC codes of conduct." David Bazay, CBC Ombudsman and a former head of CBC-TV News, reported in November 2001 that the codes had not been compromised but that Penna's complaints of bias were nonetheless justified. Anti-war and "anti-American" sentiments expressed during the broadcast, he wrote, had failed to adequately reflect Canadians' varied opinions:

I would have to say—on the basis of the way the speakers introduced themselves—that they could not be described as "a broadly representative group of citizens, a rough cross-section of Canadians." Almost a third of the speakers were university students. And many others who came to the microphones appeared to be employed in the public or voluntary sector of the economy. A government employee, a public school principal, an aid worker, a university professor and so on. There appeared to be little representation from the private sector, and this in a city that's at the centre of Canada's important economic relationship with the United States.[43]

Bazay claimed that of 23 audience members who spoke during the broadcast, eleven had either criticized the idea of using military force or blamed American foreign policy for the attacks. (The conflation in the Ombudsman's report of the anti-war and "anti-American" content of such contributions is noteworthy.) The real problem, apparently, was that these contributors received applause, giving "many viewers the impression that their opinions were the prevailing views of the studio audience." A participant who had insisted Canada "solidly stand behind America" received no applause, nor did another who had argued: "The fact is, in a thousand ways, we are more like the Americans than I think any other country.... We have a web of family relationships, of business relationships, a long-shared history. And this country has benefited in unimaginable ways from that relationship, at least over the last century."[44]

Tony Burman, executive director of CBC news, defended the Town Hall's producers against the Ombudsman's charge that they had perhaps inadvertently packed the audience:

CBC News [had] made every effort to be sure the audience represented a wide spectrum of opinion. We put out a general call for participation on CBC Radio, CBC Newsworld and cbc.ca. We went to universities. We called legion halls, firefighter and police associations, several ethnic community groups and PC and Alliance riding associations in Toronto. The result was a wide spectrum of opinion being expressed. *That some people were anti-American is hardly surprising, but most were not.* (emphasis added)[45]

This was not good enough for right-leaning critics of the CBC, some of whom used the Ombudsman's report as a pretext to go after the public broadcaster for its "left-wing" bias generally. Lydia Miljan, director of the National Media Archive at the Fraser Institute, for example, cited the incident as evidence of a broader pattern: "the CBC is typically Toronto-centric and refuses to admit that its programming is generally left of centre."[46] Borrowing from the Ombudsman's report (it is not clear whether he actually viewed the broadcasts), Eli Schuster of the *Albert Report* claimed that the "studio audience seemed to revel in kicking Uncle Sam when he was down. Statements that either ridiculed the option of using force against terrorism or that supported the 'America-had-it-coming' thesis were even greeted with applause."[47] At least one "left-wing" pundit refused to take this critique lying down. Writing in the *Toronto Star* on the Fraser Institute's enthusiasm for "America's War," Dalton Camp observed sardonically of the CBC program: "I heard part of the town hall meeting and what I heard came mostly from Michael Bliss, the historian, who impressed me as a man on the edge of joining the United States Marines."[48]

Many aspects of the CBC Town Hall controversy are noteworthy but I shall limit myself to two. The first is to observe that this broadcast—however "packed" the audience may or may not have been—was one of the only instances in which any of the dominant televisual Canadian media allowed the airing of unvarnished dissent. Certainly no criticism of the United States was allowed, even momentarily, to intrude upon the programming of Canada's private broadcasters—the best evidence for which is that there were no controversies in that quarter like the one that consumed the CBC. (It is noteworthy in this respect that the Asper family was later rumoured to have fired award-winning *Vancouver*

Sun reporter David Beers for his defence of Sunera Thobani.)[49] The argument may be easily made that even if "balance" *within* the Town Hall was lacking, the counterweight this broadcast might have brought to a national conversation in which dissent had become largely silenced ought to have made it all the more valuable.

A second and related point is the matter of the Ombudsman's (undoubtedly correct) demographic analysis. That it was university students, public and voluntary sector employees, professors and teachers, etc., who were voicing criticism of the United States should come as no surprise since, as noted in Chapter Six, these are precisely the social groups whose opinions and status positions are tied to a strong "statist" political orientation. What is surprising, therefore, is not that such individuals might have expressed opinions that could be construed as "anti-American" but that the Ombudsman would explicitly suggest that "the private sector" was inadequately represented. That such a claim should come from within the CBC clearly illustrates the extent to which the orthodox view of September 11th had put even the public broadcaster on the defensive.

The CBC Town Hall controversy paled in comparison with the fury UBC Professor Sunera Thobani unleashed across Canada, however. On 1 October 2001, Thobani spoke at an Ottawa conference on violence against women. She framed her presentation in the form of a question: "If we in the West are all Americans now, what are Third World women and Aboriginal women to do?" Thobani's remarks centred on the relatively well-rehearsed claim that "there can be no women's emancipation, in fact no liberation of any kind for women... unless it seeks to transform the fundamental divide between the north and the south...." The statements for which she would become infamous, however, took direct aim at American foreign policy:

> Today in the world the United States in the most dangerous and the most powerful global force unleashing prolific levels of violence all over the world. From Chile to El Salvador, to Nicaragua to Iraq, the path of U.S. foreign policy is soaked in

blood. We have seen, and all of us have seen, felt, the dramatic pain of watching those [September 11th] attacks and trying to grasp the fact of the number of people who died. We feel the pain of that every day we have been watching it on television. But do we feel any pain for the victims of U.S. aggression? ... [T]he people, the American nation that Bush is invoking, is a people which is bloodthirsty, vengeful, and calling for blood. They don't care whose blood it is, they want blood. And that has to be confronted.[50]

News of Thobani's remarks spread instantly, mobilizing a broadly based campaign of vilification in the national press and even in the House of Commons. The *Globe and Mail* called Thobani's speech "virulently anti-American."[51] *Globe* columnist Margaret Wente added: "Ms. Thobani is an idiot."[52] The *National Post* said that she had "condensed her febrile misandry and vicious anti-Western hatred into a spitball aimed squarely at the memory of those who died on Sept. 11."[53] The *Vancouver Sun* ran an "angry" 1994 photograph of Thobani under the headline "Feminist's Anti-U.S. Speech Causes Uproar," later claiming that "[t]he photos fit with what she was saying."[54] Well-known liberal journalist and broadcaster Ian Brown commented on Thobani's "stupidity and bottomless self-regard."[55] Foreign Affairs Minister John Manley called the speech "simply outrageous."[56] BC Premier Gordon Campbell called her speech "hateful and disgraceful."[57] The *Alberta Report* called Thobani "an angry, wild-eyed radical feminist, denouncing Western culture and spitting hatred at our good neighbours to the south."[58] In the United States, *The New Republic* cited Thobani in its "Idiocy Watch," the journal's "ongoing attempt to keep up with the dumbest, most outrageous comments made about the terrorist attacks on America and our response."[59] Reports circulated that she might have breached Canada's "hate speech" laws.

The firestorm quickly moved to the House of Commons. It came to light that the conference had received $80,000 in federal funding and also that Liberal cabinet minister Hedy Fry and Landon Pearson,

a Liberal Senator and the daughter-in-law of the late Prime Minister
Lester B. Pearson, had sat on the podium with Ms. Thobani. Opposition
parties leapt to impugn the Liberal government on both counts. On 1
October—the same day as Thobani's speech—Alliance MP Chuck
Strahl (then sitting with the Tories) demanded that "the Prime Minister
immediately refute these outrageous statements" and explain why Fry
had not "walk[ed] off the stage." Deputy Prime Minister John Manley
responded by saying that the government had "made it repeatedly plain
that we view any kind of attempt to create moral equivalency between
anyone's policies and what happened on September 11 to be utterly unthinkable, outrageous and indefensible." Alliance MP Grant Hill called
the speech "a terrible thing for all of Canada." Hedy Fry defended herself: "People in this country are allowed to say what they want. I did not
support it. I did not applaud it. I got up and left immediately following
it." She added: "I thought the speech... to be incitement. I condemned
it continually and I stand in the House right now and say that I condemn
that speech."[60]

The next day NDP MP Svend Robinson defended Thobani's right
to freely express her opinion: "Surely one of the most precious and
fundamental rights in a civilized and democratic society is freedom of
speech.... [I]t is inappropriate and unfair to attack the Secretary of
State for Multiculturalism [Fry] for not criticizing comments that were
made by Sunera Thobani during that conference." Alliance MP Howard
Hilstrom responded: "I personally stand behind the charter of rights to
freedom of speech, but I certainly want to publicly declare that I do not
agree with the position that she took. Nor do I agree that she should
receive any government moneys to advance causes that are not in keeping with the majority of Canadians' opinions." Alliance MP Keith Martin
agreed: "No longer can we use taxpayer money or the money of any
public group to further that type of hatred and disaffection." Alliance
MP Betty Hinton asked of the Prime Minister: "It cost Canadians...
$80,000 to fund a conference where outrageous anti-American remarks
were made. We support freedom of speech. However, why does this
government force taxpayers to pay for this kind of drivel?" Chrétien

explained that the main subject of the conference had been "violence against women," and that leading defenders of women's rights were present, including Justice Louise Arbour and Senator Pearson. "Of course we condemn the statement that was made there," he said, "but we will not apologize to the people of Canada because we are helping organizations like that to fight for those who are experiencing difficulties in our society."[61]

Three weeks after her speech in Ottawa, Thobani published a short essay in response to her critics. There was little contrition in it. She defended her critique of American foreign policy and of President Bush's "racialized construction of the American nation"; and she reiterated the "urgent necessity for the women's movement in Canada to oppose the war" in Afghanistan. "It has been fascinating to observe," she continued, "how my comments regarding American foreign policy—a record well documented by numerous sources whose accuracy or credentials cannot be faulted—have been dubbed 'hate speech'. To speak about the indisputable record of U.S.-backed coups, death squads, bombings and killings ironically makes me a 'hate-monger'." Thobani was unapologetic about her claim that the United States is "the largest and most dangerous global force," insisting that her "use of the words 'horrific violence' and 'soaked in blood' is very deliberate and carefully considered. I do not use these words lightly." The controversy generated by her remarks, she correctly noted, "has surprisingly not addressed the veracity of [her] assessment of the U.S. record. Instead, it has focused on my tone and choice of words (inflammatory, excessive, inelegant, un-academic, angry, and so on)." She concluded by placing her remarks in the tradition of anti-colonialism: "Anti-colonial and anti-imperialist movements and theorists have long insisted on placing the bodies and experiences of marginalized others at the centre of our analysis of the social world. To fail to do so at this moment in history would be unconscionable."[62]

Thobani's defenders were few and far between. Judy Rebick, like Thobani a past president of the National Action Committee on the Status of Women (NAC), asserted that her critique of US foreign policy was "unassailable," however indelicately it had been put. Rebick was appalled but not surprised by the smear campaign against Thobani, since the latter had "always enraged the chattering classes for her refusal to play the submissive role they expect from immigrant women of colour."[63] *Toronto Star* columnist Michele Landsberg went even further, placing her impassioned defence of Thobani in the context of the "brazen lies" that were being propagated about her speech by "conservative commentators." "What a pack of cowards," said Landsberg explicitly of Margaret Wente, Gordon Campbell, John Manley and myriad editorialists, for "rushing to climb onto a propaganda bandwagon about a speech they clearly neither heard nor read." For Landsberg, the central point of the furor was not Thobani's "right to free speech" but the question of "our ability to sustain a little complexity, and bear with the intellectual discomforts of ambiguity, despite George Bush's dicta about black and white, good and evil." Taking square aim at all who had deliberately or erroneously misquoted her, Landsberg noted that Thobani had not accused the American people of being "bloodthirsty and vengeful." Rather, "she vigorously rejected that depiction, which, she pointed out, was 'invoked by Bush'." Concluded Landsberg:

> [A] sinister demand for groupthink has dominated the media. It has proven terrifyingly easy to whip up a public hate campaign against one woman, based entirely on a few out-of-context and distorted quotes. These attacks, sadly, do serve one cautionary purpose: they show us how slickly we can all be duped, and how glibly bigotry can hide behind the Canadian mask of tolerance.[64]

That the CBC Town Hall broadcast and the Thobani speech had achieved an unparalleled degree of infamy was evident even a full year after the terrorist attacks. By the fall of 2002, a new "sovereignty" debate had been sparked by the Prime Minister's own musings on the roots of anti-Western sentiment, by the "friendly fire" deaths of Canadians in Afghanistan, and by rumours of war in Iraq (see the Conclusion). Yet historian J.L. Granatstein continued to single out the Town Hall broadcast and the Thobani speech as evidence not only that "anti-Americanism continues to flourish" in Canada, but that "[a]fter the terrorist attacks of September 11, 2001, many Canadians were quick to suggest that the Americans 'had it coming'."[65] From this generalization, Granatstein dismissed both Canadian nationalism and anti-war protest as immature "anti-Americanism" and insisted that Canadians take "a good stiff dose of realpolitik":

> On minor issues, Canada can be as vocal as it chooses, slanging the Americans upside and down. Americans argue amongst themselves too, and they won't be offended by this. But when Americans believe that their vital interests are at stake and their security is threatened, Canadians should have sense enough to recognize that Washington is a superpower with global concerns that are different from those of our small, weak nation. Canada likes to think itself a moral superpower, motivated by higher things than the crass, materialistic United States, but this is fantasy. The Americans, when they think of us at all, see us as a nation of carping complainers that regularly fails to carry its weight in the world. Why feed this perception?[66]

The continuing resonance of the Town Hall and Thobani incidents as *causes célèbres* for anti-nationalists in Canada confirmed the hegemony of the view that September 11th existed outside of history, that pubic dissent from this hegemonic interpretation of the tragedy continued to be understood as naive and insensitive, and especially—as Dalton Camp had predicted—that the crisis marked a clear fork in the road for Canadians accustomed to thinking of their nation as sovereign. The new watchword for nationalists in Canada was clear: "It's long past time for Canadians to grow up."[67]

In his January 2002 Pierre Genest Memorial Lecture, delivered at Osgoode Hall Law School, former Canadian ambassador to the United Nations Yves Fortier succinctly summarized the new post-nationalist paradigm. Drawing explicitly upon J.L. Granatstein's analysis of "anti-Americanism" in Canada, Fortier asserted that the world had changed

irrevocably for Canadians on September 11th 2001, and the federal
Liberals had better make their peace with it:

> Over the past five or so years, the government has floated a
> number of what might be called "continentalist" ideas, including
> a common currency, a customs union, water sales and a common
> energy policy. In almost every instance, however, the mere
> utterance of such ideas is followed by qualification, denial and,
> inevitably, little or no meaningful change. I deplore the almost
> reflexive gnashing of teeth and rending of garments that often
> follows the merest suggestion of closer links with our American
> cousins. Why? Because such reactions serve only to stifle debate
> regarding the very matter which the so-called Canadian nation-
> alists, self-titled defenders of our country, purport to defend,
> namely, our identity as Canadians and the values and policies
> that we espouse.... From Sept. 11 to the present day, polls have
> demonstrated that most Canadians support the United States in
> its war on terrorism. So they should, because it is our common
> values of pluralism, secularism and democracy that have come
> under attack. Canada is as threatened by terrorism as the United
> States. As a Canadian, I am not ashamed to defend a friend, and I
> am certainly not ashamed to assist a friend whose actions, even if
> imperfect, benefit my fellow citizens.[68]

CONCLUSION

In the aftermath of the terrorist attacks on September 11th Canadians'
sympathy for their American friends, allies and trading partners was
spontaneous, heartfelt and of long duration. Expressions of criticism
of the United States were for the most part muted, even as both nations
girded for war. This was particularly true in the corridors of power.
There was nothing from the Liberal government on the scale of Lester
Pearson's 1965 Temple University speech, in which the Prime Minister
openly criticized American foreign policy, nor even of John Diefenbaker's

undiplomatic request during the Cuban Missile Crisis that the UN verify the claims of the Kennedy Administration. Cabinet "hawk" John Manley was placed in charge of a parliamentary "national security committee" to co-ordinate the Canadian response to the terrorist threat.[69] Canada fell in behind the inaugural phase of the American "War on Terror" quickly and without reservation in early October 2001, dispatching troops to Afghanistan and taking dramatic steps to "harmonize" security and border policies with the US.[70] On 9 October Jean Chrétien told Canada's NATO allies that the fight against terrorism was the "first great struggle" of the twenty-first century. "We have not picked this fight," he said, "but we will finish it and finish it well."[71] Canadians agreed. Pollster Allan Gregg summarized the national mood:

> Our natural antipathy to being drawn closer into the American orbit also seems to be evaporating. Almost 65 per cent of our citizens report a closer bond with Americans following Sept. 11 and believe our reaction to these events underscores recognition of a common set of values and interests. In addition to accepting inconvenience and the possible diminution of civil liberties, Canadians report a willingness to give up a measure of sovereignty and to harmonize certain policies in order to secure a "North American perimeter." Far from indicating a desire for a common identity with Americans, these findings merely underline an attitude that always lay just below the surface of Canadian public opinion—a grudging understanding that, for good or ill, the destinies of the two nations are inextricably linked. While this may dismay rock-ribbed nationalists, it should not shock.[72]

Even the Leader of the Opposition, Stockwell Day, publicly "applaud[ed] the Prime Minister for making the right choice," acknowledging that "the decision to send Canadian men and women into harm's way is one of the most difficult that any government can make."[73]

For some critics of the government, of course, all of this was not nearly enough. Writing in the *National Post* on 10 October 2001, Andrew

Coyne accused Prime Minister Chrétien of being "consistently out of synch" in his responses to the September 11th tragedy. Coyne did not say precisely to what or whom Chrétien ought to have been "synched," but the implication was clear: like the "magnificent" Tony Blair, he should have been in much closer step with the United States:

> It isn't that Mr. Chrétien hasn't said or done the right thing. He has, eventually. But it's always a day, a step, a gesture too late. In the immediate aftermath, with the world doubled over in grief, Mr. Chrétien emitted a few wooden remarks in the lobby of the Commons. As the public's grief hardened into resolve, Mr. Chrétien was just getting into the grieving thing.... With the public, and at least one of his Cabinet ministers, clamouring for Canada to take an honourable part in any military action overseas, Mr. Chrétien leant heavily on his "we haven't been asked yet" mantra — the same excuse, almost word for word, as that offered by the government of Saudi Arabia.

Implying that there was broad agreement in Canada that Chrétien had indeed fumbled the ball, Coyne asked what could explain the Prime Minister's "puzzling behaviour." Ruling out the possibility that Chrétien was "buying time" or "trying to avoid alarming the public," Coyne ruminated that he probably had "an eye on knee-jerk Canadian nationalists, or on isolationist opinion in Québec." In truth, Coyne concluded bluntly, "there is no plan here, no strategy.... Mr. Chrétien's supremely tone-deaf response is simply a phenomenon of the imperial prime ministership."[74]

In retrospect, the most salient element in September 11th commentaries like Robert Fulford's and Margaret Wente's came not in the form of their overwrought anti-intellectual invective, though this was plainly a dominant theme, but in the discursive assumptions that lurked below the surface. Many of these assumptions had come to be shared, in fact, by Richard Gwyn and others for whom September 11th had marked a symbolic rupture in the historic Canadian-American relationship.

Perhaps the most striking of these assumptions was that the attacks on the World Trade Centre and the Pentagon were "about values" rather than power—a claim belied by the fact that only the United States was targeted and by the even more obvious point that the targets were symbols of American military and economic might. (Polls from early October 2001 revealed that while two-thirds of Americans believed there was "a continuing threat to their and their loved ones' physical safety," in Canada the figure was only one in ten.)[75] George W. Bush was quick to seize on this distinction, claiming in his speech of 20 September: "This is the world's fight. This is civilization's fight. This is the fight of all who believe in progress and pluralism, tolerance and freedom."[76] In the United States, the emphasis on values over power provided a clear ideological framework for Americans' understanding of both the attacks and the War on Terror. In Canada, however, this emphasis clearly—and by design—raised the stakes with respect to Canadians' response to the terrorist threat. It was obvious that Canada lacked the "power" to stand meaningfully alongside its American ally, at least militarily; but because values are not quantifiable in this sense, it was possible for Canada to stand "ready-aye-ready" with the United States and thus, symbolically at least, to make as great a commitment to the defence of our common values (in much the same way that British Prime Minister Tony Blair did). If the national conversation in the wake of September 11th had centred on power, nationalists might have occupied the high ground, since, as Dalton Camp argued, Canadian and American self-interest cannot be assumed to be identical. But because this conversation was steered so adeptly onto the terrain of values, about which fewer national distinctions can be made, it became difficult to defend the proposition that an independent Canadian position was either necessary or desirable.

The blunt fact remains, however, that until the first anniversary of the terrorist attacks, when Jean Chrétien took the unexpected and truly extraordinary step of placing September 11th in the context of relations between the world's rich and poor, Canadians had every reason to believe that the continentalists in their midst had finally succeeded in driving nationalism beyond the pale. For anyone who cared to make the connection, 9/11 appeared to have fulfilled one of George Grant's most pointed prophesies in *Lament for a Nation*:

> Canada has ceased to be a nation, but its formal political existence will not end quickly. Our social and economic blending into the [American] empire will continue apace, but political union will probably be delayed. Some international catastrophe or great shift of power might speed up this process.[77]

Despite incontrovertible evidence of Canadians' overwhelming feeling of sympathy and comradeship with the United States, despite the painful honesty with which leading Canadian nationalists had responded to the crisis, and despite the fact that the few outspoken Canadian critics of American foreign policy who had dared raise their voices had been pilloried mercilessly, Canadians were presented with a picture of themselves as a people "consumed" with "anti-Americanism."[78] Seldom have Canadians been so thoroughly and unambiguously misrepresented.

NOTES

1. Gordon Barthos, "Pepping up Canada's Agenda," *Toronto Star* (14 February 2002).

2. President George W. Bush asked "Why Do They Hate Us?" in his *Speech To Congress* (20 September 2001).

3. "I view this as good versus evil—there is no middle ground, as far as I'm concerned." George W. Bush, *Speech* (31 January 2002):

4. This was the explicit view of Canadian pollster John Wright, vice-president of Ipsos-Reid. Paraphrased in Shawn McCarthy, "Most Think U.S. Partly to Blame for Sept. 11," *Globe and Mail* (7 September 2002). See also Haroon Siddiqui, "Media Missing Canadian Perspective," *Toronto Star* (12 September 2002).

5. *New York Times*, cited in Ellen Willis, "Dreaming of War," *The Nation* (15 October 2001).

6. Frank Rich, cited in ibid.

7. Rick Lyman with Bill Carter, "In Little Time, Pop Culture Is Almost Back to Normal," *New York Times* (3 October 2001).

8. Christopher Hitchens, "America More Serious? You Must Be Joking," *The Guardian* (6 March 2002).

9. David Horowitz, "The Sick Mind of Noam Chomsky," *Salon* (26 September 2001).

10. Chester E. Finn Jr., "Teachers, Terrorists, and Tolerance," *Commentary* 112:5 (December 2000), pp. 54–8.

11. David Glenn, "The War on Campus: Will Academic Freedom Survive?" *The Nation* (3 December 2001).

12. Laura Miller, "America the Ignorant," *Salon* (27 September 2001).

13. Mark Crispin Miller, "Private Censorship," *The Nation* (22 October 2001). See also "News They Won't Share," *Globe and Mail* (12 October 2001), p. A18; David Talbot "No Wonder the Media Is Cowed," *The Guardian* (17 October 2001); and Rachel Giese, "Enough Dumbing Down of the News," *Rabble* (1 November 2001).

14. Matt Wells, "CNN to Carry Reminders of US Attacks," *The Guardian* (1 November 2001).

15. See David Glenn, "The War on Campus."

16. Noam Chomsky, "On the Bombings" (13 September 2001).

17. Ibid. See also Michael Moore, "What Happened?" *MichaelMoore.com* (12 September 2001); Chalmers Johnson, "Blowback," *The Nation* (15 October 2001); Peter Beinart, "Fault Lines," *The New Republic* (10 November 2001); and Noam Chomsky "Drain the Swamp," *The Guardian* (9 September 2002).

18. "It is fair to say that, in the days and weeks following September 11th, the emotions of Canadians ranged from anger and determination to feelings of bewilderment and vulnerability." Chris Baker, "Canada after September 11th: A Public Opinion Perspective" (Canada: Environics Research Group, 2002).

19. Ibid.

20. "The Prime Minister's Words," *Globe and Mail* (15 September 2001), p. A14; see also John Ibbitson, "The World Mourns," *Globe and Mail* (15 September 2001), p. A1.

21. "Canadians Now Feel Closer to Americans: Poll," *CBC.ca* (27 September 2001).

22. Robert Fulford, "U.S. Bashing No Longer a Game," *National Post* (14 September 2001).

23. Robert Fulford, "Chaos v. Civilization? We're Neutral," *National Post* (24 November 2001).

24. On the second anniversary of the terrorist attacks, Fulford remained committed to this view. He wrote of the War on Terror: "Canada has de-

veloped its own independent strategy for this war: Help a bit, lay low, hope things will work out for the best and criticize the Americans whenever possible while co-operating with their security plans when absolutely necessary. Having lost our military strength through decades of cost-cutting and our political significance through a persistent refusal to face reality, we have placed ourselves outside the great struggle of this epoch. Our government finds this the most expedient course, and many Canadians, possibly even a majority, like it that way. We have chosen to be spectators rather than participants in history." Robert Fulford, "This War Did Not Begin In 2001," *National Post* (11 September 2003).

25. Margaret Wente, "They Had It Coming?" *Globe and Mail* (15 September 2001), p. A21.

26. "Bashing Our Friend," *National Post* (15 September 2001).

27. Naomi Klein, "Game Over," *Globe and Mail* (14 September 2001). See also Naomi Klein, "Fuel for Terror," *The Guardian* (24 September 2001).

28. Haroon Siddiqui, "It's the U.S. Foreign Policy, Stupid," *Toronto Star* (19 September 2001).

29. Haroon Siddiqui, "A Letter to Our American Friends," *Toronto Star* (13 September 2001).

30. Tamara Sulliman, "US Tragedy Stuns UTM Students," *The Medium* 28:3 (17 September 2001).

31. September Eleventh Peace Coalition, "War Is Not the Answer," (October 2001?).

32. See "Don't Surrender Sovereignty in Rush to Embrace America: Copps," *Peterborough Examiner* (7 March 2002); "Sheila Copps' Latest Embarrassment," *National Post* (22 February 2002); and David Orchard, "Critical Thought in Wake of U.S. Terror," *Edmonton Journal* (7 October 2001).

33. James Laxer, "Stand on Guard for Canada," *Globe and Mail* (9 October 2001), p. A23.

34. Richard Gwyn, *Nationalism without Walls: The Unbearable Lightness of Being Canadian* (Toronto: McClelland and Stewart, 1995).

35. Richard Gwyn, "We Must Accept the Inevitable," *Toronto Star* (29 Sept 2001).

36. Richard Gwyn, "We've Grown in the Wake of Tragedy," *Toronto Star* (17 October 2001).

37. Kevin Michael Grace, "A Nation That No Longer Believes in Itself," *Report* (22 October 2001), pp. 17–20.

38. Dalton Camp, "Canada Need Not Be Lockstep with U.S.," *Toronto Star* (29 September 2001).

39. Dalton Camp, "We Like Americans But Not Their Politics," *Toronto Star* (3 October 2001).

40. Peter Gzowski, "Being Anti-U.S. Is Like Being Anti-Winter. In the End, You Love Them Both," *Globe and Mail* (15 September 2001), p. F3.

41. "Attack on the U.S.A.: The Consequences for Canada," *CBC.ca* (n.d.).

42. Heather Sokoloff, "CBC National Town Hall Too Local: Ombudsman," *National Post* (26 November 2001).

43. David Bazay, cited in ibid.

44. Ibid.

45. Tony Burman, cited in ibid.

46. Lydia Miljan, cited in Eli Schuster, "CBC's Post-September 11 'Town Hall' Was a Toronto-Centric Exercise In U.S.-Bashing," *Report* (7 January 2002).

47. Ibid.

48. Dalton Camp, "Fraser Freedom Fighters Are a Tad Upset," *Toronto Star* (31 October 2001).

49. See Michael Posner, "You've Got to Hand It to the Aspers: They Sure Know How to Wage a Fight," *Globe and Mail* (6 March 2002).

50. Sunera Thobani, "Presentation to the Ottawa Women's Resistance Conference" (1 October 2001). This excerpt is from the transcript posted by the Cable Public Affairs Channel.

51. "The Right to Speak Out," *Globe and Mail* (11 October 2001), p. A20.

52. Margaret Wente, "Two Reasons to Thank Sunera Thobani," *Globe and Mail* (4 October 2001), p. A19.

53. "Cheap Sloganeering," *National Post* (3 October 2001).

54. See Hayley Mick, "Critics Question Media Coverage of Thobani's Speech," *UBC Journalism Review* 4:2 (December 2001).

55. Ian Brown, "Why They'll Give Thanks," *Globe and Mail* (6 October 2001).

56. John Manley, cited in "Feminist's Charge on U.S. Policy Draws Political Fire," *Globe and Mail* (2 October 2001).

57. Gordon Campbell, cited in ibid.

58. Terry O'Neill, "I Was a Victim of Sunera Thobani's Hate Speech," *Alberta Report* (5 November 2001).

59. "Idiocy Watch #2," *The New Republic* (5 October 2001).

60. *Hansard* 37th Parliament, Number 89 (1 October 2001).

61. *Hansard* 37th Parliament, Number 90 (2 October 2001).

62. Sunera Thobani, "War Frenzy," *Rabble* (24 October 2001).

63. Judy Rebick, "Soaked in Censorship," *Rabble* (October 2001).

64. Michele Landsberg, "Unmasking the Bigotry behind the Hysteria," *Toronto Star* (14 October 2001).

65. J.L. Granatstein, "Our Best Friend—Whether We Like It or Not," *National Post* (23 October 2002). See also J.L. Granatstein and Norman Hillmer, "Those Damn Yankees," *Maclean's* (22 October 2001), pp. 58–9.

66. Granatstein, "Our Best Friend."

67. Ibid. See also Yves Fortier, "Time to Grow Up," *National Post* (25 January 2002); and Shawn McCarthy, "Grow Up, Manley Tells Canada," *Globe and Mail* (4 September 2002).

68. Fortier, "Time to Grow Up."

69. Edward Greenspon, "Suddenly, We're at War," *Globe and Mail* (8 October 2001), p. A17.

70. See Stephen Clarkson, *Uncle Sam and Us: Globalization, Neoconservatism and the Canadian State* (Toronto: University of Toronto Press, 2002), pp. 401–5.

71. "'First Great Struggle of 21st Century': PM," *CBC.ca* (9 October 2001).

72. Allan R. Gregg, "Now It's Safety First," *Maclean's* (15 October 2001), p. 32.

73. Stockwell Day, "Let's Stand by Our PM," *Globe and Mail* (12 October 2001), p. A17.

74. Andrew Coyne, "Mr. Chrétien Leads from the Rear," *National Post* (10 October 2001). It was, arguably, President Bush himself who inspired such criticism of Jean Chrétien. In his speech to Congress on 20 September, references to Canada had been "deliberately cut," apparently because the President had been "annoyed that Canada had not matched British and Australian offers of military assistance." See "Canada Was Purposely Cut from 2001 Speech, Frum Says," *Globe and Mail* (8 January 2003), p. A8.

75. "Canadians weren't, and aren't, the primary target of terrorists. That sad distinction belongs to Americans." Anthony Wilson-Smith, "America, Canada and Life amidst a New Form of Cold War," *Maclean's* (24 September 2001), p. 2. See also Tonda MacCharles, "We're Both at Risk, Powell Tells Canada," *Toronto Star* (15 November 2002).

76. George W. Bush, *Speech* (31 January 2002).

77. George Grant, *Lament for a Nation* (Toronto: McClelland and Stewart, 1965), p. 86.

78. Granatstein, "Our Best Friend."

CONCLUSION

THE END OF AN ERA?

"The fight for Canadian distinctiveness is fundamentally over."
MAUDE BARLOW, CHAIRPERSON, COUNCIL OF CANADIANS (2001)

"Put bluntly, the nation-state called Canada has
become an empty shell of its former self."
JOHN GRAY, PLAYWRIGHT (2001)

Until the autumn of 2002, I confess that I was one of those who saw in Canada's breakneck accommodation to post-September 11th America the national eclipse that George Grant had prophesied in *Lament for a Nation*. The calculated silencing of nationalist voices described in the last chapter was accompanied, in what seemed to me a rather cruel irony, by the deaths of Dalton Camp and Peter Gzowski—two of English Canada's most distinguished left-nationalists and men whose love for Canada was patently obvious even to their critics. The permanent loss of these two elder patriots and the withdrawal of others (most notably Richard Gwyn) appeared to have left the leadership of the nationalist camp in the hands of those who can only be called lesser lights—Sheila Copps, David Orchard, Svend Robinson, Buzz Hargrove—individuals with vested political interests, strident personalities and limited intellectual credentials. There remained a scattering of nationalist thinkers with the credibility, the acumen and the national exposure to perhaps fill the shoes of the elders—James Laxer, Rick Salutin, John Godfrey and Tom Walkom come to mind—but they were thin on the ground. Nationalist stalwarts Maude Barlow and Mel Hurtig maintained their comparatively high visibility but their interest in Canadian sovereignty appeared to have become "diffused" and unfocused.[1] As noted in Chapter Six, nationalism appeared not to have caught the imaginations of young Canadians except in the most superficial of forms, leaving in doubt whether as an ideology it had any but the most vestigial lease on life.

There was also the fact that Prime Minister Jean Chrétien was, to borrow Stephen Clarkson's understated phrase, "comfortable with continentalism."[2] He had campaigned against NAFTA during the election of 1993, only to embrace it when in office; and as noted in Chapter Seven, his mid-Nineties conversion to neo-conservatism had gutted the very social programs and cultural subsidies that had been the hallmark of left-nationalist politics under his Liberal predecessors. Despite his undoubtedly sincere professions of love for Canada and his unimpeachable commitment to federalism, Chrétien studiously avoided what might be called visionary pronouncements on the destiny of the nation, a misstep that very nearly cost him the 1995 Quebec referendum. He appeared to adopt what he no doubt believed was a safe ideological middle ground—that is, between the uncompromisingly continentalist Alliance, on the one hand, and the uncompromisingly separatist Bloc Québécois, on the other. The overtly nationalist ministers in his cabinet, most notably Sheila Copps, he relegated to economically inconsequential portfolios; the most pro-American of his ministers, most notably John Manley, found themselves on the fast track within the most powerful federal departments. As the *Washington Post* reported in 2001, many of Canada's leading lights—"corporate chieftains, university presidents and government officials"—were "demoralised by Chrétien's failure to launch a bold program that could reinvigorate the country's sense of self."[3] Where Paul Martin, Jr., stood was anybody's guess for virtually the entirety of his tenure as Finance Minister. Although rumoured to harbour deep suspicions of continentalizing influences arising within the United States, Martin rarely said or did anything that undermined them; he served as the government's leading spokesperson for freer trade, and in 2003 he campaigned for the leadership of the Liberal party on a platform that included "strengthen[ing] the friendship between our two countries."[4]

Chrétien was, of course, in some measure a captive of the political culture of his times, notwithstanding claims that he governed like a friendly dictator. After NAFTA—and especially after September 11th—he had little choice but to accept the realities of continental trade and security priorities, and not only due to pressures emanating from south of the border. Throughout 2002 polls showed that the great majority of Canadians wanted "even closer economic ties to the United States to increase their standard of living."[5] The number of Canadians "adamantly opposed" to greater economic integration with the US—once the benchmark for economic nationalists in Canada—had dropped to a meagre 5 per cent.[6] Almost half of Canadians expressed support for an "integrated defence policy," while almost two-thirds said they would like to see "environmental policies developed in an integrated and coordinated manner."[7] As noted in the last chapter, the term *nationalism* was routinely paired in the press with the adjective *knee-jerk*, while the defence of Canadian sovereignty was mocked as little more than "recreational bitching at the United States."[8]

Moreover, although Chrétien faced a weak and divided opposition in the House of Commons, it cannot have escaped his notice that, outside of his own caucus, English-Canadian nationalists were almost to a person crowded into the beleaguered New Democratic Party. The conflation of nationalism with socialism in Canada had, in fact, become a running joke among commentators intoning the NDP's pathetic backwardness and irrelevance.[9] Certainly as a species the venerable "red Tory" appeared extinct; this was the not-so-subtle meaning of Joe Clark's observation that David Orchard, the outspoken opponent of free trade who ran for the Tory leadership in 2003, was a "tourist" in the party.[10] Meanwhile on the neo-conservative Right, newly minted Alliance leader Stephen Harper calculated that his party's best hope for defeating the Liberals would be to adopt an aggressively continentalist platform, the likes of which Canadians had never seen. In March 2002, in his inaugural speech in the House of Commons as Leader of the Opposition, Harper made Canadian support for the United States a defining issue for himself and his party, embracing American missile-defence policies, rejecting the international land-mines treaty, and trumpeting the commonsense wisdom that Canada and the United States were inextricably bound: "If the United States prospers, we prosper. If the United States hurts or is angry, we will be hurt. If it is ever broadly attacked, we will surely be destroyed."[11]

To an extent that seems astonishing even now, this formidable post-nationalist consensus on Canada's relationship with the United States was shattered on the first anniversary of the September 11th terrorist attacks. In a CBC interview aired on that evening, Prime Minster Jean Chrétien calmly and unambiguously stated his view that the West bore some responsibility for the socio-economic conditions that nurture international terrorism:

> You cannot exercise your powers to the point of humiliation for the others. That is what the Western world—not only the Americans, the Western world—has to realize. Because they are human beings too. There are long-term consequences. And I do think that the Western world is getting too rich in relation to the poor world and necessarily will be looked upon as being arrogant and self-satisfied, greedy and with no limits. The 11th of September is an occasion for me to realize it even more.[12]

In one fell swoop, Chrétien undermined the orthodox view within Canada that September 11th existed outside history and, with it, the prohibition on critical analysis of US foreign policy.

Within hours, Chrétien's remarks were making headline news throughout Canada, igniting a fervent national debate which, seen in retrospect, must have been smoldering below the guarded silence of the previous year. For some, the Prime Minister's comments were tantamount to "urinating on the graves" of the September 11th victims, as one radio host put it.[13] Stephen Harper expressed outrage: "Chrétien's comments, particularly coming on the anniversary of 9-11, blaming the victim, are shameful. What was behind the events of Sept. 11 are the forces of evil and hatred."[14] Some prominent Liberals defended their leader unequivocally. Foreign Affairs Minister Bill Graham said: "I think the prime minister's comments were right on."[15] Allan Rock, the Industry Minister, agreed, issuing a statement urging "responsible leaders" to "ask themselves some hard questions. Questions about whether the exercise of foreign policy has been just. Or whether the concentration of power and wealth in the hands of a few serves to abandon the less fortunate to the despair, resentment and hatred which fuels extremism."[16] Deputy Prime Minister John Manley equivocated but fell in behind his leader:

> I reject any kind of suggestion that there's a moral equivalency between somebody's views on U.S. foreign policy or on the environment or on poverty and saying that justifies using an aircraft as a bomb. [But] we need to work on the causes of despair. You can't have a world of peace unless you deal with the world of need. And as long as large parts of the world are living on less than $1 a day, there's going to be unrest, discontent and some people—just out of sheer frustration—are going to become suicide bombers or whatever.[17]

What, exactly, Jean Chrétien meant by his remarks or how he expected Canadians (and others) to interpret them are not yet matters of the public record but, canny and cautious politician that he is, he must have known that he was venturing onto extremely sensitive ground. That the Prime Minister had in fact taped the interview the preceding July—giving him many weeks to ponder, reconsider or even retract his comments—implies not only considerable forethought but also a calculated political gambit that on the anniversary he would be speaking on behalf of a good many Canadians. Two days after the airing of the interview, presumably in response to the firestorm that had followed, the Prime Minister's Office issued the following clarification: "It is a gross misconstruction of his remarks to suggest that he was blaming the United States for the attacks."[18] Yet the Prime Minister did not prevaricate, affirming on the same day that he "he meant every word of his comments...."[19] On 16 September 2002, speaking in New York to the United Nations General Assembly special session on Africa, Chrétien reiterated his concern about poverty and desperation in the developing world, explicitly telling reporters afterwards that although Osama bin Laden is not poor, he "use[s] people who are the products of misery."[20] As columnist Chantal Hébert noted, Chrétien's remarks "put him squarely in the mainstream of G-8 leadership" — no less critical of western selfishness than British Prime Minister Tony Blair, and far less so than either German Chancellor Gerhard Schroeder or French President Jacques Chirac.[21]

Pollsters disagreed about the extent to which Canadians concurred with Chrétien's statement. An Ipsos-Reid poll taken on 7 September 2002 — several days prior to the airing of the Prime Minster's remarks — found that "84 per cent of Canadians believe the United States bore at least some responsibility for the stunning attacks."[22] A *National Post*/COMPAS poll taken just after the airing of the interview, in contrast, found that "[o]nly 22% of Canadians believe Jean Chrétien's statements linking Western policies and terrorism are essentially right."[23] Whether, in fact, the Prime Minster did speak for Canadians became one of the burning questions in the national debate. On September 13, American TV-news anchor Shepard Smith asked Stephen Harper to comment on the Ipsos-Reid poll. Harper responded: "I think Canadians have been frankly shocked and outraged by the comments of the Prime Minister. I just want to make it clear... that Canadians understand that the responsibility for the attacks in New York last year were 100 per cent, and no less, the responsibility of the kind of dark, evil and hateful forces that represent organizations like al-Qaeda."[24] In contrast, *Toronto Star* columnist Haroon Siddiqui ventured the observation that "Prime Minister Jean Chrétien has been reflecting the public mood better than our media." Whether or not Canadians agreed with the Prime Minister, wrote Siddiqui, there was a larger question at stake: "The issue here is not whether Canadians and Europeans are right or wrong in, in effect, blaming the victim. Rather, it is that they do hold such views; that they are entitled to such views in their free and democratic societies; and that their views deserve to be heard and debated in their free and open media...." [25]

There is evidence to suggest that Chrétien had indeed gauged Canadians' sentiments astutely, notwithstanding the patent defeatism in the ranks of nationalists noted above. In January 2002, for example, a handful of Liberal "backbenchers" (including Bonnie Brown, Steve Mahoney, Carolyn Bennett, John Harvard and John Godfrey) openly urged the government "to remind Americans that Canada has its own priorities and its own values." [26] They worried not only that the hasty erection of the "North American security perimeter" might have irrevocable consequences for Canadian sovereignty but that the government had rushed far too precipitously to join George W. Bush's War on Terror. John Godfrey was quoted as saying: "George Bush has declared that the war on terrorism is the cause of his generation. National sovereignty will be the cause of ours." [27] Recognizing that such statements threatened the full-blown continentalism that it had done so much to promote since September 11th, the *National Post* responded to these renegade Liberal nationalists with unvarnished contempt:

After a rocky start in the days after Sept. 11, the federal government is doing and saying more or less the right things. But some of its backbenchers are still hiding resentfully in their Trudeau-era redoubt. Oh, they are happy to be lobby fodder when the government proposes sluicing billions of dollars into "job creation" or some other sinkhole. But when it comes to a really important task—the defeat of a murderous conspiracy—they dig in their heels and refuse to get on the right side of history. [28]

Godfrey—himself a former *National Post* editor—responded to this invective directly. While he considered the September 11th attacks "despicable" and believed that Canada's joining the War on Terror was "consistent with the exercise of our national sovereignty," he insisted that "by linking the war on terrorism so closely with keeping the border open for trade and investment, we run the risk of undermining Canadian sovereignty in the long run."[29]

In the months that followed this exchange, with an American-led war against Iraq increasingly likely, the question of whether or not Canada ought to fall in behind the United States became linked, albeit tentatively, with a more generalized discussion of Canadian sovereignty.[30] George W. Bush's invocation of an "axis of evil" (Iran, Iraq and North Korea)—a turn of phrase which raised hackles even within the United States—abetted this process.[31] So, too, did several undiplomatic remarks about Canadians from the Bush Administration. In March 2002, for example, the US Ambassador to Canada, Paul Cellucci, remarked that he did not think "the average Canadian wakes up every morning worried about sovereignty."[32] The same month it was revealed that "White House officials" used the nickname "Dino" (as in dinosaur) to refer to Prime Minster Jean Chrétien, apparently because he was perceived to be an "unreconstructed guy who hasn't quite changed with the world...."[33] *Toronto Star* columnist Gordon Barthos noted perceptively that "Jean Chrétien's government is finding its nationalist voice again, after months of soft-pedalling policy differences with Washington out of deference for our neighbours' grief and rage."[34] Cabinet "hawk" John Manley called Bush's pronouncements "bellicose."[35] Bill Graham, who was anxious to re-establish the primacy of the External Affairs Department in Canada's dealings with the United States, put the new spirit of independence in Canadian foreign policy in the context of the changed political climate since 9/11: "Immediately after Sept. 11 there was a natural, tremendous rallying around the United States. But we've always said 'We stand beside you, but we don't jump how high you tell us to jump.'"[36]

On 18 April 2002, four members of the Princess Patricia's Canadian Light Infantry were killed by a 250-kilogram American bomb in a "friendly fire" incident. "On radio call-in shows, in coffee shops and on news Web sites," announced the front page of the *Globe and Mail* the next day, Canadians "voiced their rage" at the tragedy.[37] Whether, in fact, Canadians were more angry than shocked and grieved is difficult to gauge. It is clear, however, that despite overtures from Defence Minister Art Eggleton to the effect that the incident would have no bearing on Canada's "long-range defence and security co-operation with the United States," the government was sufficiently anxious about "anti-U.S. feelings by the public" that it cancelled a Defence Department presentation "seeking permission for a mandate to negotiate greater military co-operation with the United States."[38] In what appears to have been an unplanned coincidence, U.S. Defence Secretary Donald Rumsfeld announced the creation of a new continental "Northern Command" on the same day as the friendly fire incident. Described as "the biggest reform to America's military command since the Second World War," the "area of operations" of the new command structure was to include Canada, Mexico and parts of the Caribbean. That the American head of Northern Command was also to be given authority over NORAD suggests the that the Bush Administration may have taken Canadian participation for granted, though this was never stated explicitly. In any case, there was little ambiguity in Jean Chrétien's response to the proposal:

> The sovereignty of Canada cannot be taken away by this decision made by the administration of the United States. This decision by the American administration about their own defence, it is their own business. The defence of Canada will be assured by the Canadian government and not by the American government.[39]

By the time of Jean Chrétien's 9/11 anniversary remarks, in short, Canadians' post-September 11th support for American defence initiatives at home and abroad appeared to be waning, so much so that the Prime Minister could openly resist continentalizing pressures in the name of "Canadian sovereignty" even when it aggravated the Bush Administration and frustrated his own defence advisers.[40] The "Canadian question" had again—unexpectedly—become a subject of national debate. As *Globe and Mail* columnist John Ibbitson observed, somewhat pejoratively:

Iraq. Kyoto. Health care. Any one of these issues could keep the capital humming for months. But this is a once-in-a-generation autumn, a political season dominated by no fewer than three large, complex and highly controversial issues. And they are linked. Each reflects the determination of a retiring prime minister to reassert Canadian independence from the United States, even if it means risking our political and economic future.[41]

As it has turned out, Ibbitson was not correct on all counts. Anxiety about threats to Canadian sovereignty — and the nationalist impulse that anchored it — was not merely the peccadillo of a retiring Prime Minister, but a powerful sentiment that seemed to be shared by many of the people of Canada. In May 2003, Foreign Affairs Minister Bill Graham completed a three-month "cross-country dialogue on Canada's role in the world," and found, apparently to his own surprise and consternation, that "[c]itizens are willing to pay a price for standing up to the United States on the world stage. They believe that pursuing an independent foreign policy is fundamental to Canadian sovereignty, whatever the economic repercussions."[42] Polls revealed that, far more than Americans or most Europeans, Canadians "really like" themselves.[43] Richard Gwyn confidently reclaimed his role as a left-nationalist standard-bearer, and others fell in behind him.[44] Most surprisingly of all, perhaps, Tory "tourist" David Orchard cut a secret deal with new party leader Peter MacKay in which the latter "agreed not to seek a merger with the Canadian Alliance and to review Brian Mulroney's hailed free-trade agreement."[45] To paraphrase Mark Twain, rumours of the death of Canadian nationalism turned out to be greatly exaggerated.

Although sorting out the myriad nuances of this unexpected ideological twist in the post-9/11 Canadian story must await a longer view, it is already apparent that the sovereignty debate will not be thwarted by insult and insinuation the way it was after September 11th. Undeniably, *bona fide* anti-Americanism has reared its head — most notably when Liberal communications director Françoise Ducros was overheard calling George W. Bush a "moron" and when Liberal MP Carolyn Parrish remarked: "Damn Americans, hate those bastards." Yet it is also clear that despite the continuing efforts of continentalist politicians and editorialists in Canada to dismiss all anxiety about Canadian sovereignty as "immature" anti-Americanism, Canadians will no longer accede to such partisan over-simplification. This refusal became especially pointed when Canadians had to decide whether to fall in behind George W. Bush's war on Iraq. The question was not merely whether or not Canadians and Americans were "family," to borrow Ambassador Cellucci's phrase, or whether Canadians had "let Americans down." This was a debate about first principles, about whether Canadian "human security initiatives" had any place in a post-9/11 world of American *realpolitik*, about whether multilateralism — as seen in Canada's support for a land-mines ban, the Kyoto Protocol and the International Criminal Court — could survive a in a world more polarized than it had been at any time since the Cold War. In March 2003, just days before the start of the US bombing campaign over Baghdad and other Iraqi cities, a *La Presse*/EKOS poll found that 71 per cent of Canadians supported the decision of the Liberal government not to participate in the conflict. The same poll also noted an "almost unprecedented awareness and interest among Canadians in the war and this country's role."[46] Canadians led by Jean Chrétien had refused to be cowed; they had decided for themselves.

NOTES

1. See Terry Goldie, "Blame Canada," *Essays on Canadian Writing* 71 (Fall 2000), pp. 224–31.

2. Stephen Clarkson, *Uncle Sam and Us: Globalization, Neoconservatism and the Canadian State* (Toronto: University of Toronto Press, 2002), p. 389.

3. Stephen Pearlstein, "Canada, USA?" *Washington Post* (29 January 2001).

4. Paul Martin, cited in Anne Dawson, "'Strengthening Friendship' with U.S. a Priority," *National Post* (29 April 2003). See also Lawrence Martin, "Future PM Is No Fan of Mr. Bush," *Globe and Mail* (26 September 2002), p. A19; and Clarkson, *Uncle Sam and Us*, pp. 286–7.

5. Robert Fife, "66% Favour Stronger Ties To US," *National Post* (21 October 2002). See also Alan Toulin, "Canadians Want Closer U.S. Ties:

Poll," *National Post* (18 June 2002); and Alanna Mitchell, "Canadians Support Closer Ties with U.S.," *Globe and Mail* (29 April 2002).

6 . Fife, "66% Favour Stronger Ties to US."

7. Toulin, "Canadians Want Closer U.S. Ties: Poll."

8. Margaret Wente, "They Had It Coming?" *Globe and Mail* (15 September 2001), p. A21.

9. See, for example, Allan Fotheringham, "NDP Hero Finds Party in Shambles," *Globe and Mail* (2 March 2002), p. A2.

10. See Jane Taber, "Rise Of 'Tourist' No Accident," *Globe and Mail* (2 June 2003), p. A5; and Andrew McIntosh, "Orchard 'Should Be Running for the NDP'," *National Post* (27 May 2003).

11. Stephen Harper, cited in Brian Laghi, "Harper Adopts Strong Stance in Favour of the U.S.," *Globe and Mail* (29 May 2002), p. A5.

12. Jean Chrétien, cited in Sheldon Alberts, "PM Links Attacks to 'Arrogant' West," *National Post* (12 September 2002).

13. Cited in "PM's 9/11 Comments Spark Lively Debate," *Toronto Star* (13 September 2002).

14. Stephen Harper, cited in Allison Dunfield, "PMO Blames Media for Misreporting Sept. 11 Comments," *Globe and Mail* (13 September 2002).

15. Bill Graham, cited in "PM's 9/11 Comments Spark Lively Debate."

16. Allan Rock, cited in Steven Edwards, "PM Adds Fuel to Sept. 11 Debate," *National Post* (17 September 2002).

17. John Manley, cited in "PM's 9/11 Comments Spark Lively Debate."

18. PMO, cited in Allison Dunfield, "PMO Blames Media for Misreporting Sept. 11 Comments."

19. "PM's 9/11 Comments Spark Lively Debate."

20. Jean Chrétien, cited in Allan Thompson, "PM Repeats Poverty Message," *Toronto Star* (17 September 2002).

21. Chantal Hébert, "PM Not Unique in Terror Analysis," *Toronto Star* (18 September 2002). A six-country poll conducted on behalf of the Chicago Council on Foreign Relations and the German Marshall Fund showed that a majority of people in France, Britain, Germany, Holland, Italy and Poland believed that "U.S. foreign policy was partly to blame for Sept. 11." Cited in Haroon Siddiqui, "Media Missing Canadian Perspective," *Toronto Star* (12 September 2002).

22. Ipsos-Reid poll, cited in Shawn McCarthy, "PM Says U.S. Attitude Helped Fuel Sept. 11," *Globe and Mail* (13 September 2002).

23. *National Post*/COMPAS poll, cited in Bill Curry, "Canada Divided on PM's 9/11 View," *National Post* (16 September 2002).

24. Stephen Harper, cited in "PM 'Outraged' Canadians, Harper Tells U.S. Network," *National Post* (14 September 2002). Ipsos-Reid responded to Harper's slur that "Liberal pollsters get Liberal results" by threatening to sue the Canadian Alliance, following which Harper publicly retracted the statement. See Shawn McCarthy, "Ipsos-Reid Takes Issue With Harper Criticism," *Globe and Mail* (18 September 2002); and Allison Dunfield, "Harper Apologizes To Ipsos-Reid," *Globe and Mail* (24 September 2002).

25. Siddiqui, "Media Missing Canadian Perspective."

26. Joan Bryden, "Liberal MPs Grow Tired of Unity with U.S.," *Southam News* (24 January 2002). See also Campbell Clark, "Grit MPs Worried over Deal with U.S.," *Globe and Mail* (15 December 2001), p. A15.

27. John Godfrey, cited in Bryden, "Liberal MPs Grow Tired of Unity with U.S."

28. "Forget Terrorism. Where's Our 'Payoff'?" *National Post* (25 January 2002).

29. John Godfrey, "Afghan Prisoners a Test for Our Sovereignty," *National Post* (30 January 2002).

30. See, for example, William Thorsell, "Cause for A Rebel: Vive l'Amérique du Nord," *Globe and Mail* (11 February 2002), p. A15; Barry Cooper and David Bercuson, "Finding Our Place in the U.S. Orbit," *Calgary Herald* (9 January 2002); and "Don't Surrender Sovereignty in Rush to Embrace America: Copps," *Peterborough Examiner* (7 March 2002).

31. See John Ibbitson, "Bush's Tough Talk Stirs Allies, Foes," *Globe and Mail* (31 January 2002), p. A12; and Jim Travers, "Go-Slow Approach Makes Sense," *Toronto Star* (21 February 2002).

32. Paul Cellucci, cited in Steven Chase, "Canadians Concerned about Threats, Cellucci Says," *Globe and Mail* (27 March 2002), p. A9.

33. Christopher Sands, director of the Canada Project at the Centre for Strategic and International Studies, cited in Mike Trickey and Sheldon Alberts, "Chrétien and Bush Remain Chilly Allies," *National Post* (13 March 2002).

34. Gordon Barthos, "Pepping up Canada's Agenda," *Toronto Star* (14 February 2002).

35. John Manley, cited in ibid.

36. Bill Graham, cited in Allan Thompson, "Graham Keen to Take on U.S.," *Toronto Star* (6 June 2002). See also Allan Thompson, "Canada to Chart Own Course, Graham Vows," *Toronto Star* (22 January 2002); and Jeff Sallot, "Canada Won't Cede Priority to the U.S., Graham Vows," *Globe and Mail* (2 March 2002), p. A8.

37. Murray Campbell, "Nation's Grief Turns to Anger," *Globe and Mail* (19 April 2002), p. A1.

38. See Tim Harper, "Deaths Won't Affect U.S. Ties: Eggleton," *Toronto Star* (22 April 2002); and Mike Trickey, "Plans for Closer Ties with U.S. Stalled," Southam News (30 April 2002).

39. Jean Chrétien, cited in Allan Thompson, "PM Undecided on New Defence Link," *Toronto Star* (18 April 2002).

40. "For months, Washington and senior Canadian military officials have been putting pressure on the federal cabinet to join the North American command." Shawn McCarthy and Paul Koring, "Canada Opts out of American Plan to Defend Continent," *Globe and Mail* (18 April 2002), p. A1.

41. John Ibbitson, "Don't Look Now, But Canadian Nationalism Is Back," *Globe and Mail* (9 September 2002), p. A13.

42. Carol Goar, "Willing to Pay for Our Sovereignty," *Toronto Star* (3 May 2003). See also "Canadians Feel Stronger World Ties vs. U.S.: Study," *Toronto Star* (18 April 2003).

43. Michael Adams, "Good News for Canada," *Globe and Mail* (30 December 2002), p. A13.

44. See, for example, Richard Gwyn, "It's Not Our Fault We're Morally Superior to U.S.," *Toronto Star* (8 December 2002). See also Ken Kalturnyk, "Canadian Nationalism and the Struggle for Popular Sovereignty," *Canadian Dimension* (September/October 2002); James Laxer, "Wake Up Time," *Canadian Dimension* (November/December 2002); and Thomas Walkom, "Time to Get into a U.S. State of Mind," *Toronto Star* (10 June 2003).

45. Taber, "Rise of 'Tourist' No Accident."

46. Tim Harper, "Canadians Back Chrétien on War, Poll Finds," *Toronto Star* (24 March 2003). See also Lawrence Martin, "A Declaration of National Integrity," *Globe and Mail* (11 September 2003).

BIBLIOGRAPHY

Achieving Excellence: Investing in People, Knowledge and Opportunity. Ottawa: Industry Canada, 2002.

Adams, Ian, Lamar Carson and Goffredo Parise. "Our War." *Maclean's* (February 1968).

Adams, Mary Louise. *The Trouble with Normal: Postwar Youth and the Making of Heterosexuality*. Toronto: University of Toronto Press, 1997.

Adams, Michael. "Good News for Canada." *Globe and Mail* (30 December 2002).

_____. *Sex in the Snow: Canadian Social Values at the End of the Millennium*. Toronto: Viking/Penguin, 1997.

Alberts, Sheldon. "PM Links Attacks to 'Arrogant' West." *National Post* (12 September 2002).

_____. "PM 'Outraged' Canadians, Harper Tells U.S. Network." *National Post* (14 September 2002).

Allahar, Anton L. and James E. Coté. *Richer & Poorer: The Structure of Inequality in Canada*. Toronto: Lorimer, 1998.

Alliance Atlantis Communication Inc. *Investors' Overview*. Posted at allianceatlantis.com.

Alphonso, Caroline. "Canadians Are Now World's Best Educated." *Globe and Mail* (12 March 2003).

Anderssen, Erin. "Paycheques Show Generational Split." *Globe and Mail* (12 March 2003).

Angus, Ian. *A Border within: National Identity, Cultural Plurality and Wilderness*. Montreal: McGill-Queen's University Press, 1997.

Anisef, Paul and Paul Axelrod, eds. *Transitions: Schooling and Employment in Canada*. Toronto: Thompson, 1993.

Arnason, H.H. *History of Modern Art*, second edition. New York: Prentice-Hall, 1977.

"Attack on the U.S.A.: The Consequences for Canada." CBC.ca.

Attali, Jacques. *Noise: The Political Economy of Music*. Minneapolis: University of Minnesota Press, 1985.

Atwood, Margaret. *Survival: A Thematic Guide to Canadian Literature*. Toronto: Anansi, 1972.

_____. *Wilderness Tips*. Toronto: Bantam, 1996.

Audley, Paul. *Canada's Cultural Industries: Broadcasting, Publishing, Records and Film*. Toronto: Lorimer, 1983.

Augaitis, Daina, ed. *Eye of Nature*. Banff: Walter Phillips Gallery, 1991.

Axworthy, Thomas S. and Pierre Elliot Trudeau, eds. *Towards a Just Society*. Toronto: Penguin, 1990.

Ayres, Jeffrey M. "From National to Popular Sovereignty? The Evolving Globalization of Protest Activity

in Canada." *International Journal of Canadian Studies* 16 (Fall 1997).
_____. "National No More: Defining English Canada." *American Review of Canadian Studies* 25:2–3 (Summer-Fall 1995).

Bailey, Sue. "Program to Ease Student Debt Falls Short: Official." *Canadian Press* (27 February 2002).

Baker, Chris. "Canada after September 11th: A Public Opinion Perspective." Canada: Environics Research Group, 2002.

Baker, Maureen. *Canadian Family Policies: Cross-National Comparisons.* Toronto: University of Toronto Press, 1995.

Ballantyne, Morna, Dave Meslin, Judy Rebick, Svend Robinson and Jim Stanford. "The Left Needs New Voices." *Globe and Mail* (7 June 2001).

Bangs, Lester. "Review of *Canned Heat.*" *Rolling Stone* (7 February 1970).

Barclay, Michael, Ian A.D. Jack and Jason Schneider. *Have Not Been the Same: The CanRock Renaissance, 1985–1995.* Toronto: ECW Press, 2001.

Barlow, Maude and Bruce Campbell. *Straight Through the Heart: How the Liberals Abandoned the Just Society and What Canadians Can Do about It.* Toronto: HarperCollins, 1996.

Barthos, Gordon. "Pepping up Canada's Agenda." *Toronto Star* (14 February 2002).

Bashevkin, Sylvia B. *True Patriot Love: The Politics of Canadian Nationalism.* Toronto: Oxford University Press, 1991.

"Bashing Our Friend." *National Post* (15 September 2001).

Bateman, Jeff. "FACTOR Vetting Quality over Quantity." *The Record* (8 October 1990).

Batten, Jack. "Canada's Rock Scene: Going, Going…" *Maclean's* (February 1968).
_____. "The Guess Who." *Maclean's* (June 1971).

Beaujot, Roderic. *Population Change in Canada: The Challenges of Policy Adaptation.* Toronto: McClelland and Stewart, 1991.

Beauvais, Caroline, et al. *A Literature Review on Youth and Citizenship.* Ottawa: Canadian Policy Research Networks, 2001.

Beinart, Peter. "Fault Lines." *The New Republic* (10 November 2001).

Belz, Carl. *The Story of New Rock.* New York: Oxford, 1972.

Benzie, Robert. "A Scripted Appeal to Older Voters." *National Post* (28 March 2003).

Bercuson, David Jay, Robert Bothwell and J.L. Granatstein. *Petrified Campus: The Crisis in Canada's Universities.* Toronto, Random House, 1997.
_____. *The Great Brain Robbery: Canada's Universities on the Road to Ruin.* Toronto: McClelland and Stewart, 1984.

Berger, Carl. *The Sense of Power: Studies in the Ideas of Canadian Imperialism 1867–1914.* Toronto: University of Toronto Press, 1970.

Berger, John. *Ways of Seeing.* London: Penguin, 1972.

Berland, Jodi. "Locating Listening: Technological Space, Popular Music, Canadian Mediations." *Cultural Studies* 2 (1998).
_____. "Politics after Nationalism, Culture after 'Culture'." *Canadian Review of American Studies* 27: 3 (1997).

Bernstein, Robin and Seth Clark Silberman. *Generation Q: Gays, Lesbians and Bisexuals Born around 1969's Stonewall Riots Tell Their Stories of*

Growing up in the Age of Information.
Los Angeles: Alyson, 1996.

Bevilacqua, Maurizio. "Youth and Employment—the Issues." (1996). Retrieved from the Human Resources and Development Canada website: http://www.hrdc-drhc.gc.ca.

Bibby, Reginald W. and Donald C. Posterski. *Teen Trends: A Nation in Motion.* Toronto: Stoddart, 1992.

Bibby, Reginald W. *Canada's Teens: Today, Yesterday and Tomorrow.* Toronto: Stoddart, 2001.

_____. *The Bibby Report: Social Trends Canadian Style.* Toronto: Stoddart, 1995.

Bickley, Claire. "Fascist Immersed in Soapy Froth." *Toronto Sun* (13 November 1998).

_____. "Nominated Documentaries Air before Oscars." *Toronto Sun* (17 February 1998).

_____. "Shedding a Little Lite on the Past." *Toronto Sun* (3 December 1997).

Black, Conrad. "I Dreamt of Canada." *National Post* (16 November 2001).

Bliss, Michael. "Is Canada a Country in Decline?" *National Post* (30 November 2001).

_____. "'None of the Above'—On Coping with Political Alienation." *National Post* (9 September 2003).

_____. "Privatizing the Mind: The Sundering of Canadian History, The Sundering of Canada." *Journal of Canadian Studies* 26 (1991–2).

Bloom, Allan. *The Closing of the American Mind.* New York: Simon & Schuster, 1987.

Bordo, Jonathan. "Jack Pine: Wilderness Sublime or the Erasure of the Aboriginal Presence from the Landscape." *Journal of Canadian Studies* 27:4 (Winter 1992–3).

Botchford, Jason. "Canadians Flunk out in War History: Poll." *Toronto Sun* (11 November 1998).

Bothwell, Robert, Ian Drummond and John English. *Canada Since 1945: Power, Politics and Provincialism.* Toronto: University of Toronto Press, 1981.

Broadfoot, Barry. *Ten Lost Years 1929–1939: Memories of Canadians Who Survived the Depression.* Markham: Paperjacks, 1975.

Brooke, Jeffrey. *Hard Right Turn.* Toronto: HarperCollins, 1999.

Brown, Ian. "Why They'll Give Thanks." *Globe and Mail* (6 October 2001).

Bryden, Joan. "Liberal MPs Grow Tired of Unity with U.S." *Southam News* (24 January 2002).

Bunner, Paul. "Globalization or Canadianization: Take Your Pick." *Alberta Report* (14 May 2001).

Bush, George W. *Speech to Congress* (20 September 2001).

_____. *Speech* (31 January 2002).

Byfield, Ted. "How Come We're Paying People to Inflict Social Amnesia on Us?" *Alberta Report/Western Report* (12 June 1995).

_____. "We Don't Teach Canadian History Because It's Incompatible with Canadian Culture." *Alberta Report/Western Report* (4 May 1998).

Byfield, Virginia. "History, Beaten to Death by a Gang." *Alberta Report/Western Report* (4 May 1998).

"Cable Companies Plan History Networks." *American History Illustrated* 28:4 (September/October 1993).

Campbell, Murray. "Nation's Grief Turns to Anger." *Globe and Mail* (19 April 2002).

Camp, Dalton. "Canada Need Not Be Lockstep with U.S." *Toronto Star* (29 September 2001).

_____. "Fraser Freedom Fighters Are a Tad Upset." *Toronto Star* (31 October 2001).

_____. "We Like Americans But Not Their Politics." *Toronto Star* (3 October 2001).

"Canada among Top 5 in World Education Tests." *Canadian Press* (16 September 2003).

"Canada Was Purposely Cut from 2001 Speech, Frum Says." *Globe and Mail* (8 January 2003).

"Canadian Artists Resort to Re-Recording Songs." *The Record* (23 July 1990).

Canadian Association of Broadcasters. *A Submission to the Canadian Radio-Television and Telecommunications Commission with Respect to Public Notice.* CRTC 1998-44 (18 November 1998).

_____. "CRTC's Arbitrary Decision to Hike Canadian Content Hurts Listeners and Broadcasters Alike." Press Release (30 April 1998).

Canadian Independent Film Caucus. *A Level Playing Field for the Documentary* (29 June 1998).

"Canadians Feel Stronger World Ties vs. U.S.: Study." *Toronto Star* (18 April 2003).

"Canadians Now Feel Closer to Americans: Poll." *CBC.ca* (27 September 2001).

"Cancon Reg Has Industry Seeing Red." *The Record* (23 July 1990).

Cantin, Paul. *Alanis Morissette: You Oughta Know.* Toronto: Stoddart, 1997.

Carey, Elaine. "Jobs Elude Most Teens, Report Says." *Toronto Star* (19 January 1999).

_____. "Poor Economy Hit Young Hard, Analysis Says." *Toronto Star* (22 January 1999).

Carrick, Rob. "Four Years of University Education Will Cost You $92,292." *Globe and Mail* (30 August 2003).

CBC Press Release. "CBC Announces BCE Sponsorship of Season Two of *Canada: A People's History*." (7 August 2001).

_____. "CBC Delighted by Response to *Canada: A People's History*." (2 January 2001).

_____. "Season Two Fact Sheet." (1 September 2001).

Chase, Steven. "Canadians Concerned about Threats, Cellucci Says." *Globe and Mail* (27 March 2002).

"Cheap Sloganeering." *National Post* (3 October 2001).

Cherney, Elena. "Families Can't Afford 'Luxury' of Kids." *National Post* (23 December 1999).

Chomsky, Noam. "Drain the Swamp." *The Guardian* (9 September 2002).

_____. "On the Bombings." (13 September 2001).

"Chrysler Sponsors Céline Dion in Las Vegas." *Chrysler Corporation News Release* (16 January 2003).

Chwialkowska, Luiza. "Canada Tougher on Youth Crime than U.S." *National Post* (8 May 2000).

CIRPA. "Canadian Content." Toronto: CIRPA, 2000.

"CIRPA Study Recommends Ontario Support Program." *The Record* (15 October 1990).

Claridge, Thomas. "McMichael Agreement in Force." *Globe and Mail* (26 November 1996).

Clark, Campbell. "Grit MPs Worried over Deal with U.S." *Globe and Mail* (15 December 2001).

_____. "Immigration Targets Virtually Unchanged for 2003." *Globe and Mail* (31 October 2002).

Clarkson, Stephen. *Uncle Sam and Us: Globalization, Neoconservatism and the Canadian State.* Toronto: University of Toronto Press, 2002.

Cohen, Jason, and Michael Krugman. *Generation Ecch!* New York: Simon & Schuster, 1994.

Cole, Douglas. "Artists, Patrons and Public: An Inquiry into the Success of the Group of Seven." *Journal of Canadian Studies* 13 (1974).

Cole, Stephen. "Saying No to Zero Tolerance." *Globe and Mail* (30 August 2003).

Collins, Robert. *You Had to Be There: An Intimate Portrait of the Generation That Survived the Depression, Won the War and Re-Invented Canada.* Toronto: McClelland and Stewart, 1997.

"The Commission Approves the Applications by Alliance Atlantis Communications Inc...." CRTC Public Notice 1999-48 (20 May 1999).

Conlogue, Ray. "CanLit Gets Shot in the Arm as Thomas Allen Shows It Cares." *Globe and Mail* (14 February 2000).

Conway, John F. *The Canadian Family in Crisis.* Toronto: Lorimer, 1993.

Cooke, Stephen. "Adams Makes the Best of It." *The Halifax Herald* (4 January 2000).

Cooper, Barry and David Bercuson. "Finding Our Place in the U.S. Orbit." *Calgary Herald* (9 January 2002).

Coupland, Douglas. *Generation X: Tales for an Accelerated Culture.* New York: St. Martin's, 1991.

Coyne, Andrew. "Mr. Chrétien Leads from the Rear." *National Post* (10 October 2001).

Crane, David. "Banks Have Role to Play in Nation's Success." *Toronto Star* (18 December 2001).

Currie, Dawn H. *Girl Talk: Adolescent Magazines and their Readers.* Toronto: University of Toronto Press, 1998.

Curry, Bill. "Canada Divided on PM's 9/11 View." *National Post* (16 September 2002).

Dallaire, Christine and Claude Denis. "'If You Don't Speak French, You're Out': Don Cherry, the Alberta Francophone Games, and the Discursive Construction of Canada's Francophones." *Canadian Journal of Sociology* 25:4 (Fall 2000).

Danesi, Marcel. *Cool: The Signs and Meanings of Adolescence.* Toronto: University of Toronto Press, 1994.

Dawson, Anne. "'Strengthening Friendship' with U.S. a Priority." *National Post* (29 April 2003).

Day, Stockwell. "Let's Stand by Our PM." *Globe and Mail* (12 October 2001).

Decision. CRTC 99-106 (19 March 1999).

deGroot-Maggetti, Greg. "Putting the National Children's Agenda on Hold? Citizens for Public Justice Responds to the Federal Budget." (2 March 2000). Retrieved from the Citizens for Public Justice website: http://www.cpj.ca/budget/00/NCAhold.html.

Diamond, Beverley. "What's the Difference? Reflections on Discourses of Morality, Modernism and Mosaics in the Study of Music in Canada." *Canadian University Music Review* 21:1 (2000).

Dickinson, Paul and Jonathan Ellison. "Plugged into the Internet." *Canadian Social Trends* 55 (Ottawa: Statistics Canada, Winter 1999).

"Don't Surrender Sovereignty in Rush to Embrace America: Copps." *Peterborough Examiner* (7 March 2002).

Doob, Anthony N. et al. *Youth Crime and the Youth Justice System in Canada: A Research Perspective.* Toronto: University of Toronto Centre of Criminology, 1995.

Dunfield, Allison. "Harper Apologizes to Ipsos-Reid." *Globe and Mail* (24 September 2002).

_____. "PMO Blames Media for Misreporting Sept. 11 Comments." *Globe and Mail* (13 September 2002).

Edmunds, Nancy. "Review of *Wheatfield Soul*." *Rolling Stone* (14 June 1969).

Edwards, Steven. "PM Adds Fuel to Sept. 11 Debate." *National Post* (17 September 2002).

EKOS Research Associates. *Making Ends Meet: The 2001–2002 Student Financial Survey* (March 2003).

Elliot, Louise. "Ontario Rekindles Debate over Repeating Grades." Canadian Press (29 April 2001).

Emberley, Peter C. *Zero Tolerance: Hot Button Politics in Canada's Universities*. Toronto: Penguin, 1996.

Evaluation of the Sound Recording Development Program. Ottawa: Department of Canadian Heritage, Corporate Review Branch, April 2000.

"Executive Directors Report." *CIRPA Newsletter* (August 1990).

Farrell, David. "FM Regs Help Promote Fool's Gold." *The Record* (6 August 1990).

Feihl, John. "The Impact of the Canadian Content Regulations on the Canadian Recording Industry." *Association of Canadian Studies Newsletter* 12:3 (Fall 1990).

"Feminist's Charge on U.S. Policy Draws Political Fire." *Globe and Mail* (2 October 2001).

Fife, Robert. "66% Favour Stronger Ties to US." *National Post* (21 October 2002).

Finkel, Alvin et al. *History of the Canadian Peoples: 1867 to the Present*. Toronto: Copp Clark Pitman, 1993.

Finn Jr., Chester E. "Teachers, Terrorists, and Tolerance." *Commentary* 112: 5 (December 2000).

"'First Great Struggle of 21st Century': PM." *CBC.ca* (9 October 2001).

Flavelle, Dana. "Firms Ignore Jobless Youth." *Toronto Star* (25 June 1999).

Flynn, John. "It's All History Now." *Adweek* 46:18 (29 April 1996).

Foot, David K. with Daniel Stoffman. *Boom, Bust and Echo: How to Profit from the Coming Demographic Shift*. Toronto: Macfarlane Walter and Ross, 1996.

"Forget Terrorism. Where's Our 'Payoff'?" *National Post* (25 January 2002).

Fortier, Yves. "Time to Grow Up." *National Post* (25 January 2002).

Fotheringham, Allan. "NDP Hero Finds Party in Shambles." *Globe and Mail* (2 March 2002).

Freedland, Jonathon. "The Rise of the Non-Voter." *The Guardian* (12 December 2001).

Freiler, Christa and Paul Zarnke. "Putting the Poor Back on the Political Agenda." *Toronto Star* (26 August 2002).

Frum, David. *What's Right: The New Conservatism and What It Means for Canada*. Toronto: Random House, 1996.

Fulford, Robert. "Chaos v. Civilization? We're Neutral." *National Post* (24 November 2001).

_____. "The Young in History's Stream: Generation X and the Survival of Tradition." (Lecture presented at the University of Chicago, 16–18 May 1997).

_____. "This War Did Not Begin in 2001." *National Post* (11 September 2003).

_____. "U.S. Bashing No Longer a Game." *National Post* (14 September 2001).

_____. "1960s Prophet Saw the Internet Vision, But Not Its Scale." *Globe and Mail* (29 October 1999).

Gallaway, Burt and Joe Hudson, eds. *Youth in Transition: Perspectives on Research and Policy*. Toronto: Thompson, 1996.

Giese, Rachel. "Enough Dumbing Down of the News." *Rabble* (1 November 2001).

"Gilliland Proposes 30% Music Content for Daily Newspapers and Consumer Magazines." *The Record* (13 August 1990).

Glenn, David. "The War on Campus: Will Academic Freedom Survive?" *The Nation* (3 December 2001).

Goar, Carol. "Willing to Pay for Our Sovereignty." *Toronto Star* (3 May 2003).

Goddard, Peter. "A Maple Leaf on Every Turntable Means Made-in-Canada Pop Stars." *Maclean's* (November 1970).

_____. "Pop Record Makers Ignore Borders." *Toronto Star* (15 November 1980).

Godfrey, John. "Afghan Prisoners a Test for Our Sovereignty." *National Post* (30 January 2002).

Goldie, Terry. "Blame Canada." *Essays on Canadian Writing* 71 (Fall 2000).

Government Expenditures on Culture. Ottawa: Statistics Canada, October 1999.

Grace, Kevin Michael. "A Nation That No Longer Believes in Itself." *Report* (22 October 2001).

Granatstein, J.L and Norman Hillmer. "Those Damn Yankees." *Maclean's* (22 October 2001).

Granatstein, J.L "Our Best Friend—Whether We Like It Or Not." *National Post* (23 October 2002).

_____. *Who Killed Canadian History?* Toronto, HarperCollins, 1998.

Grant, George. *Lament for a Nation: The Defeat of Canadian Nationalism.* Toronto: McClelland and Stewart, 1965.

Gray, John. *Lost in North America: The Imaginary Canadian in the American Dream.* Vancouver: Talonbooks, 1994.

Greenspon, Edward. "Suddenly We're at War." *Globe and Mail* (8 October 2001).

Gregg, Allan R. "Brave New Époque." *Maclean's* 11:114 (6 April 1998).

_____. "Now It's Safety First." *Maclean's* (15 October 2001).

Griffiths, Franklin. *Strong and Free: Canada and the New Sovereignty.* Toronto: Stoddart, 1996.

Grossberg, Lawrence. *We Gotta Get Out of This Place: Popular Conservatism and Postmodern Culture.* New York and London: Routledge, 1992.

The Guess Who. "American Woman." Cirrus Music, 1970.

Gwyn, Richard. "It's Not Our Fault We're Morally Superior to U.S." *Toronto Star* (8 December 2002).

_____. *Nationalism without Walls: The Unbearable Lightness of Being Canadian.* Toronto: McClelland and Stewart, 1995.

_____. "Ottawa Fails to Lead Border Debate." *Toronto Star* (28 November 2001).

_____. "We Must Accept the Inevitable." *Toronto Star* (29 September 2001).

_____. "We've Grown in the Wake of Tragedy." *Toronto Star* (17 October 2001).

Gzowski, Peter. "Being Anti-U.S. Is Like Being Anti-Winter. In the End, You Love Them Both." *Globe and Mail* (15 September 2001).

Halstead, Ted. "A Politics for Generation X." *Atlantic Monthly* (August 1999)

Hamilton, Graeme. "Quebec's Baby Incentives Cost a Bundle." *National Post* (25 January 2002).

Hansard Number 3 (24 September 1997).

Hansard Number 72 (12 March 1998).

Hansard Number 89 (1 October 2001).

Hansard Number 90 (2 October 2001).

Harding, Katherine and Virginia Galt. "Job Market Prospects Chill Young Adults." *Globe and Mail* (14 December 2002).

Harper, Tim. "Alliance under Day Losing New Young Backers: Poll." *Toronto Star* (4 June 2001).

_____. "Canadians Back Chrétien on War, Poll Finds." *Toronto Star* (24 March 2003).

_____. "Deaths Won't Affect U.S. Ties: Eggleton." *Toronto Star* (22 April 2002).

"Harris Hits Back at His Critics in Academia." *National Post* (11 February 2000).

Heath-Rawlings, Jordan. "Third of Boomers Worry about Retirement Assets." *Globe and Mail* (3 September 2003).

Hébert, Chantal. "PM Not Unique in Terror Analysis." *Toronto Star* (18 September 2002).

Henighan, Tom. *The Presumption of Culture: Structure, Strategy and Survival in the Canadian Cultural Landscape*. Vancouver: Raincoast, 1996.

"Hire More Full-Time Federal Workers: Auditor General." CBC.ca (5 December 2001).

"History Channel Dumps Corporate Profile Series." *Advertising Age* (10 June 1996).

"History Channel to Debut." *History Today* 29:6 (February 1995).

"History Plan Rewritten." *Advertising Age* (7 June 1996).

Hitchens, Christopher. "America More Serious? You Must Be Joking." *The Guardian* (6 March 2002).

Hobsbawn, Eric. *Age of Extremes*. London: Abacus, 1994.

Hodgins, Bruce and Margaret Hobbs, eds. *Nastawgan: The Canadian North by Canoe and Snowshoe*. Toronto: Betelgeuse, 1985.

Hoffman, Tod. "Making History." *McGill News Alumni Quarterly* (Fall 2001).

Horowitz, David. "The Sick Mind of Noam Chomsky." *Salon* (26 September 2001).

Housser, F.B. *A Canadian Art Movement: The Story of the Group of Seven*. Toronto: Macmillan, 1926.

Howard, Victor. *We Were the Salt of the Earth! A Narrative of the On-to-Ottawa Trek and the Regina Riot*. Regina: Canadian Plains Research Centre, 1985.

Howell, Bill. "Upper Canada Romantic." *Maclean's* (May 1972).

Human Resources Development Canada. "Summative Evaluation of Youth Service Canada." (18 October 2000).

Hurst, Linda. "Are Young Voters Down for the Count?" *Toronto Star* (15 September 2003).

Hurtig, Mel. *Pay the Rent or Feed the Kids: The Tragedy and Disgrace of Poverty in Canada*. Toronto: McClelland and Stewart, 1999.

Ibbitson, John. "Bush's Tough Talk Stirs Allies, Foes." *Globe and Mail* (31 January 2002).

_____. "Don't Look Now, But Canadian Nationalism Is Back." *Globe and Mail* (9 September 2002).

_____. "The World Mourns." *Globe and Mail* (15 September 2001).

"Idiocy Watch #2." *The New Republic* (5 October 2001).

Johnson, Chalmers. "Blowback." *The Nation* (15 October 2001).

"Joni Mitchell." *Rolling Stone* (17 May 1969).

"Joni Mitchell Hangs It Up." *Rolling Stone* (13 December 1969).

Justus, Martha and Mike McCracken. "Securing the Future of Canadian Youth: A Review of the Landscape."

Monthly Economic Review 16:6 (27 November 1997).

Kallmann, Helmut et al., eds. *Encyclopedia of Music in Canada*. Toronto: University of Toronto Press, 1981.

Kalturnyk, Ken. "Canadian Nationalism and the Struggle for Popular Sovereignty." *Canadian Dimension* (September/October 2002).

Kaplan, William, ed. *Belonging: The Meaning and Future of Canadian Citizenship*. Montreal: McGill-Queen's University Press, 1993.

Kasinsky, Renee G. *Refugees from Militarism: Draft-Age Americans in Canada*. New Brunswick: Transaction Books, 1976.

Kealey, Gregory S. "Class in English-Canadian Historical Writing: Neither Privatizing, Nor Sundering." *Journal of Canadian Studies* 27:2 (Summer 1992).

Kealey, Linda, Ruth Pierson, Joan Sangster and Veronica Strong-Boag. "Teaching Canadian History in the 1990s: Whose 'National History' are We Lamenting." *Journal of Canadian Studies* 27:2 (Summer 1992).

Kershaw, Ian. *Hitler*, volume 1. London: Penguin, 1998.

Kerstetter, Steve. *Rags and Riches: Wealth Inequality in Canada*. Toronto: Canadian Centre For Policy Alternatives, December 2002.

Kettle, John. *The Big Generation*. Toronto: McClelland and Stewart, 1980.

Killan, Gerald. *Protected Places: A History of Ontario's Provincial Park System*. Toronto: Dundurn, 1993.

Klein, Naomi. "Game Over." *Globe and Mail* (14 September 2001).

_____. "Fuel for Terror." *The Guardian* (24 September 2001).

_____. *No Logo: Taking Aim at the Brand Bullies*. Toronto: Vintage, 2000.

Kostash, Myrna. *Long Way from Home: The Story of the Sixties Generation in Canada*. Toronto: Lorimer, 1980.

_____. *No Kidding: Inside the World of Teenage Girls*. Toronto: McClelland and Stewart, 1987.

_____. *The Next Canada: In Search of Our Future Nation*. Toronto: McClelland and Stewart, 2000.

_____. "The Pure, Uncluttered Spaces of Bruce Cockburn." *Saturday Night* (June 1972).

Kuper, Adam and Jessica Kuper, eds. *The Social Science Encyclopedia*, second edition. London: Routledge, 1989.

Lacey, Liam. "Little Labels Can Make a Big Mark." *Globe and Mail* (4 April 1986).

Laframboise, Donna. "The Sky Isn't Falling." *National Post* (16 May 2000).

Laghi, Brian. "Harper Adopts Strong Stance in Favour of the U.S." *Globe and Mail* (29 May 2002).

Landsberg, Michele. "Unmasking the Bigotry behind the Hysteria." *Toronto Star* (14 October 2001).

Laver, Ross. "The 'Lost Generation'." *Maclean's* 110:22 (2 June 1997).

Laxer, James. *False God: How the Globalization Myth has Impoverished Canada*. Toronto: Lester, 1993.

_____. *In Search of a New Left: Canadian Politics after the Neoconservative Assault*. Toronto: Viking, 1996.

_____. "Stand on Guard for Canada." *Globe and Mail* (9 October 2001).

_____. "The Left Reinvents the Zeal." *Globe and Mail* (26 July 2001).

_____. *The Undeclared War: Class Conflict in the Age of Cyber Capitalism*. Toronto: Viking, 1998.

_____. "Wake Up Time." *Canadian Dimension* (November/December 2002).

Lefebvre, Pierre and Philip Merrigan. "Assessing Family Policy in Canada:

A New Deal for Families and Children." *Choices* 9:5 (June 2003).

Leppert, Richard and Susan McClary, eds. *Music and Society*. London and New York: Cambridge University Press, 1987.

Levant, Ezra. *Youthquake*. Vancouver: The Fraser Institute, 1996.

Little, Bruce. "Ethnicity, Marriage Trends Causing Fertility Disparity with U.S." *Globe and Mail* (30 September 2002).

Litt, Paul. *The Muses, the Masses and the Massey Commission*. Toronto: University of Toronto Press, 1992.

Lorimer, Rowland and Donald Wilson, eds. *Communications Canada: Issues in Broadcasting and New Technologies*. Toronto: Kagan and Woo, 1988.

Luffman, Jackie. "Variations on a Theme: The Changing Music Scene." *Quarterly Bulletin from the Culture Statistics Program* (Statistics Canada) 11:4 (Winter 1999).

Lyman, Rick with Bill Carter. "In Little Time, Pop Culture Is Almost Back to Normal." *New York Times* (3 October 2001).

MacCharles, Tonda. "We're Both at Risk, Powell Tells Canada." *Toronto Star* (15 November 2002).

Macfarlane, John. "What if Anne Murray Were an American?" *Maclean's* (May 1971).

MacGregor, Roy. "The Extended Teen Generation: Why It's Sticking So Close to the Many Comforts of Home." *Globe and Mail* (8 September 2003).

MacInnis, Craig. "High Price of Selling Rock." *Toronto Star* (29 December 1987).

MacKinnon, Mark. "Young Voters Feel Disaffected." *Globe and Mail* (6 November 2000).

MacMillan, Ernest, ed. *Music in Canada*. Toronto: University of Toronto Press, 1955.

Males, Mike A. *The Scapegoat Generation: America's War on Adolescents*. Maine: Common Courage Press, 1996.

Mallan, Caroline. "McGuinty, Eves Chase 'Gray' Vote." *Toronto Star* (16 September 2003).

Markle, Robert. "Early Morning Afterthoughts." *Maclean's* (December 1971).

Marquardt, Richard. *Enter at Your Own Risk: Canadian Youth and the Labour Market*. Toronto: Between the Lines, 1998.

Martin, Lawrence. "A Declaration of National Integrity." *Globe and Mail* (11 September 2003).

_____. "Future PM Is No Fan of Mr. Bush." *Globe and Mail* (26 September 2002).

McBride, Stephen. *Paradigm Shift: Globalization and the Canadian State*. Halifax: Fernwood, 2001.

McCarthy, Shawn and Paul Koring. "Canada Opts Out of American Plan to Defend Continent." *Globe and Mail* (18 April 2002).

McCarthy, Shawn. "Grow Up, Manley Tells Canada." *Globe and Mail* (4 September 2002).

_____. "Ipsos-Reid Takes Issue With Harper Criticism." *Globe and Mail* (18 September 2002).

_____. "Most Think U.S. Partly to Blame For Sept. 11." *Globe and Mail* (7 September 2002).

_____. "PM Says U.S. Attitude Helped Fuel Sept. 11." *Globe and Mail* (13 September 2002).

McGill University. *Giving the Past a Future: Conference on the Teaching and Learning of Canadian History* (January 1999).

McIntosh, Andrew. "Orchard 'Should Be Running For the NDP'." *National Post* (27 May 2003).

McKay, John. "Four New Cable Outlets Getting Ready to Launch." Canadian Press (11 May 1997).

McKillop, A.B. "Who Killed Canadian History? A View from the Trenches." *Canadian Historical Review* 80:2 (1999).

McLaren, Leah. "Leah McLaren Looks Both Left and Right." *Globe and Mail* (13 September 1999).

McMichael, Robert. *One Man's Obsession*. Toronto: Prentice-Hall, 1986.

McQuaig, Linda. *Shooting the Hippo: Death by Deficit and Other Canadian Myths*. Toronto: Penguin, 1996.

Mick, Hayley. "Critics Question Media Coverage of Thobani's Speech." *UBC Journalism Review* 4:2 (December 2001).

Miller, Laura. "America the Ignorant." *Salon* (27 September 2001).

Miller, Mark Crispin. "Private Censorship." *The Nation* (22 October 2001).

Milrad, Aaron. "What Does the McMichael Collection Do Now?" *Globe and Mail* (26 November 1996).

Mitchell, Alanna. "Canadians Support Closer Ties with U.S." *Globe and Mail* (29 April 2002).

Modderno, Craig. "Guess Who: Good Business Partners." *Rolling Stone* (7 January 1971).

Moore, Christopher. "History Television: Stay Tuned." *Beaver* 78:1 (February/March 1998).

Moore, Michael. "What Happened?" *MichaelMoore.com* (12 September 2001).

Nasgaard, Roald. *The Mystic North: Symbolist Landscape Painting in Northern Europe and North America 1890–1940*. Toronto: University of Toronto Press, 1984.

National Council on Welfare. "Serious Concerns about the Levels of Poverty in Canada." (29 June 2003).

National Report—Canada: Ten-Year Review of the World Summit for Children. Ottawa: Government of Canada, 2002.

Nelson, Rob and John Cowan. *Revolution X: A Survival Guide for Our Generation*. New York: Penguin, 1994.

Newman, Peter C. *The Canadian Revolution: From Deference to Defiance*. Toronto: Viking, 1995.

"News They Won't Share." *Globe and Mail* (12 October 2001).

Nolan, Nicole. "Isn't It Ironic?... The Slickest New Nationalism Is in the Latest Wave of Beer Ads." *This Magazine* 30:3 (November/December 1996).

O'Neill, Brenda. "Generational Patterns in the Political Opinions and Behaviour of Canadians." *Policy Matters* 2:5 (October 2001).

O'Neill, Terry. "I Was a Victim of Sunera Thobani's Hate Speech." *Alberta Report* (5 November 2001).

Orchard, David. "Critical Thought in Wake of U.S. Terror." *Edmonton Journal* (7 October 2001).

Osborne, Ken. "Review of Granatstein, *Who Killed Canadian History?*" *Canadian Historical Review* 80:1 (1999).

Ostroff, Joshua. "A Hip Homecoming." *Ottawa Sun* (4 July 1998).

"Ottawa to Help Record Industry Change Its Tune." *Globe and Mail* (10 May 1986).

"Ottawa Wants Kane Painting to Remain Here." *Toronto Star* (3 May 2003).

Owram, Doug. *Born at the Right Time: A History of the Baby Boom Generation*. Toronto: University of Toronto Press, 1996.

Palmer, Bryan D. "Of Silences and Trenches: A Dissident View of

Granatstein's Meaning." *Canadian Historical Review* 80:4 (1999).

Paul, Karen. "*EL* Takes You to the Movies." *Emergency Librarian* 25:2 (November/December 1997).

Pearlstein, Stephen. "Canada, USA?" *Washington Post* (29 January 2001).

Pendakur, Krishna. "Consumption Poverty in Canada 1969 to 1998." *Canadian Public Policy* (June 2001).

Pevere, Geoff and Greig Dymond. *Mondo Canuck: A Canadian Pop Culture Odyssey*. Toronto: Prentice Hall, 1996.

Picot, Garnett. *What Is Happening to Earnings Inequalities and Youth Wages in the 1990s?* Ottawa: Statistics Canada, July 1998.

"PM's 9/11 Comments Spark Lively Debate." *Toronto Star* (13 September 2002).

"Policies Encourage Growing Inequity." *Toronto Star* (17 May 2003).

Posner, Michael. "You've Got to Hand It to the Aspers: They Sure Know How to Wage a Fight." *Globe and Mail* (6 March 2002).

Postman, Neil. *Amusing Ourselves to Death: Public Discourse in the Age of Show Business*. New York: Viking, 1985.

_____. *Technopoly: The Surrender of Culture to Technology*. New York: Random House, 1992.

Potter, Mitch and Betsy Powell. "Agonizing over Ecstasy." *Toronto Star* (20 November 1999).

"The Prime Minister's Words." *Globe and Mail* (15 September 2001).

Quill, Greg. "Record Industry Needs New Deal." *Toronto Star* (1 December 1984).

_____. "What Do Most Indies Want?" *Toronto Star* (21 February 1986).

Rawlyk, George A. "Lament for Canadian-American Relations?" *Journal of Canadian Studies* 26:2 (Summer 1991).

Rebick, Judy. "Soaked in Censorship." *Rabble* (October 2001).

Reid, Angus. *Shakedown: How the New Economy Is Changing Our Lives*. Toronto: Doubleday, 1996.

Reid, Dennis. *A Concise History of Canadian Painting*, second edition. Toronto: Oxford University Press, 1988.

Resnick, Phillip. *The Land of Cain: Class and Nationalism in English Canada 1945–1975*. Vancouver: New Star Books, 1977.

Revenues in the Sound Recording Industry. Ottawa: Statistics Canada, 1997.

"The Right to Speak Out." *Globe and Mail* (11 October 2001).

Ritchie, Karen. *Marketing to Generation X*. New York: Lexington, 1995.

Robertson, Heather-jane. *No More Teachers, No More Books: The Commercialization of Canada's Schools*. Toronto: McClelland and Stewart, 1998.

Rodriguez, Juan. "Jesse Winchester's Trip to Canada." *Rolling Stone* (19 March 1970).

Ross, Alexander. "Colour Them Big Pink." *Maclean's* (February 1969).

Ruddy, Jon. "How to Become a Rock Star without Really Trying." *Maclean's* (November 1969).

_____. "The Pit and the Star." *Maclean's* (November 1970).

Rutherford, Paul. *When Television Was Young: Prime Time Canada 1952–1967*. Toronto: University of Toronto Press, 1990.

Sallot, Jeffrey. "Canada Won't Cede Priority to the U.S., Graham Vows." *Globe and Mail* (2 March 2002).

_____. "Canada Mourns with U.S., PM Tells Bush." *Globe and Mail* (12 September 2003).

Salloum, Habeeb. "Pierre Trudeau's Visionary Prime Minister." *Contemporary Review* 277 (December 2000).

Sanford, Jeff. "Blame the Boomers." *Financial Post* (6 September 2003).

Saul, John Ralston. *Reflections of a Siamese Twin: Canada at the End of Twentieth Century*. Toronto: Penguin, 1998.

Schiller, Herbert I. *Culture Inc.: The Corporate Takeover of Public Expression*. New York: Oxford University Press, 1989.

Schissel, Bernard. *Blaming Children: Youth Crime, Moral Panics and the Politics of Hate*. Halifax: Fernwood, 1997.

Schuster, Eli. "CBC's Post-September 11 'Town Hall' Was a Toronto-Centric Exercise in U.S.-Bashing." *Report* (7 January 2002).

Seo, Danny. *Generation React: Activism for Beginners*. New York: Ballantyne, 1997.

September Eleventh Peace Coalition. "War Is Not the Answer." (October 2001).

Shecter, Barbara. "Radio Fears Canadian Content Boost." *Financial Post* (4 April 2003).

"Sheila Copps' Latest Embarrassment." *National Post* (22 February 2002).

Shepherd, John. *Music as a Social Text*. Oxford: Basil Blackwell, 1990.

_____. "Music Studies in the New Millennium: Perspectives from Canada." *Canadian University Music Review* 21:1 (2000).

Siddiqui, Haroon. "A Letter to Our American Friends." *Toronto Star* (13 September 2001).

_____. "It's the U.S. Foreign Policy, Stupid." *Toronto Star* (19 September 2001).

_____. "Media Missing Canadian Perspective." *Toronto Star* (12 September 2002).

Sokoloff, Heather and Siri Agrell. "Student Loans Fall Short of Needs: Study." *National Post* (11 March 2003).

Sokoloff, Heather. "Canadian Students Among Top in UN Test." *National Post* (2 July 2003).

_____. "CBC National Town Hall Too Local: Ombudsman." *National Post* (26 November 2001).

Stewart, Walter. "Proudly We Stand the 'Butcher's Helper' in Southeast Asia." *Maclean's* (May 1970).

St. Germain, Pat and Bill Brioux. "Sex Charge Kills Pioneer Dream." *Sun Media* (7 June 2000).

Struthers, James. *No Fault of Their Own: Employment and the Canadian Welfare State 1914–1941*. Toronto: University of Toronto Press, 1983.

Sulliman, Tamara. "US Tragedy Stuns UTM Students." *The Medium* 28:3 (17 September 2001).

Taber, Jane. "Rise of 'Tourist' No Accident." *Globe and Mail* (2 June 2003).

_____. "The Threat of Zero Tolerance." *National Post* (27 November 2001).

Talbot, David. "No Wonder the Media Is Cowed." *The Guardian* (17 October 2001).

Tapscott, Don. *Growing up Digital: The Rise of the Net Generation*. New York: McGraw-Hill, 1998.

Taylor, G. "The Serene Teens." *Maclean's* (15 April 1991).

Teeple, Gary. *Globalization and the Decline of Social Reform*. Toronto: Garamond Press, 1995.

Théberge, Paul. "The Project Ahead: Some Thoughts on Developing a Popular Music Curriculum." *Canadian University Music Review* 21:1 (2000).

Thobani, Sunera. "Presentation to the Ottawa Women's Resistance Conference." (1 October 2001).

————. "War Frenzy." *Rabble* (24 October 2001).

Thompson, Allan. "Canada to Chart Own Course, Graham Vows." *Toronto Star* (22 January 2002).

————. "Food Bank Users Double in Decade." *Toronto Star* (17 October 2002).

————. "Graham Keen to Take on U.S." *Toronto Star* (6 June 2002).

————. "PM Repeats Poverty Message." *Toronto Star* (17 September 2002).

————. "PM Undecided on New Defense Link." *Toronto Star* (18 April 2002).

Thompson, John Herd with Allen Seager. *Canada 1922–1939: Decades of Discord*. Toronto: McClelland and Stewart, 1985.

Thorsell, William. "Cause For a Rebel: Vive l'Amérique du Nord." *Globe and Mail* (11 February 2002).

Tippett, Maria. *Making Culture: English-Canadian Institutions and the Arts before the Massey Commission*. Toronto: University of Toronto Press, 1990.

"Tin Soldiers and Nixon's Coming." *Rolling Stone* (25 June 1970).

Toulin, Alan. "Canadians Want Closer U.S. Ties: Poll." *National Post* (18 June 2002).

Tower, Courtney. "The Heartening Surge of New Canadian Nationalism." *Maclean's* (February 1970).

Transcript of Proceedings for the Canadian Radio-Television and Telecommunications Commission Canadian Television Policy Review 14:9 (14 October 1998).

Travers, Jim. "Go-Slow Approach Makes Sense." *Toronto Star* (21 February 2002).

Trickey, Mike and Sheldon Alberts. "Chrétien and Bush Remain Chilly Allies." *National Post* (13 March 2002).

Trickey, Mike. "Plans For Closer Ties With U.S. Stalled." Southam News (30 April 2002).

Trudeau, Gary. "*Amistad* Is Important. Discuss." *Time Canada* 150:27 (December 1997–January 1998).

Trudeau, Pierre Elliot. *Conversation With Canadians*. Toronto: University of Toronto Press, 1972.

"True Patriot Love." *National Post* (17 December 2001).

Vipond, Mary. *The Mass Media in Canada*. Toronto: Lorimer, 1992.

Vital Links: Canadian Cultural Industries. Ottawa: Government of Canada, Department of Communications, 1987.

Vittert, Mark. "Thankful for History." *Triangle Business Journal* 13:13 (28 November 1997).

Walkom, Thomas. "Time to Get into a U.S. State of Mind." *Toronto Star* (10 June 2003).

Wallis, Roger and Krister Malm. *Big Sounds from Small People: The Music Industry in Small Countries*. New York: Pendragon, 1984.

Walton, Paul H. "The Group of Seven and Northern Development." *RACAR: Revue d'art canadien/Canadian Art Review* 17:2 (1990).

Watson, William G. *National Pastimes: The Economics of Canadian Leisure*. Vancouver: The Fraser Institute, 1998.

Webber, Marlene. *Street Kids: The Tragedy of Canada's Runaways*. Toronto: University of Toronto Press, 1991.

Wells, Matt. "CNN to Carry Reminders of US Attacks." *The Guardian* (1 November 2001).

Wente, Margaret. "Two Reasons to Thank Sunera Thobani" *Globe and Mail* (4 October 2001).

————. "They Had It Coming?" *Globe and Mail* (15 September 2001).

Westell, Anthony. "Who's Winning the War on Terror? Sorry, George." *Globe and Mail* (9 September 2003).

Westfall, William. "Pop Counter-Revolution?" *Canadian Forum* (August 1969).

"What American Involvement in Vietnam Is Doing to Canadian Business." *Financial Post* (14 October 1967).

Whitburn, Joel, ed. *Top Pop, 1955–1982*. Wisconsin: Record Research, 1983.

Williams, Robert. "Pioneers Press On." *Winnipeg Sun* (27 June 2000).

Willis, Ellen. "Dreaming of War." *The Nation* (15 October 2001).

Wilson-Smith, Anthony. "America, Canada and Life amidst a New Form of Cold War." *Maclean's* (24 September 2001).

Wistow, David. *The Mystic North*. Toronto: Art Gallery of Ontario, 1983.

Wong, Jan. "Party Animals." *Globe and Mail* (12 July 2003).

Wright, Robert. *Hip and Trivial: Youth Culture, Book Publishing and the Greying of Canadian Nationalism*. Toronto: Canadian Scholars' Press, 2001.

_____. "I'd Sell You Suicide: Pop Music and Moral Panic in the Age of Marilyn Manson." *Popular Music* 19:3 (Autumn 2000).

"The Year for Kids." *Maclean's* (21 December 1992).

York, Ritchie. *Axes, Chops, and Hot Licks*. Edmonton: Hurtig, 1971.

_____. "I'd Rather Be Burned in Canada." *Rolling Stone* (13 December 1969).

Young, Scott. *Neil and Me*. Toronto: McClelland and Stewart, 1984.

Youth '71: An Inquiry into the Transient Youth and Opportunities for Youth Programs in the Summer of 1971. Ottawa: Canadian Council on Social Development, 1971.

Zemans, Joyce. "Establishing the Canon: Nationhood, Identity and the National Gallery's First Reproduction Program of Canadian Art." *Journal of Canadian Art History* 16:2 (1995).

"99.5% Should Be So Lucky." *National Post* (7 February 2002).

INDEX

293